Reinhold Niebuhr (1892–1971) was a major American theologian and political thinker of the mid-twentieth century. He has received much attention from biographers and historians in recent years, but, since his thought remains very relevant for contemporary ethics, a reassessment is due of what he might contribute to current thinking about politics and society. This book is intended to present Niebuhr's ideas about 'Christian Realism' in a way that will be useful to people who are thinking about today's social issues.

REINHOLD NIEBUHR AND CHRISTIAN REALISM

Reinhold Niebuhr (photograph courtesy of the Archives of the Burke Library at Union Theological Seminary, New York City).

REINHOLD NIEBUHR AND CHRISTIAN REALISM

ROBIN W. LOVIN

Dean, and Professor of Ethics,
Perkins School of Theology,
Southern Methodist University

CAMBRIDGE
UNIVERSITY PRESS

Published by the Press Syndicate of the University of Cambridge
The Pitt Building, Trumpington Street, Cambridge CB2 1RP
40 West 20th Street, New York, NY 10011–4211, USA
10 Stamford Road, Oakleigh, Melbourne 3166, Australia

© Cambridge University Press 1995

First published 1995

Printed in Great Britain at the University Press, Cambridge

A catalogue record for this book is available from the British Library

Library of Congress cataloging in publication data

Lovin, Robin W.
Reinhold Niebuhr and Christian Realism / Robin W. Lovin.
p.   cm
Includes bibliographical references and index.
ISBN 0 521 44363 6 (hardback) ISBN 0 521 47932 0 (paperback)
1. Niebuhr, Reinhold, 1892–1971.
2. Sociology, Christian – History – 20th century.
3. Christianity and politics – History – 20th century.
4. Christian ethics – History – 20th century.
I. Title.
BX4827.N5L68 1995
261.8′092–dc20   94–6809   CIP

ISBN 0 521 44363 6 hardback
ISBN 0 521 47932 0 paperback

CE

Contents

Acknowledgments

This book has been a long time in the making, and many people have contributed to it. Preston Williams launched my serious study of Christian Realism at Harvard, nearly two decades ago. After that, a succession of students at Emory, Chicago, and Drew encouraged my work with their own enthusiasm, and sometimes sharpened my points on their own resistance. Good collegiality, which always survives time and changing institutional loyalties, has helped, too. I am especially grateful to James Gustafson, Michael Perry, William Schweiker, and Douglas Ottati, and more recently to Neal Riemer and Peter Ochs. David Heim provided regular encouragement and occasional footnotes. Phil Blackwell provided quiet space and strong Bedouin coffee during a crucial phase of the writing.

Indispensable contributions were made by a series of research assistants. William C. French, Christine Firer Hinze, Todd Whitmore, and Dan Malotky all helped at Chicago, as did Gary Matthews at Drew. These persons are now, or are about to become, recognized scholars in their own right, but at an earlier stage in their careers I got to claim their talents for my own purposes. My debt to each of them is immense.

Institutions have helped, too. The University of Chicago Divinity School and Yale Divinity School provided forums for lectures that found their way into these pages, and a version of Chapter Four appeared in the *Journal of Religion*. The John Simon Guggenheim Foundation supported a year of research at the beginning of the project, and Cambridge University Press has coaxed and goaded it to completion.

A final word of thanks is due to the students, clergy, and laity across the country who have listened to the speeches, sermons, workshops, study groups, and impromptu lectures that I have spun out of this material over the last decade. Their discovery of Christian Realism has kept it new for me, too; and their interest, more than anything else, sustains my confidence that Reinhold Niebuhr was saying something that we still need to hear.

An introduction to Christian Realism

During the first half of the twentieth century, Protestant theologians in the United States gave new attention to the social forces that shape and limit human possibilities. Like the leaders of the Social Gospel movement before them, these writers were concerned with the gap between the biblical vision of God's rule and the realities of modern industrial society. For the new generation, however, a Christian conscience informed by scientific study would not suffice to close the gap. The biblical ideal stands in judgment not only on the social reality, but also on every attempt to formulate the ideal itself.

Therefore, social achievements provide no final goal. The dynamics of history are driven by the human capacity always to imagine life beyond existing limitations. Biblical faith gives vision and direction to that capacity for self-transcendence, but we are best able to challenge and channel our powers when we also understand what is really going on.

'Christian Realism' is the name that has been given to that way of thinking. It is a term closely associated with Reinhold Niebuhr, when it is not exclusively identified with his thought. It is, however, important to remember that the theological movement originated before Niebuhr took it up as his own. From the early 1930s, D.C. Macintosh and Walter Marshall Horton wrote about "religious realism" or "realistic theology" in ways that influenced Niebuhr's call for a church that would produce "religious or Christian realists."[1] The term 'Christian

[1] Reinhold Niebuhr, "When Will Christians Stop Fooling Themselves?" *Christian Century* 51 (May 16, 1934), 659. See also Douglas Clyde Macintosh, ed., *Religious Realism* (New York: Macmillan, 1931); Walter Marshall Horton, *Realistic Theology*

Realism' belongs perhaps as much to John C. Bennett as to Niebuhr, and certainly others both in Christian ethics and in political philosophy have adopted the idea and developed it in their own ways.[2]

Reinhold Niebuhr was the most important voice of this movement. His ideas eventually dominated and directed it, and his thought will be the key to our understanding of it. Nevertheless, Christian Realism is not simply the set of ideas and opinions that Niebuhr held on the questions of his day. Niebuhr always understood himself to be speaking for a larger movement, if not for Christianity as a whole.[3] If others found his analyses of contemporary events and his prescriptions for policy and action uniquely illuminating and persuasive, Niebuhr was clear that the analytical power came from a "Christian view of human nature" which is "involved in the paradox of claiming a higher stature for man and taking a more serious view of his evil than other anthropology."[4] Niebuhr's major works were devoted to a validation of this Christian understanding of human nature, and his assessments of political choices and issues rested on it, even when they did not

(New York: Harper and Brothers, 1934). For this period generally, see Martin E. Marty, *Modern American Religion, 2: The Noises of Conflict, 1919–41* (Chicago: University of Chicago Press, 1991), pp. 303–40. The best accounts of Reinhold Niebuhr's life and times are Richard W. Fox, *Reinhold Niebuhr: A Biography* (New York: Pantheon, 1985), and Charles C. Brown, *Niebuhr and His Age: Reinhold Niebuhr's Prophetic Role in the Twentieth Century* (Philadelphia: Trinity Press International, 1992).

2 John C. Bennett, *Christian Realism* (New York: Charles Scribner's Sons, 1941). See also Glenn Bucher, "Christian Political Realism After Niebuhr: The Case of John C. Bennett," *Union Seminary Quarterly Review*, 41 (1986), 43–58.

3 One of the subtle manifestations of this sense that he is speaking for a broad tendency in Christian thought is Niebuhr's reluctance to treat 'Christian Realism' as a proper name. In his printed works, it nearly always appears as a generic noun qualified by a proper adjective, viz. 'Christian realism.' We will shortly see, however, that Niebuhr's thought depends on a distinctive combination of several quite different kinds of realism. For this study, I have chosen to use the term 'Christian Realism' to denominate that complex of ideas as a whole, reserving the lower-case 'realism' for reference to a variety of realisms – moral, political, metaphysical, etc. – which may or may not figure in Niebuhrian Christian Realism. Where it is possible or necessary to refer to a distinctively Christian version of one or another of these realisms, I will speak of 'Christian moral realism,' or 'Christian political realism,' etc., without any necessary implication that the idea under discussion is part of Christian Realism.

4 Reinhold Niebuhr, *The Nature and Destiny of Man* (New York: Charles Scribner's Sons, 1964), I, 18.

explicitly discuss it. The subject of this book is that broader set of ideas which provides the conceptual center from which many of Niebuhr's more specific ideas can be understood. We want to know what the key elements of that Christian Realism were for Niebuhr and his generation, and, just as important, we want to know what use those elements might be in our thinking about Christian ethics today.

POLITICAL REALISM

Niebuhr gives little time to definitions in his work. His aims are synthetic, linking related ideas into a complex whole, rather than strictly delimiting the individual elements. His method is dialectical, in the sense that concepts are clarified by stating what they exclude, and positions are explained by specifying what they reject.

This is especially apparent in the terminology of Christian Realism itself. Niebuhr's position emerges as a complex of theological conviction, moral theory, and meditation on human nature in which the elements are mutually reinforcing, rather than systematically related. The "logic" of the biblical doctrine emerges as we carefully distinguish it from other views and come to appreciate "the adequacy of its answer for human problems which other views have obscured and confused."[5] We understand what Christian Realism is largely by identifying the many less adequate views that it is not.

One of the rare points at which this dialectical method yields almost definitional specificity occurs when Niebuhr distinguishes political from metaphysical realism at the beginning of an essay on "Augustine's Political Realism."

The terms "idealism" and "realism" are not analogous in political and in metaphysical theory; and they are certainly not as precise in political as in metaphysical theory. In political and moral theory "realism" denotes the disposition to take all factors in a social and political situation, which offer resistance to established norms, into account, particularly the factors of self-interest and power ... "Idealism" is in the esteem of its proponents, characterized by loyalty

---

[5] Niebuhr, *The Nature and Destiny of Man*, I, 151.

to moral norms and ideals, rather than to self-interest, whether individual or collective. It is, in the opinion of its critics, characterized by disposition to ignore or be indifferent to the forces in human life which offer resistance to universally valid ideals and norms.[6]

The frustration and illumination of reading Reinhold Niebuhr are neatly packaged in that quotation. The meaning of "realism" emerges primarily in a negative assessment of "idealism," while the political meaning here considered is to be distinguished from another "metaphysical" meaning, which, however, is not specified at all. Yet we do emerge from the paragraph with a sense of the forces with which political realism will be concerned, while the identification of those forces by contrast to "universally valid ideals and norms" warns us, significantly, that idealism does not rest entirely upon illusions.

We may begin to understand Christian Realism, then, by taking it seriously as a version of political realism. The reality in question is the multiplicity of forces that drive the decisions that people actually make in situations of political choice. The desire to reward one's friends and punish one's enemies, convictions about the justice of a cause, the hope to advance one's own interests through the success of one's group or party, the need to demonstrate one's power over events, and the wish to acquire more of it, fear of the loss of power, fear of the consequences of failure – all of these, and more, shape the responses of individuals and groups to choices about use of public resources and about institutions that serve public purposes. To be "realistic" in this context is, Niebuhr suggests, to take all of these realities into account. None should be overlooked, and each should be assigned a weight that reflects its real effect on the course of events, rather than its place in our own scale of values.

This formulation of political realism suggests that we should not rely on moral argument alone to decide on political action, nor should we overestimate the power of moral suasion to

[6] Reinhold Niebuhr, "Augustine's Political Realism," in *Christian Realism and Political Problems* (New York: Charles Scribner's Sons, 1953), pp. 119–20.

determine the course of events. During World War II and the tense decades which followed, this Niebuhrian counsel had a powerful influence on political leaders and diplomats, who were caught between the moral idealism of democracy and the brutal realities of international politics. Niebuhr's warnings were, however, initially directed to religious idealists, who still held to the hope of American Protestantism's Social Gospel.

At the beginning of the twentieth century Social Gospel preachers and theologians were confident that a new age of social Christianity was about to begin, transforming the raw realities of life in industrial cities and ushering in an era of international peace by the application of Christian love. Biblical scholars were rediscovering the social dimensions of the original Christian ethic, which had been lost to sight under centuries of superstitious accretions. Advances in scientific knowledge promised that this rediscovered ethic could be put into practice in a way that it could not have been in an earlier day. "For the first time in religious history," Walter Rauschenbusch exulted, "we have the possibility of so directing religious energy by scientific knowledge that a comprehensive and continuous reconstruction of social life in the name of God is within the bounds of human possibility."[7]

Rauschenbusch's call for social reconstruction that would be both Christian and scientific was far more attentive to the complexities of life in an industrial society than some of his nineteenth-century predecessors. For Reinhold Niebuhr, however, Rauschenbusch's writings shared with these sentimental pieties one fundamental confusion: the moral vision of the New Testament is treated as a "simple possibility."[8] It becomes a key point of Christian Realism that the ethics of Jesus cannot provide a social ethics. For Niebuhr, the most difficult problems lie not between the Gospel profession and present practice, but between what the ethics of Jesus demands and any possible social organization.

[7] Walter Rauschenbusch, *Christianity and the Social Crisis* (Louisville: Westminster/John Knox, 1992), p. 209.
[8] Reinhold Niebuhr, "Walter Rauschenbusch in Historical Perspective," in *Faith and Politics*, ed. Ronald H. Stone (New York: George Braziller, 1968), pp. 33–46.

The ethic of Jesus does not deal at all with the immediate moral problem of every human life – the problem of arranging some kind of armistice between various contending factions and forces. It has nothing to say about the relativities of politics and economics, nor of the necessary balances of power which exist and must exist in even the most intimate social relationships.[9]

The point is made at first against a particular kind of Christian idealism, but in the end, the warning applies to idealisms of every kind: Given the complexities of the human situation, a moral ideal alone cannot dictate what we ought to do and will not settle the outcomes of history. To devote oneself exclusively to determining and proclaiming the right thing to do is most probably to render oneself powerless in the actual course of events, and it may – in the unlikely event that the proclamation is heeded – prove horribly destructive, abolishing the necessary balances of power and unleashing potent fanaticisms. Attentiveness to the "factions and forces" at work in each specific situation is the key to effective resolution of conflicts, although the shifting equilibrium of power insures that each solution is only temporary and the creative work will shortly have to begin again.

REALISM AND SUSPICION

Realism implies recognition of the limits of purely moral solutions to political problems and calls for attention to the realities that shape social, political, and economic conflicts. Niebuhr's realism also includes attention to the ways in which these realities may be hidden. It is not simply that we must not overestimate the political force of moral ideals. We must also be alert to the fact that professions of ideals frequently conceal more limited, selfish interests, and the pursuit of justice may mask a ruthless exercise of power. The mechanisms of concealment here are so effective that those who use them often deceive themselves. Paradoxically, it is the victims of moral idealism and the demand for justice who are most likely to

---

[9] Reinhold Niebuhr, *An Interpretation of Christian Ethics* (New York: Seabury Press, 1979 [first published 1935]), p. 23.

detect the fraud. Those who find their aspirations consistently frustrated by the power of another group are less likely to believe that this frustration is what justice requires than those who find the situation congruent with their own desires.

Niebuhr's political realism thus introduces into the discourse of American religious social ethics what a later generation would call the "hermeneutics of suspicion." We must not accept what people say about a social situation at face value, even when they apparently believe it themselves. We will be more likely to find the truth among those who have experienced injustice and repression than by listening to the explanations of the powerful.

Especially in his early work, Niebuhr relied on Marxist thought as the starting point for this analysis. Laws, customs, and traditions that justify the privileges of a ruling elite arc the product of underlying economic forces that derive their power from control of productive resources. The virtues of thrift and industry to which the powerful attribute their special position will not tell us what is going on in a society. An analysis of the realities of economic power will. In 1933, Niebuhr wrote that Marxism provides "the key to the real facts of capitalistic civilization."[10] In later years, he was more pragmatic in his assessment of socialism, and he became a harsh critic of Soviet communism, but exposure of the group and class interests that retard (or in some cases accelerate) demands for change remained a staple of his writing. Dennis McCann's assessment that Niebuhr later in his career becomes a "post-Marxist" rather than an "anti-Marxist" is surely correct.[11]

Niebuhr's assessment of social realities was also guided by attention to the psychological forces at work. Here, he was less influenced by theory than by his own insights.[12] Anxiety about

[10] Reinhold Niebuhr, "A Reorientation of Radicalism," *The World Tomorrow*, 16 (July, 1933), 444.
[11] Dennis McCann, "Reinhold Niebuhr and Jacques Maritain on Marxism: A Comparison of Two Traditional Models of Practical Theology," *Journal of Religion*, 58 (April, 1978), 140–68.
[12] Niebuhr believed that Freudian psychology made too sharp a distinction between the rational center of personality in the ego and the driving forces of the id, and promised too easy a release from those drives and desires. Later in life, he became acquainted with Erik Erikson and developed an interest in that psychologist's

the insecurity of our position in the world and guilt about the things we have done to achieve and hold it lead us to fashion images of our own invulnerability and purity and provide powerful incentives to believe in what we have made. The ideals and values to which social classes and political interest groups appeal to justify their claims are thus more than ideological smokescreens to conceal their real economic interests. They also defend against the threats posed by our own anxiety, and they protect our illusions from the reality of ourselves and our past.

Christian Realism combines these critical tools of social and psychological analysis and applies them consistently to all groups and classes. Marxism identifies the rationalizations of privilege that conceal the interests of the elite, but it overlooks the element of envy that also distorts the egalitarian ideals of the poor.[13] Psychological theories explain the distorted perceptions and self-defeating illusions that mental suffering generates, but psychology expects too much from the healthy mind, which may have a more objective view of its circumstances, but which will never be entirely free of the interests and anxieties that generate more acceptable illusions and yield benign self-satisfactions.

Niebuhr's "hermeneutics of suspicion" thus draws on both Marxian and Freudian interpretations, but it corresponds to neither of them. Niebuhr applies his criticism more consistently to all parties in social controversy because his analysis rests in the end on a theological insight.[14] The root cause of our illusions lies deeper than economic interest or psychic vulnerability to particular fears and losses. The root cause is anxiety over the finitude which is necessarily part of every human situation. We trust distorted visions of ourselves because we

---

revisions of Freud. See Niebuhr, *The Nature and Destiny of Man*, I, viii; also *The Self and the Dramas of History* (New York: Charles Scribner's Sons, 1955), pp. 20–23.

[13] Reinhold Niebuhr, *Moral Man and Immoral Society* (New York: Charles Scribner's Sons, 1960), pp. 160–61.

[14] For an extended discussion of this point, see Louis H. Tietje, "Was Reinhold Niebuhr Ever a Marxist? An Investigation Into the Assumptions of His Early Interpretation and Critique of Marxism," Ph.D. Dissertation, Union Theological Seminary, 1984.

fear to trust the only real source of security, which lies outside ourselves, in God.[15]

While we may expect that poor and marginalized persons will be less susceptible to the specific illusions by which the prosperous center of society explains its comfortable circumstances, they are subject to other characteristic exaggerations of their own virtue. Because the source of these illusions is neither social location nor psychic accident, but the human condition itself, a realist will expect to find these forces at work among all parties. The political realist's commitment to "take all factors in a social and political situation ... into account" requires that we identify the interests and fears behind all the values that are professed, even – or especially – when those professions seem to be entirely sincere.

THE LIMITS OF POLITICAL REALISM

Self-interest is pervasive in politics. Niebuhr's realism requires that we face that fact candidly, but he did not believe that self-interest is the only reality. Realism is a matter of taking self-interest into account, as a reality that resists norms that are also real. This sets Niebuhr apart from a more rigid sort of political realist, who insists that to be realistic about politics, one must deny the reality of "values," "goods," or "norms." This realism insists that concrete objects of desire and the material relationships that create and control them are the only realities that impinge on politics. Moral concepts, in particular, may have a reality in individual consciousness, but since they are themselves reflections of the realities of power and interest, nothing will be gained by studying these abstractions, which provide no practical guidance for the affairs of government.

There are interpreters who read Reinhold Niebuhr as a political realist in this more narrow sense. Niebuhr, the theologian and preacher, convinced a nation that was all too

---

[15] Niebuhr, *The Nature and Destiny of Man*, I, 178–79. I will provide a more detailed examination of Niebuhr's understanding of the relationships between finitude, anxiety, and sin in Chapter Three of this volume.

confident of its Christian ideals to lay them aside and face the
stark realities of politics within and between nations. His criticism of the sentimentalities of the Social Gospel became generally relevant when he directed them at more broadly shared
illusions of American virtue. Summing up Niebuhr's influence
on public life, the political scientist Hans Morgenthau said,
"Reinhold Niebuhr has shown that … this relationship
between a concealed political reality and a corrupted ethic is
the very essence of politics; that, in other words, political
ideologies are an inevitable weapon in the struggle for power
which all participants must use to a greater or lesser extent."
That insight marks Niebuhr as the greatest American political
philosopher of his time, and "perhaps the only creative political philosopher since Calhoun."[16]

Niebuhr was puzzled by this accolade, and he found Morgenthau's analysis one-sided. Ideology is inevitably an element
in political controversy, but it is not the only element. The
moral ambiguities of politics cannot be neglected, but the
terms of moral evaluation are not simply reducible to individual and group interests.[17] The political reality to which
Niebuhr wants to be attentive thus includes both the "established norms" and the "factors of self-interest and power"
which offer resistance to them. Moral standards and ideals
direct our attention to human aspirations that are present in
political life along with the more particular conflicts of interest.
It is a mistake in purely descriptive terms to adopt a version of

[16] Hans J. Morgenthau, "The Influence of Reinhold Niebuhr in American Political
Life and Thought," in Harold R. Landon, ed., *Reinhold Niebuhr: A Prophetic Voice in
Our Time* (Greenwich, Conn.: Seabury Press, 1962), p. 109.

[17] Niebuhr put this mildly in a response to Morgenthau's summary which we have just
cited. "I do not think we will sacrifice any value in the 'realist' approach to the
political order," Niebuhr said "… if we define the moral ambiguity of the political
realm in terms which do not rob it of moral content." See "The Response of
Reinhold Niebuhr," in Landon, ed., *Reinhold Niebuhr*, p. 122. His response in a
letter to June Bingham, quoted by Daniel F. Rice, is more pointed, rejecting the
comparison between Calhoun's "rather amoral conception of politics" and his own
"conviction of the moral ambiguity of the political order." See Daniel F. Rice,
Reinhold Niebuhr and John Dewey: An American Odyssey (Albany: SUNY Press, 1993),
p. 333 n. 5. Niebuhr offers a more extended criticism of Morgenthau in *Man's
Nature and His Communities: Essays on the Dynamics and Enigmas of Man's Personal and
Social Existence* (The Scribner Lyceum Editions Library; New York: Charles Scribner's Sons, 1965), pp. 71–75.

political realism that treats values and ideals as irrelevant to
political choices, even as it is a mistake to suppose that we
could create a situation in which these norms were the only
determinants of action.[18] A generation that believed it could
create a situation in which the Christian norms alone would be
relevant needed to be attentive to the stubborn realities and
hidden distortions of self-interest, but a generation that saw
only the stubborn realities and hidden distortions was as
"unrealistic" as its sentimental predecessors.[19] Each ignored
something that is irreducibly real in the political situation,
something that has its own distinctive power to shape political
conflict.

MORAL REALISM

Moral ideas have political consequences simply because many
people believe in them. The cultural significance and psychological power of "established norms" gives them a political
reality that must be considered even by those who think they
are false. The sentimental devotion of Christians to what they
regard as the "pure ethics of Jesus" is also real in its social
impact. It is unrealistic in that it cannot be lived by persons
who must struggle with multiple demands and against the
finite limits of human life and individual history. The devotion
of revolutionaries to their cause is real enough, but it is unrealistic because the goals they espouse will not finally end social
conflict and usher in the age of peace they promise. Moral
ideas may be fervently held and actively practiced, and to that

---

[18] A more balanced version of political realism is found in some recent writers on
international politics who view moral standards as relevant, but not determinative,
for foreign policy. See the essays by Arthur M. Schlesinger, Jr., Joseph Nye, and
Robert Jervis in Robert J. Myers, ed., *International Ethics and the Nuclear Age* (Ethics
and Foreign Policy Series, IV; Lanham, Md.: University Press of America, 1987),
and also my Introduction to that volume, pp. 8–11.

[19] In his recent account of Reinhold Niebuhr's career as a teacher, Ronald H. Stone
notes that in lectures on Christian ethics at Union Theological Seminary after 1943,
Niebuhr emphasized the contemporary relevance of the unrealizable demands of
Jesus' moral teaching more than he had in his early work, *An Interpretation of
Christian Ethics*. See Ronald H. Stone, *Professor Reinhold Niebuhr: A Mentor to the
Twentieth Century* (Louisville: Westminster/John Knox Press, 1992), p. 63.

extent they will have real effects. To be realistic in Niebuhr's sense, however, they must also be true.

In the parlance of contemporary philosophy, this is to say that Christian Realism is a version of moral realism. Moral ideas can be true or false. Moral statements are not only expressions of emotion or reports of the speaker's attitudes and preferences, as non-cognitivist theories would have it. Moral statements make claims about what is the case, independently of our ideas about what is the case and of the evidence we marshal to support those ideas.[20]

A political realist who is not a moral realist need not deny that moral statements appear to be claims about what is the case, but he or she could deny that this is the meaningful sense in which the claims are true or false. What matters, he or she might say, is whether the moral statement conforms to the way that moral language is ordinarily used in this community, whether it accurately reports the moral beliefs of the persons for and to whom the speaker claims to speak. For this political realist, the statement, "Justice requires that innocent people not be punished for crimes committed by others," uttered in a court of law, is true. The statement, "Justice requires that everyone be paid the same rate for each hour of labor given to the company," uttered in the board room at General Motors, is false. This political realist is a cognitivist. He or she clearly believes that moral statements can be true or false, but also believes that the relevant criteria of truth or falsity are embedded in the moral beliefs and practices of the community in question. In recent ethics, certain sophisticated forms of cultural relativism provide a theoretical formulation of this sort of political realism.[21] From this point of view, it makes no sense to say that a moral claim might be true, even if nobody believes it. Whether a particular moral claim conforms to what people

---

[20] Cf. David Brink, *Moral Realism and the Foundations of Ethics* (Cambridge: Cambridge University Press, 1989), pp. 14–23. For a useful collection of articles on the varieties of moral realism, see Geoffrey Sayre-McCord, ed., *Essays on Moral Realism* (Ithaca: Cornell University Press, 1988).

[21] See, for example, Gilbert Harman, "Moral Relativism Defended," *Philosophical Review*, 84 (1975), 3–32.

generally believe about morality is precisely what determines whether or not it is true.

The moral realist, by contrast, holds that whether a moral statement is true or false depends on a state of affairs that exists independently of the ideas that the speaker or the speaker's community holds about the appropriate use of moral terms. A moral claim might thus be true, even if nobody believes it. If, for example, the truth or falsity of a moral claim depends on what God has commanded, and God has commanded that no person be held in slavery, then slavery is wrong, even if everyone in a slave-holding society, including the slaves, believes that it is morally right. Or, to formulate an example closer to the point of most moral realist arguments, if the truth or falsity of a moral claim depends on the conditions that enable persons to live well, and conditions of poverty create such danger and disorder that everyone suffers a significant loss of freedom, then it is true that poverty should be eliminated, whether or not prevailing moral beliefs about justice, initiative, and personal responsibility support the action.

The important distinction, then, is between a political realism that is mostly concerned with how claims relate to what people believe, and a moral realism that is concerned with moral truths independent of these beliefs. It is important, however, to recognize that different versions of moral realism may differ significantly about what makes a moral belief true or false. The two examples above, which turn respectively on divine commands and on human well-being, illustrate this point well.

The moral realist holds that the truth of moral claims depends on a state of affairs that exists independently of our moral beliefs. This does not necessarily imply that the moral realist holds that true statements somehow "correspond" to a state of affairs in the world. The moral realist must hold that moral statements are true of the world, and not just true of our beliefs about morality. But the moral realist may hold any one of a number of theories of truth to explain that relationship. Many contemporary versions of moral realism employ pragmatic or coherentist theories of truth and argue that theories of truth which depend on a simple correspondence between true statements and reality are incoherent.[22] I will argue that Christian Realism is linked to some of these contemporary moral realisms by its use of a pragmatic method, although the early Christian Realists often qualified their commitments to pragmatism, and almost never worked their own pragmatic method out in detail.

Just as moral realists are not required to hold a correspondence theory of truth, so they are not committed to the metaphysical claim that "good" and "evil," or "right" and "wrong" are metaphysical properties that exist apart from the natural, empirical properties of things. A moral realist *may* hold that moral predicates refer to non-natural properties,[23] but he or she may also hold that moral properties are supervenient on the natural properties of things.[24]

Moral realisms of this latter sort are versions of *ethical naturalism*. In the example above, the moral realist who is an ethical naturalist could say that poverty is evil just because it has the corrosive effects on human well-being that characterize its natural features. It is right to act against situations of poverty, and wrong to create or to perpetuate them, not because we intuit some non-natural property of rightness or wrongness in those acts, but because the conditions of poverty have the natural properties which they have.

Ethical naturalism explains the appropriate use of moral terms by reference to the natural properties of "good" or "bad" persons, situations, and actions, though the ethical naturalist tries to avoid *reductive naturalism*, which holds that the moral terms mean nothing but the natural properties.[25] Human intentions and responses are intrinsic to moral

---

[22] Cf. Brink, *Moral Realism*, pp. 100–43.

[23] The most famous example of this position is the view in G. E. Moore, *Principia Ethica* (Cambridge: Cambridge University Press, 1903).

[24] For further development of this point, see Brink, *Moral Realism*, p. 160; Sayre-McCord, ed., *Essays on Moral Realism*, pp. 12–14; 270–77.

[25] On this distinction see Morton O. White, *What Is and What Ought to Be Done* (New York: Oxford University Press, 1981). When Reinhold Niebuhr, especially in his early writings, criticizes "naturalism," he means some version of reductive naturalism, not the ethical naturalism we are discussing here. Compare, for example, Niebuhr, *An Interpretation of Christian Ethics*, pp. 42–43.

meanings. Moral realism, in holding that moral truths are independent of particular moral beliefs, does not imply that moral truths could be meaningfully defined for a universe of natural properties in which there were no human beings to know and respond to them.[26]

Christian Realism, as we shall see more fully in Chapter Two, is an ethical naturalism of this sort. Theoretical agreement on ethical naturalism may, however, cover wide differences over just which natural properties and human experiences are significant for moral assessment. Utilitarian theories focus on human happiness and the natural properties that elicit this response in ways that allow it to be shared among the largest number of persons. Eudaimonistic theories call attention to natural circumstances that maximize the development of valued human characteristics, or virtues. More socially oriented theories of virtue stress the development of human characteristics that allow constructive responses to a range of recurrent social problems. Natural law theories stress human functioning in accordance with an order that can be discerned in nature and progress toward states of affairs that mark the full development of that nature.

A comprehensive survey of these types of ethical naturalism is beyond the scope of this introduction, though we will have occasion to examine many of them as the argument of this book unfolds. Niebuhr, following his usual method, formulates his own naturalism by explaining his disagreements with other versions, and in Chapters Two and Three we will continue that approach in a critical comparison of the naturalism of Christian Realism to other naturalisms found in the literature today.

Niebuhr's own attention focuses on natural law ethics as formulated in the Catholic tradition. He brings to this examination a Protestant prejudice against natural law which he never entirely loses.[27] As a result, he sometimes fails to see how much his own Christian Realism depends on natural law

---

[26] See David Wiggins, "Truth, Invention, and the Meaning of Life," in Sayre-McCord, ed., *Essays on Moral Realism*, pp. 127–65.

[27] Niebuhr, *Man's Nature and His Communities*, p. 19. John C. Bennett has a more balanced Christian Realist's assessment of the natural law tradition. See his *Christian Realism*.

premises, and he would no doubt be surprised to see how closely the revisions of natural law that have developed in Catholic ethics since Vatican II have paralleled his own criticisms of the lack of contextual flexibility and the overemphasis on biological function in previous moral theology.

What Christian Realism chiefly shares with the natural law tradition is the conviction that right action is action that conforms to human nature. The good person acts in ways that develop the capacities human beings have, rather than defeating them. The good person does not settle for less than human possibilities allow, but he or she also avoids demands and expectations that exceed a realistic estimate of those possibilities or strain our human powers to the point that they are apt to break. Conformity to nature characterizes individual morality, but Niebuhr is especially concerned to point out that it provides guidance for appropriate forms of social life. In a foreword to *The Children of Light and the Children of Darkness*, written in 1959, Niebuhr said:

> [A] free society prospers best in a cultural, religious and moral atmosphere which encourages neither a too pessimistic nor too optimistic view of human nature. Both moral sentimentality in politics and moral pessimism encourage totalitarian regimes, the one because it encourages the opinion that it is not necessary to check the power of government, and the second because it believes that only absolute political authority can restrain the anarchy, created by conflicting and competitive interests.[28]

There is, of course, room for substantial disagreement about just which views of human nature are "too optimistic" or "too pessimistic," but the key point is that moral and political systems are to be formulated in relation to that realistic assessment of human nature, not imposed on it from some other source.

Moral systems fail when their norms become unrelated to human nature or, more usually, when they are formulated in relation to only a part of it. The moral inadequacies of American Protestantism relate to its tendency to err in one of

[28] Reinhold Niebuhr, *The Children of Light and the Children of Darkness* (New York: Charles Scribner's Sons, 1972), p. viii.

two ways on this point: "An ethic of sacrificial love, relevant only to the summit experiences of life, which tends to persuade Christians that they are saints, contrasts with an individualistic–economic ethic of self-reliance which teaches us how to be prosperous."[29]

Christian Realism agrees with the broad and basic premise of natural law that the moral life is life lived in accordance with nature. Persons and societies fail morally when they attempt to ignore these requirements, and they stand in gravest danger when their moral systems and political institutions do not truthfully represent the possibilities and limitations of human life.

Just at that point, however, attentiveness to the realities of human nature introduces a significant complication into the usual formulations of ethical naturalism, for there is in human nature an element that cannot be reduced to a determinate set of requirements and resists conformity to any set of expectations.

To the essential nature of man belong, on the one hand, all his natural endowments, and determinations, his physical and social impulses, his sexual and racial differentiations, in short his character as a creature imbedded in the natural order. On the other hand, his essential nature also includes the freedom of his spirit, his transcendence over natural process and finally his self-transcendence.[30]

No account of human nature that omits this freedom can be adequate, but none which includes it can formulate the requirements of human nature as a determinate set of rules, goals, or virtues.

To live according to human nature is to have an imaginative grasp of possibilities for one's life as well as an accurate picture of its realities. We envision ways in which our world and ourselves could be better than they are. Some of the possibilities we envision will be immediate, personal, and rather easily realized. Others will require social cooperation, more time, and larger transformations – if, indeed, they can be realized at all. We may argue about the possibilities, just as we

---

[29] Niebuhr, *Man's Nature and His Communities*, pp. 16–17.
[30] Niebuhr, *The Nature and Destiny of Man*, I, 270.

argue about the requirements of nature, but we cannot ignore their importance in the shaping of the moral lives of individuals and cultures.

What should be apparent, then, is that there is an element of idealism in the moral life of each individual and an element of utopianism in every attempt to think normatively about the life of society. Reinhold Niebuhr's criticism of the sentimentalities of the Social Gospel and his sensitivity to the self-deceptions involved in moral crusades makes him wary of these moral ideals, but his attentiveness to the facts of human experience will not allow him to eliminate them from consideration. In an early work, which nonetheless provides his only systematic treatment of Christian ethics, Niebuhr argues for "the relevance of an impossible ethical ideal."[31] Christian Realism is about defining an appropriate role for these ideals, especially in the moral deliberations of groups and nations.

One question, however, requires further attention: what is the relationship between these "impossible ethical ideals" and the commitment to moral realism? The freedom in which we hold these ideas in judgment over the facts of present experience is part of human nature, but if the ideals guide our choices, in what sense are those choices *realistic*? To answer that question, we must determine whether reality is known in the imaginative apprehension of the possibilities of love, as well as in the sober judgments of experience on human nature.

THEOLOGICAL REALISM

In freedom, persons apprehend alternatives to their present ways of life. In freedom, they also lay claim to these possibilities in various ways. Sometimes these claims are made by commitments of one's own effort, or by commitment to another person. By committing myself to the effort of study, and the isolation of research, and the cost of education, I will realize my dream of becoming a scholar. By committing myself to another person, despite the irreducible differences in our characters and the

---

[31] Niebuhr, *An Interpretation of Christian Ethics*, pp. 62–63.

changes time may bring, I will realize the stability and security of family life, and experience the fulfillments that it offers. Sometimes, too, the claims persons make on different possibilities for living are moral claims. These claims do not pledge one's own effort or offer commitment to a common project. They make demands on others for opportunities and resources. Justice, we say, requires that I not be denied the education I need because of my race. I have a right, we say, to shelter, to food, to basic medical care, even though I lack the resources to pay for them.

These moral claims seem to presuppose a relationship between persons which, while not as personal as the relationships of marriage or mentoring, is irreducibly different from the relationships between persons and things, persons and other animals, or persons and the environment. What I claim from you as a moral right, I do not wrest from you by labor as I coax a crop from the soil. What I ask in justice, I do not obtain by hitching you to my cart as a beast of burden. We may, of course, resort to coercion or to violence if our moral claims are denied, but the fact that we make the moral claims at all bespeaks a relationship in which we have more to do with each other than to defend our interests against incursions.

The fact of that relationship implies, of course, that others may also make claims on me. Not everything that I claim in justice or as a matter of right will survive these counterclaims. At some point, I may have to concede that what I have claimed as a matter of justice is simply something that I want.

Indeed, not all claims that I make will survive my own scrutiny, for there will always be possibilities I must myself reject because they conflict with more compelling visions. "Life must not be lived at cross-purposes," Niebuhr wrote. "The self must establish an inner unity of impulses and desires and it must relate itself harmoniously to other selves and other unities."[32]

In the life of a whole society this process of claim and counterclaim yields agreement on a minimal set of recognized

[32] *Ibid.*, p. 23.

rights and standards of justice, and it is to those arrangements that most persons have recourse in their claims against others. They adjust their conflicts of interest through recognized judicial and legislative procedures, and for the most part they regard law and ethics as nothing more than established means for adjudicating disputes.

In experience, it is impossible to say whether the resolution of a particular conflict points the way to the harmony of all interests, or merely opens the way for new and different conflicts, possibly involving larger groups and interests and higher levels of destructiveness. Theories of justice point the way to adjudication of future conflicts on the basis of moral claims, but there is no way of knowing in advance that they will be successful. The obligation to pursue justice must rest on some commitment other than predictable success.

One form that commitment takes is the belief that God is love and that love requires justice. To say that is not to claim that one's idea of God provides, even implicitly, a formula of justice that would enable us to say in detail how all moral conflicts should be resolved. It is, rather, to claim that justice and love have a reality beyond the ideas that we happen to hold about them.

Every truly moral act seeks to establish what ought to be, because the agent feels obligated to the ideal, though historically unrealized, as being the order of life in its more essential reality. Thus the Christian believes that the ideal of love is real in the will and nature of God, even though he knows of no place in history where the ideal has been realized in its pure form. And it is because it has this reality that he feels the pull of obligation.[33]

At this point, Niebuhr links theological realism and moral realism. Statements about God are not simply expressions of emotion or acts of personal commitment. Theological claims have cognitive content. They may be true or false. True statements about God are true because they accurately represent a reality independent of the concepts, theories, and evidence we have pertaining to that reality.

[33] *Ibid.*, p. 5.

A moral realist who is not also a theological realist could affirm the adjudication of divergent interests that moral judgments make possible. It is precisely the point of moral realism that moral claims are not just a more emphatic way of asserting one's own desires. Moral claims are based on knowledge of needs and constraints which are essential to human life, individual and social. Moral principles resolve conflicts between different wants and values by identifying the aims and purposes we are obliged to support, regardless of our preferences. What the moral realist might well doubt is the theological claim that this harmonization of aims and purposes can be carried on indefinitely, and that each person's ultimate interest lies in that final harmony of life with life, and not in any of the relationships, plans, or commitments he or she values more immediately. The moral realist can affirm moral truths without joining in the theological realist's affirmation that the law of life is love.[34]

Many contemporary philosophers, in fact, hesitate to affirm any realism that claims such comprehensive knowledge. The problem with the older metaphysical realism, these critics suggest, is precisely that it promises this "God's-eye point of view" of reality.[35] Realism fell into disrepute because it seemed to require that there be one and only one true account of reality, which presents things exactly as they are, and not as they are related to any particular observer's point of view. Moral realism is doubly suspect, because it not only claims that there is one and only one correct view of moral reality, but also – because it is *moral* reality that is under consideration – claims moral authority to impose the imperatives that the one correct view dictates on those who hold to other interests and opinions. For those who reject the authoritarianism of such moral commitments as immoral in themselves, any credible form of moral realism must adopt a more pragmatic theory of moral truth, offering its account of moral reality as the best

[34] Cf. Niebuhr, "The law of [human] nature is love, a harmonious relation of life to life in obedience to the divine centre and source of . . . life," *The Nature and Destiny of Man*, I, 16.

[35] Cf. Hilary Putnam's critique in *Reason, Truth, and History* (Cambridge: Cambridge University Press, 1981), pp. 49–74.

guide to human living among the alternative accounts in a particular historical situation, rather than as a universal law of life. For some, that means that credible moral realism must avoid theological realism.

To speak theologically of "the will and nature of God" as a reality in which the conflicting impulses and purposes that rend individual lives and human communities are unified, or as a law according to which all persons could live in harmony is not, however, to claim that we can give a complete account of that reality or that we know everything that law requires. To claim that God is real is not to claim for oneself a "God's-eye point of view" of either the natural or the moral world. Indeed, the religious conviction that such a perspective belongs to God alone may be the best way to insure that no person or group can lay a claim to it.

From an early point in his work, Niebuhr adopts this sort of theological realism. Indeed, it is for him the key to understanding the theological and moral language of scripture and a guide to Christian proclamation today. Niebuhr contrasts the prophetic faith of Christianity and Judaism both to rational religion, which treats knowledge of God like any other knowing, and to mysticism, which locates God in an incomprehensible mystery beyond history. Christianity speaks in myths and symbols which relate God to the realities of our own experience. The mythic representation is always incomplete and partial. By the criterion of rational coherence, it always fails as knowledge. Yet the myth apprehends a coherence in God which the reason of the myth-maker cannot completely formulate.

In this sense the myth alone is capable of picturing the world as a realm of coherence and meaning without defying the facts of incoherence. Its world is coherent because all facts in it are related to some central source of meaning; but [it] is not rationally coherent because the myth is not under the abortive necessity of relating all things to each other in terms of immediate rational unity.[36]

[36] Niebuhr, *An Interpretation of Christian Ethics*, p. 16. Niebuhr gives considerable attention to the role of myth in Christian thought in the mid-1930s, and the theme reappears periodically throughout his later works. An important early statement is found in "The Truth in Myths," in *The Nature of Religious Experience: Essays in Honor*

Clearly, the important feature of myth for Niebuhr is neither its narrative structure nor its literal meaning, but its paradoxical relationship to the patterns of rational coherence by which we usually identify a statement as true. The myth is not coherent as a literal representation of the known facts, but it deals with aspects of the world in which ignorance, uncertainty, and conflict render the facts themselves incoherent. By pointing to the possibility of a resolution beyond the present conflicts, the myth represents a world that is more coherent than the world of the facts, though of course the myth cannot hold up as a statement of what those facts are.

Someone who understands theological language in this way is more concerned with the cognitivist claim of theological realism that theological propositions can be true than with the truth value of specific traditional theological formulations. Moral realists assert that moral statements can be true or false as a necessary condition for their more important claim that some specific moral statement is true. Theological realists may have to acknowledge that, by these tests of truth, many of their statements about "the will and nature of God" are false.

Niebuhr acknowledges this paradox in a famous sermon on Paul's claim that the ministers of God will always be known "by honor and dishonor, by evil report and good report; as deceivers, yet true ..." (2 Corinthians 6:8). "For what is true in the Christian religion can be expressed only in symbols which contain a degree of provisional and superficial deception. Every apologist of the Christian faith might well, therefore, make the Pauline phrase his own. We do teach the truth by deception. We are deceivers, yet true."[37]

The point clearly extends to the moral claims that Christians make about God. To speak of the requirements of God's justice

of D. C. *Macintosh* (New York: Harper and Bros., 1937), pp. 117–35. See also "Coherence, Incoherence, and Christian Faith," in *Christian Realism and Political Problems* (New York: Charles Scribner's Sons, 1953), pp. 175–203. For a recent interpretation of Niebuhr's work which considers the role of myth in ethics, see Kenneth Durkin, *Reinhold Niebuhr* (Harrisburg, Pa.: Morehouse Publishing, 1991), pp. 75–94.

[37] Reinhold Niebuhr, *Beyond Tragedy: Essays on the Christian Interpretation of History* (New York: Charles Scribner's Sons, 1937), p. 3.

is to demand justice with a specificity and certainty that we cannot, in fact, provide in particular cases. To say that love is the law of life asserts a unity of human purposes that we cannot demonstrate. Yet these propositions are more true than an account of the moral life that reduces it to the partial perspectives and intractable conflicts of which we can give an accurate account.

MYTH AND MORAL TRUTH

Closer attention to the symbolic or mythic use of moral language should clear up the misconception that theological realism necessarily involves a "God's-eye point of view" of moral truth. It still requires an account of how this moral language relates to the truth claims of moral realism.

The simplest answer is that Niebuhr's theological realism provides an explanation of how moral language is meaningful, rather than a set of specific moral claims that it holds to be true. Niebuhr articulates the point of relating an ultimate moral law of love to the reality of God by saying that morality requires a meaningful universe. We will have to explore this at much greater length in Chapter One, but the point can be put briefly by recalling that, in a theological realism which culminates in the divine nature as love, a moral resolution unifies all human aims and interests in a harmony of life with life which conforms to the unity and love of the divine nature itself. This is an impossible ideal, not only in the sense that we can never fully achieve it, but also in the sense that we cannot fully grasp it by reason. Although we affirm that any specific conflict between persons is susceptible to a resolution in accordance with the law of love, we cannot argue directly from the law of love to the requirements of love for that situation. What we can determine is a resolution to conflicts, perhaps in accordance with the moral realities of human nature, that reconciles some interests, but not others; a resolution that creates some human unity, but perhaps at the ironic cost of setting that new unity at odds with other groups and interests.

Those who reject a "God's-eye point of view" of moral

reality may suggest that this is, in fact, all that our moral solutions ever come to. Moral answers are distinguishable from – and preferable to – continued conflict or the imposition of a solution by brute force, but there is no guarantee that the moral answers will all be compatible with one another, or that there will not be tragic conflicts in which equally valid moral claims require contradictory courses of action.

The theological realist suggests that this minimal moral realism is simply inadequate to the meaning we give to moral obligation. When we require the suppression of intense desires and the sacrifice of long-sought personal goals to moral requirements, it is not simply because the moral requirements represent a wider interest group. We cannot account for the difference in our language and in our lives between a sober prudence and moral courage without the assumption that the meanings of our moral terms are linked to claims of ultimate significance, rather than to a better calculation of proximate interests. "All life stands under responsibility to this loving will. In one sense the ethic which results from this command of love is related to any possible ethical system; for all moral demands are demands of unity."[38]

The minimal moral realist will no doubt want to offer another way to understand the meaning of moral terms. Indeed, he or she will argue that if there is no ultimate unity in reality, then there will have to be another way to understand the meaning of moral terms, lest moral language be literally meaningless. Niebuhr's account of moral meaning is not evidence for the truth of theological realism, although he sometimes writes as though he thinks it is. Rather, the Niebuhrian account offers a distinctive way to relate moral meaning to theological realism.

Unlike divine command metaethics, for example, Christian Realism does not argue that moral imperatives are meaningful only insofar as they can be understood as commands of God.[39]

---

[38] Niebuhr, *An Interpretation of Christian Ethics*, p. 23.
[39] Cf. Robert M. Adams, "A Modified Divine Command Theory of Ethical Wrongness," in Gene Outka and John P. Reeder, eds., *Religion and Morality* (Garden City: Anchor, 1973), pp. 318–47; "Divine Command Metaethics Modified Again," *Journal of Religious Ethics* 7 (Spring, 1979), 66–79.

Moral language, rather, resolves conflicts between persons and groups by overruling interests and preferences in favor of considerations that are basic to the human life that all share. Those moral reference points in the realities of human nature have the same moral meaning whether they are articulated by a minimal moral realist or by a theological realist. The theological realist argues in addition that the overriding character of moral obligations, and especially their power to require the sacrifice of even the most essential personal interests, cannot be understood unless we suppose that the resolutions to conflict that moral considerations impose are not themselves in conflict, but bespeak an ultimate unity. The minimal moral realist and the theological realist share an understanding of what it means to say that something is morally required. Unlike, say, a divine command theorist and a reductive naturalist, they do not differ from the outset over what it means to say that an act is moral. But the theological realist asserts that an ultimate unity is essential to these proximate moral meanings, even though it cannot be grasped except in mythic and symbolic terms.

Niebuhr's interest in this ultimate meaning of morality centers on the way it affects proximate moral choices. The Christian ideal of love cannot directly guide ordinary moral choices, because it has no place for the prudent balancing of competing interests that most of these decisions are about. Trying to apply it directly yields only confusion, or illusions about our own virtue. Still, there are differences between the decisions of those who attend to the ideal and those who ignore it. The differences may become apparent only over time, in the persistence and courage that shapes the search for moral solutions, or in an unwillingness to settle for obvious answers.

In his later writings, Niebuhr speaks of these ethical ideals as "regulative principles" of moral and political choice.[40] Ideals which cannot possibly be met in ordinary experience nonetheless shape daily moral choices by setting limits within which the choices must fall, or more to the point, pulling the choices in a

---

[40] Reinhold Niebuhr, "Liberty and Equality," in *Pious and Secular America* (New York: Charles Scribner's Sons, 1958), pp. 185–98.

certain direction. If each moral choice falls well below the ideal of love, there is still the possibility that the ideal will make any particular choice more attentive to the needs of the neighbor than it otherwise would be; and there is the realistic hope that though every choice must fall below the demands of the ideal, it need not fall below the level of our previous choices.

Niebuhr's discussion of moral ideals focuses on the idea of love, and specifically on the self-sacrificial love or *agape* that he regards as the highest expression of divine goodness.[41] It appears, however, that the concept of a "regulative principle" also explains the normative role of many general moral ideas, such as justice and equality.[42]

Regulative principles are needed because moral and theological realism do not provide a single, determinate account of what our moral obligations are. Even with a highly developed understanding of the possibilities and constraints of human nature, it is likely that more than one set of plausible claims will emerge in concrete situations of moral choice, particularly where these choices regard complex social and political situations. One need not be a moral cynic, using moral language only as a cloak for the pursuit of self-interest, to find a moral framework that fits one's own purposes rather comfortably. Homeowners can act to protect property values and community standards with the satisfaction that they are protecting real social goods. The claims of those who want a halfway house or sheltered workshop in the neighborhood may have to be passed over for the sake of the greater good. A business proprietor can reject taxation to aid the homeless or to improve the local schools in favor of maintaining a climate more favorable to enterprise. That, too, is a choice for which moral reasons can be given.

[41] Niebuhr, *The Nature and Destiny of Man*, II, 68–76.

[42] Niebuhr in fact suggests at points that these norms can be arranged in a hierarchy in which mutual love is regulated by the ideal of sacrificial love (*The Nature and Destiny of Man*, II, 69), or in which love is the regulative principle of liberty and equality, which in turn serve as regulative principles of justice. While the reader needs to pay attention to the use Niebuhr makes of these hierarchies in each presentation of them, I do not think that a systematic development of them is a good vehicle for the exposition of Niebuhr's ethics. Formally, the hierarchical structure is too rigid, and

What, then, might require a little further searching of the limits of one's own interests? Not the moral considerations themselves. They rule out the grosser forms of self-service at the expense of others, and in the real conflicts of life it is not a negligible achievement to move from a mere opposition of wants and interests to an argument based on moral principles. But moral considerations alone do not require the generosity and spirit of self-sacrifice that might allow persons who have to balance a variety of considerations to move from moral argument to moral agreement. What prevents realistic moral disagreements from "degenerating into mere calculation of advantage"[43] is the theological realist's conviction that any understanding of these disagreements that presents them as ultimate conflicts must at some point be false. So the possibility for agreement, at whatever cost to my own aims and interests, must always be acknowledged; and where it seems essential to maintain the opposition, this must be done with both a seriousness appropriate to the issues at stake and a humility born of the recognition that since one of us, at least, must be wrong, it may be me. Thus does theological realism, which insists on an ideal of love that is real in the will and nature of God, have its effects on a situation of choice in which the reality of love may be anything but evident.

CONFIDENCE AND CRITICISM

In this introduction, we have separately considered several aspects of Christian Realism which must work closely together in the actual assessment of social and political situations. Christian Realism is a combination of different "realisms" – political, moral, and theological. The distinctive insights come as these perspectives are drawn into a relationship in which no one of their conclusions is definitive, but from which, likewise, none can be omitted. The moral truths that Christian Realism

details of the relationships vary significantly in different essays. For further discussion, see Chapter Five.

43 Reinhold Niebuhr, *Faith and History: A Comparison of Christian and Modern Views of History* (New York: Charles Scribner's Sons, 1949), p. 193.

claims depend on an attentiveness to all of the forces at work in a situation, *and* on the limits imposed by human nature, *and* on the possibilities opened by love. "Man's capacity for justice makes democracy possible; but man's inclination to injustice makes democracy necessary," Niebuhr once wrote, in what has become perhaps the most famous of his many aphorisms.[44] His deft summaries of the human situation reflect his own wisdom and a gift for well-turned phrases, but it should by now be apparent that the insights packed into this aphorism – its attentiveness to prevailing circumstances, human nature, and human aspirations – result from more than an intuitive combination of the right elements.

Niebuhr was known as a pessimist, critical of the illusions of faith and the pride of nations. *Time* magazine captured the popular impression of his message with a 1948 cover story captioned "Man's story is not a success story."[45] While that aptly summarizes his criticism of the optimism of liberal Christianity, Niebuhr was aware that the currents of Christian thought had in fact often flowed in the opposite direction. Appreciation of the human tendency to oppose God led some Christian theologians, notably Luther, to a "too consistent pessimism" about human possibilities.[46] The Christian Realist must temper this pessimism with hope in God's power to reconcile forces now opposed. Just as there can be no simple resolution that ignores self-interest and power, there can be no simple limit on the possibilities for new arrangements that achieve the real aims of both sides of old enmities.[47]

Christian Realists see the possibilities that lie in both directions from present conflicts. In their combination of political and theological realism, there are no rules that tell them how to weigh the different possibilities. Facts that demand attention must be carefully considered, and courses of action based on these considerations have to be compared to alternative pro-

---

[44] Niebuhr, *The Children of Light and the Children of Darkness*, p. xiii.
[45] Fox, *Reinhold Niebuhr*, p. 233.
[46] Niebuhr, *The Children of Light and the Children of Darkness*, p. 44. The criticism is extended to Augustine in some of Niebuhr's later works. See *Christian Realism and Political Problems*, p. 127.
[47] Niebuhr, *The Children of Light and the Children of Darkness*, pp. 48–50.

posals which may have more systematic consistency, but which incorporate less of the political, moral, and theological reality against which every choice must be made. Taken together, this combination of self-criticism and critical thinking, of political realism's skepticism and theological realism's hope, provides a more adequate understanding of contemporary events than those accounts which rest on less comprehensive visions.

These resources give us some treasures to contribute to the community in its struggle for justice. Among them are an understanding of the fragmentary character of all human virtue; the tentative character of all schemes of justice, since they are subject to the flow of history; the irrevocable character of the "moral law" transcending all historical relativities; and the hazardous judgments which must be made to establish justice between the competing forces and interests.[48]

For Christian Realists, understandings of justice and history follow from an understanding of God's relationship to the values that spark human conflict and guide human aspirations. The reason for paying attention to the theological interpretation of events is that the theologian's beliefs about the ultimate resolution of human conflicts yield a better grasp of present possibilities. In the risks and uncertainties of modern political life, everyone seeks a realistic assessment of persons and events. Theological realism insists that when this assessment does not include the ultimate context of human choice and action, it will shortly go wrong in its dealings with people and its anticipations of current events.

These insights certainly do not "prove" the truth of Christian faith, but they provide a grasp of issues and events that is a relevant standard of comparison to other ways of understanding justice and history.[49] Niebuhr's Christian Realism was both confident and critical. It was critical because he made no absolute claims for his own perspective. Faith can be distorted by self-interest, lulled into sentimental piety, or lured into fanatical excesses. Niebuhr could analyze those errors with a clarity and urgency born of the conviction that they are never

[48] *Ibid.*, p. 66.   [49] Cf. Niebuhr, *Faith and History*, pp. 151–53.

far removed from even our most sincere efforts to find moral and political truth. Yet after all the critical insights, Niebuhr remained confident that Christian Realism made more sense of problematic historical situations than other interpretations. Niebuhr's criticism required no retreat into a language of faith that was impervious to challenge. He was confident that when subjected to those same criticisms, "the truth of faith is correlated with all truths which may be known by scientific and philosophical disciplines and proves itself a resource for coordinating them into a deeper and wider system of coherence."[50]

Today, a reinterpretation of Niebuhr's Christian Realism must capture both the criticism and the confidence. Both the Christian neo-conservatives who find in Niebuhr a prophet of triumphant liberal democracy and the Christian radicals who dismiss him as an "apologist for power" need to recover the penetrating insight that discovers the taint of self-interest in every moral position, including one's own.[51] What all sides—and perhaps most especially the Protestant liberals who are Niebuhr's direct descendants—need, however, is a recovery of the Niebuhrian confidence that acknowledges the limitations of its own perspective without reducing the moral commitment to its principal insights. Christian Realism teaches us how to do Christian theology in a modern intellectual world where critical consciousness makes us most suspicious of precisely those things we most strongly believe.

Niebuhr realized that Christianity survives in human history not as a set of clear and distinct ideas, but as a locus of possibilities that always transcend more immediate forms of thought and action. That which is clear, distinct, and definitive in human life has its day and disappears. What endures must have a measure of flexibility and ambiguity that is adaptable to the incoherences of real experience. Great truths require mythic expression, and those who articulate them in the modern world will always appear "as deceivers yet true."

---

[50] *Ibid.*, p. 152.

[51] See, for example, Michael Novak, "Reinhold Niebuhr: Model for Neoconservatives," *Christian Century* 103 (January 22, 1986), 69–71; and Bill Kellerman, "Apologist of Power: The Long Shadow of Reinhold Niebuhr's Christian Realism," *Sojourners* 16 (March, 1987), 15–20.

The myth, however, is not just an empty vessel. It draws our thinking in definite ways, serving as a "regulative principle" for more specific moral choices. Love defies reduction to a universally valid rule of action, but it enables us to make judgments about the choices that are actually before us. It allows us to distinguish those who move toward the impossible ideal from those who move away from it.

There are no doubt psychological and cultural pre-conditions that explain why Niebuhr's confidence was so easily sustained and so well received in the middle decades of the twentieth century, just as there are no doubt elements of genius in his own insights that are lost in any attempt to generalize his message. Nevertheless, this book is written with my own confidence that a systematic treatment of the main elements of Reinhold Niebuhr's Christian Realism will help us to formulate a version of it that will be adequate to the tasks of Christian ethics in our own day.

Those main elements have already been identified in this introduction. In what follows, we will treat them in reverse order of their appearance here. Chapter One will further explore Niebuhr's theological realism and its relationship to distinctive currents in American Protestant thought. Chapters Two and Three will discuss Christian Realism's moral realism, relating it more clearly to other versions of ethical naturalism and to natural law thought, and contrasting it to the dominant versions of moral rationalism and moral relativism in religious ethics today. Chapter Four will return us to the testing of theological and moral insights against the multiple demands of politics and lead us toward a more synthetic statement about justice and love with which, in Chapter Five, we will bring the study to a close.

CHAPTER I

God

STARTING WITH THEOLOGY

Reinhold Niebuhr challenged both liberalism and orthodoxy with "theological realism." The American theologians who formulated "theological realism" did not expect to provide a conclusive argument for their beliefs, but they did offer what Niebuhr would call "a limited rational validation of the truth of the Gospel." Niebuhr's contribution was both to show how closely this pragmatic theological realism could be related to other moral discourses, and to illuminate the specific difference that it makes to affirm that God is the center of meaning in a morally coherent universe.

Christian Realism concentrates on the assessment of specific political situations and social choices. It does not always speak explicitly of God. Larry Rasmussen observes that Reinhold Niebuhr "was at his very best in his ability to render a theological interpretation of events for a wide audience, as a basis for common action. But precisely because of the audience's diverse beliefs, Niebuhr often cast his case in ways which left his Christian presuppositions and convictions unspoken."[1] Both friends and critics have sometimes assumed that this means that the theology of Christian Realism is superfluous, a pious footnote to an analysis that can be accepted or rejected on its own terms. Political thinkers admired Reinhold Niebuhr's insights into the fundamental importance of power in democratic politics or his warnings to America not to take its

---

[1] Larry Rasmussen, "Reinhold Niebuhr: Public Theologian," *Cross Currents*, 38 (Summer, 1988), 201.

own virtues too seriously, but many thought that these insights could stand on their own, without the theological dynamics to which they were linked in Niebuhr's mind. They have been called the "atheists for Niebuhr."[2]

Theologians have also detected a gap between realistic politics and the convictions of faith, but they have supposed this means that the Christian Realist has given up theology in order to arrive at politics. A theologian critical of *Moral Man and Immoral Society* charged that Niebuhr had abandoned "the idea that Christianity has a unique function to fulfill in the process of social transformation."[3] Perhaps these critics should be called "theists against Niebuhr." If their judgment seems too harsh, many more moderate critics would agree with James Gustafson's assessment that Niebuhr's Christian Realism is "theology in the service of ethics."[4]

Whether from friends or critics, these evaluations pose in acute form a dilemma that faces all theological reflections in an age of many faiths or no apparent faith: If one aims to speak about problems and choices that affect everyone in a society, the analysis must be made in terms that are widely accepted and understood, and it may be difficult to say anything at all about God. But if one tries to exercise the theologian's vocation to speak a distinctive word about God, those of other faiths or no faith may dismiss it as a private meditation, an esoteric religious idea that has no relevance for their lives and choices.

A realistic appeal for racial justice, or arms control, or care for the poor must convince us that its author knows the facts of the case, comprehends the motivations of those who must decide and act, and understands what is at stake for society in the choices at hand. A religious statement that does this well, whether it be a papal encyclical on economic development, a theologian's essay on church and state, or a pastor's letter to the editor about the plight of the homeless, may make an

---

[2] See Daniel F. Rice, *Reinhold Niebuhr and John Dewey: An American Odyssey*, p. 217.
[3] Francis Pickens Miller directed this criticism to Niebuhr in 1933. Quoted in Fox, *Reinhold Niebuhr*, p. 142.
[4] James Gustafson, "Theology in the Service of Ethics: An Interpretation of Reinhold Niebuhr's Theological Ethics," in Richard Harries, ed., *Reinhold Niebuhr and the Issues of Our Time* (Grand Rapids: Eerdmans, 1986), pp. 24–45.

important difference in the public discussion. It is just when these statements are most effective, however, that they elicit the question that Jeffrey Stout puts to contemporary theologians who begin their work with an interpretation of common human experience: What does the idea of God add to this account?[5] What new claims about the human situation do we make by saying that God is present in the needs or goals that we all understand? What motives emerge that were not already available to us? What actions are we permitted or required to take that a non-religious analysis would not also permit or require? Does belief in God make it reasonable for us to do or to risk things that a reasonable person who did not believe in God would not do or risk?

While God must be known in images and metaphors drawn from all aspects of human experience, the idea of God must refer to more than just those experiences if the theologian has anything to say that cannot also be said by the psychologist, the political scientist, or the literary critic.[6] It may ask too much to require that each and every aspect of our human circumstances be altered by an immediate relationship to divine reality. (It strains the point to think that a theistic choice of painting contractors should be much different from a responsible secular one.) If the reality of God has any practical meaning, however, it should make some difference to the ways we understand our choices on the whole in the major activities of human life – in economics, politics, and family life, as well as in religion.

On this point, Reinhold Niebuhr's realistic politics was matched by theological realism. The complex interactions of interest groups, historical forces, and persistent human needs for power and security each demand their own elaborate theoretical explanations, and Niebuhr can be eloquent in his analysis of the social strains imposed by class conflicts or the ideological justifications that palliate inequalities of wealth and privilege. In the end, however, human conflict and human

---

[5] Jeffrey Stout, *Ethics After Babel* (Boston: Beacon Press, 1988), p. 183.
[6] For a more developed statement of this point, see Janet M. Soskice, *Metaphor and Religious Language* (Oxford: Oxford University Press, 1985), pp. 104–8.

aspirations must be understood in relation to God, who sets limits on the conflict and affirms human unity, while at the same time judging every particular attempt to formulate that unity and every claim to have achieved it.

CONFIDENCE

The idea that God is love is a symbol for an ultimate unity of lives and interests in which all proximate conflicts are resolved. "The ultimate confidence in the meaningfulness of life, therefore, rests upon a faith in the final unity, which transcends the world's chaos as certainly as it is basic to the world's order."[7]

For the Christian Realist, God is what H. Richard Niebuhr would later call "the center of value," the One in whom every real value must cohere and from whose perspective every human community must be evaluated.[8] So understood, 'God' cannot be just a name for the complex of values that I hold or that my culture teaches. God is not a program that I, or my party, or my faith has designed to settle conflicts on our own terms. Any resolution of conflict that is more than the simple capitulation of one side to another involves transcending the conflict toward a new harmony. The resolution of all conflicts, however, exceeds not only the practical limits of our circumstances, but also the creative possibilities of human consciousness. A unity that gives meaning to all particular purposes "transcends the world beyond [our] own capacity to transcend it."[9]

The Christian Realist argues that belief in this transcendent center of value makes a difference in the way persons respond to aspirations and conflicts. The possibility of unity is known by faith and not by sight. Experience is, in fact, uncertain about this "final unity which transcends the world's chaos."[10]

---

[7] Niebuhr, *An Interpretation of Christian Ethics*, pp. 22–23.
[8] H. Richard Niebuhr, "The Center of Value," in *Radical Monotheism and Western Culture* (New York: Harper and Row, 1960), pp. 100–13.
[9] Niebuhr, *The Nature and Destiny of Man*, I, 164.
[10] Niebuhr occasionally writes as though human beings have an instinctive conviction that "there is only one world and that it is a cosmos" (*Christian Realism and Political Problems*, p. 176). That is, he presents a Christian *interpretation* of experience as if it

There is no conclusive evidence that it *is* so, and any believable assertion of unity will have to deal with the abundant evidence of chaos. Our own aims and desires and those we recognize in persons around us cannot all be satisfied. Perhaps, as one line of political realism has insisted since the beginning of the modern age, when the necessary choices are made, the final unity is not God, but bare survival. People will agree only on those constraints they must accept if they are not to be destroyed in their pursuit of goods they cannot share.[11]

If there is a final unity that goes beyond this mutual restraint, we will have to say that some of the things that people want are wrong – bad for themselves as well as for others. But if there is a final unity, we must also insist that people will recognize their own good in it, that they will choose it, or that they could choose it, over the partial and incomplete goods that satisfy their own interests at the expense of the final unity.

The Christian Realist does not stubbornly assert unity in the face of conflict, or sentimentally dwell on the "harmony of life with life" while everyone else is seething with rage. Where aims and goals are radically opposed, as between a wealthy, urban elite and the revolutionary movements of the poor in Central America, or between the nuclear power industry and ecological movements in the United States, political realism requires us not to underestimate the depth of the conflict, and not to overlook the possibility that either side will employ distorted moral appeals and subvert established moral standards in order to achieve its goals. Ringing appeals to freedom combined with terroristic repression of dissent, or appeals to

---

were simply a *report* of experience. Clearly these claims, and the similar claim that "The self feels itself in dialogue with God," are more than uninterpreted statements of what everyone, in fact, experiences (see Niebuhr, *The Self and the Dramas of History*, p. 96). We will do well to be more clear from the outset than Niebuhr was on this point. What we must also insist, however, is that to acknowledge that a formulation is a Christian interpretation of experience does not *a priori* render it unintelligible to those who do not share Christian convictions. The issue of how interpretations of experience in one community or tradition are related to the interpretations of others remains a question for discussion.

[11] The classic statement of this minimal condition for political unity is found in Thomas Hobbes, *Leviathan*, ed. C.B. Macpherson (Harmondsworth: Penguin Books, 1968 [first published in 1651]).

scientific objectivity combined with suppressed data and the intimidation of researchers are exactly what we should expect.

But we also expect something else. We expect that the forces which prevail in the end will be those that aim to make the resources for a good life available to everyone, and that use the earth's resources in ways that enhance the lives of future generations. We do not suppose that any one group has the whole truth about this future. We are suspicious of those whose vision of a just and sustainable society corresponds too closely to their own present interests, and we look for anticipations of a better future especially among the people whose lives are diminished and whose hopes are thwarted by the way things are done now.

Nevertheless, our confidence does not rest in particular plans and goals, but in a morally coherent universe, in which we may discover human aims and goals that do not set us in ultimate conflict with one another, and in which our aspirations for unity are not mocked. Our confidence rests in God.

CRITICISM

Answering Jeffrey Stout's question this way, however, appears to bring us around to face the other half of the modern theologian's dilemma.[12] Have we interpreted events in a way that can make sense only to those who share our faith? Are those who do not share it justified in ignoring what we have to say and going on about the business of acquiring power and pursuing interests?

The answer to these questions is complex, and it requires further investigation of the American theological movement that identified itself as "theological realism" or "religious realism" during the 1930s. Reinhold Niebuhr participated in these discussions, and the understanding of religious truth that the movement developed became the presupposition of his own notion of a "limited rational validation" of the claims of Christianity.[13]

---

[12] See page 34 above.   [13] Niebuhr, *Faith and History*, p. 152.

In the aftermath of World War I, the American realists shared with Karl Barth and other European theologians a strong sense of the need for a Christian response to the failures of Western culture and politics. In place of progressive, liberal convictions about the links between Christianity and social progress, these theologians believed that Christian truth will contradict the hopes and presumptions of modern society. Christian claims about the ultimate unity of human life do not simply anticipate the assurances of modern social science. The empirical evidence regarding human destiny is decidedly ambiguous. "The points of reference for the structure of the meaning of history in the Christian faith are obviously not found by an empirical analysis of the observable structures and coherences of history. They are 'revelations,' apprehended by faith, of the character and purposes of God."[14] However one understands the meaning of revelation, the final unity of human life that is central to the Christian's moral confidence is not demonstrable by methods of argument and investigation that proceed simply on the basis of generally acknowledged facts about the world. To suggest otherwise would eliminate the tension between Christian faith and human wisdom that is central to the theological critique of the world's injustice, violence, and lack of harmony. On this key point, the Protestant theologies that emerged in the decades after World War I were generally in agreement.

The American theological realists, however, had available a philosophical system that provided more persuasive links between experience and action than the dominant European philosophies. Beginning with the works of Charles Sanders Peirce (1839–1916) and William James (1842–1910) in the nineteenth century, and continuing in the twentieth with John Dewey (1859–1952) and George Herbert Mead (1863–1931), the philosophy that Peirce named 'pragmatism' developed a method for assessing ideas in terms of their coherence with the other ideas by which we guide actions and make choices. For the theological realists a modified pragmatism opened the way

14 *Ibid.*, p. 136.

to a distinctive form of the apologetic theology which Barth rejected root and branch.[15] While there is no proof of Christian truth "which would compel conviction on purely rational grounds," Niebuhr wrote, "there is nevertheless a positive apologetic task. It consists in correlating the truth, apprehended by faith and repentance, to truths about life and history gained generally in experience."[16]

Like other religious thinkers, the theological realists were wary of pragmatic philosophy because it seemed to imply cognitive relativism, a plurality of mutually incompatible, yet equally workable, accounts of reality. Instead of completely rejecting pragmatism, however, these theologians employed its criteria of coherence and fruitfulness for action as a method of testing rival interpretations of human nature and history. Pragmatism cannot demonstrate that ideological systems, social theories, or religions are true, but it can show that one or another of them provides a better way of anticipating future events and making choices in light of the likely outcomes. Since that is a large part of the interest people have in any comprehensive account of human life, they can hardly be indifferent to an argument that Christianity provides such an account more adequately than other systems, even if that pragmatic demonstration fails to "prove" that all human claims and interests are limited in the way that the Christian idea of God implies.[17]

So the Christian Realist denies that those who do not share

---

[15] The Barthian rejection of apologetics is echoed by theologians who argue that there is no generally shared discourse in which the claims of a religious tradition can be objectively evaluated. See William Placher, *Unapologetic Theology: A Christian Voice in a Pluralistic Conversation* (Louisville: Westminster/John Knox Press, 1989). It would take us too far afield to provide a complete response to these current developments in American theology here, though our discussion of the work of Stanley Hauerwas in Chapter Two will suggest a Christian Realist response.

[16] *Ibid.*, p. 165.

[17] Thus the theological realists understood their claims about God not as rational demonstrations, but as what Charles Taylor has recently called "an articulation of what is crucial to the world in one's best account." See Charles Taylor, *Sources of the Self: The Making of the Modern Identity* (Cambridge, Mass.: Harvard University Press, 1989), p. 76. Cf. the concept of a "relatively adequate" interpretation in David Tracy, *Plurality and Ambiguity* (San Francisco: Harper and Row, 1987), pp. 22–23.

faith in the final unity of human life are intellectually free to go about the business of acquiring power and pursuing interests. And the Christian Realist denies with equal vigor that the Christian is free to abandon the effort to make sense of faith in practical terms and to leave the world to its own devices. It is not possible to prove that there is a "final unity, which transcends the world's chaos as certainly as it is basic to the world's order," but it is possible to disturb those who find the pursuit and protection of their own interests amidst a chaos of irreconcilable conflict a fully adequate account of the circumstances of human life. That modest goal was sufficient to engage Reinhold Niebuhr's tremendous energies.

The method of this "Christian pragmatism"[18] is implicit in the argument of *The Nature and Destiny of Man*, which makes a case for the adequacy of a Christian or biblical understanding of human nature and history against a variety of modern interpretations.[19] It is argued explicitly in *Faith and History*.[20] The origins, however, can be seen in Niebuhr's earliest work, in the influences of his mentors and colleagues, and in a group who for a couple of decades called themselves "The Younger Theologians."

THE SEARCH FOR REALISM

The theologians' search for more adequate ways of speaking about God and about human society was part of a broader reassessment of Western civilization that began during World War I. After several decades of rapid industrial development, colonial expansion, and missionary extension of Christianity, the states of Europe and North America were plunged into a bloody conflict that halted processes of development and expansion, and shook confidence in the progress of civilization itself.

The brutality of trench warfare and the loss of a generation

[18] See page 48 below.
[19] See Niebuhr's preface to *The Nature and Destiny of Man*, I, vii.
[20] See especially chapter 10, "The Validation of the Christian View of Life and History," *Faith and History*, pp. 151–70.

of youth raised questions about Western society that cut deeper than the poverty and corruption that accompanied change and growth. One had to ask not only whether these social evils could be avoided, but whether the very things regarded as social values had not become corrupt and destructive. The human capacity for goodness seemed less reliable than it had before, and the propensity to evil seemed more insidious.

Liberal Protestant theology, which since the early nineteenth century had based many of its theological claims on human consciousness of value and awe as experiences of the presence of God, had now to contend not only with a skepticism which suggested that these experiences were merely projections of human wants and needs, but also with a nihilism that argued that the values attributed to God are not values at all. Ludwig Feuerbach had suggested nearly a century earlier that Christians mistakenly disvalue themselves by supposing that the best qualities they can conceive belong only to God, whereas these virtues really originate in themselves.[21] In the twentieth century, the question came to be whether the virtues themselves are the source of our problems. Fidelity elicits blind loyalty to race and nation, and justice provokes a rigid, self-righteous moralism that too quickly takes up arms to extirpate the unrighteous enemy.

Faced with these challenges, theologians proposed that divine reality challenges and shatters our claims to virtue, instead of confirming and fulfilling them. The claim to find God in human experience had been mistaken. The reality of God transcends that experience. The theologians' attempt to be politically realistic about the faded hopes of Western civilization required a realistic theology, affirmed boldly or cautiously against their liberal predecessors' emphasis on human experience.

In North America, Douglas Clyde Macintosh provided one of the more cautious formulations. In his introduction to a collection of essays titled *Religious Realism*, Macintosh wrote:

[21] Ludwig Feuerbach, *The Essence of Christianity*, trans. George Eliot (New York: Harper and Row, 1956).

Religious Realism, as the term is used in this volume, means centrally the view that a religious Object, such as may appropriately be called God, exists independently of our consciousness therefor, and is yet related to us in such a way that through reflection on experience in general and religious experience in particular, and without any dependence upon the familiar arguments for epistemological idealism, it is possible for us to gain either (as some would maintain) adequately verified knowledge or (as others would be content to affirm) a practically valuable and theoretically permissible faith not only that that religious Object exists but also, within whatever limits, as to what its nature is.[22]

Macintosh shared many of the hopes and commitments of the Social Gospel movement.[23] He had no wish to link Christianity to the isolationism and conservative political beliefs that enjoyed a new popularity in the United States after World War I. As a professor at Yale Divinity School, he became the center of a group of students and younger colleagues who did give new attention to the obstacles to the religious transformation of society, especially to the obstacles that reflect the Christians' own ambivalence toward the values they profess.

This loosely constituted group of "Younger Theologians" included both Reinhold Niebuhr, who had joined the faculty of Union Theological Seminary in New York in 1928, and his younger brother, H. Richard Niebuhr, who was himself already well established on the faculty at Yale. In one sense, their generational identification was correct, for though the Younger Theologians inevitably aged along with everyone else, they were distinguished from their predecessors in American theology by skepticism about prospects for "Christianizing the social order,"[24] and linked by that same skepticism to their European contemporaries, led by Karl Barth.

[22] Macintosh, ed., *Religious Realism*, p. v.
[23] Macintosh, a Canadian who had been a chaplain in World War I, became a pacifist. When his application to become a citizen of the United States was refused because he would not take an oath to defend the country, he initiated a legal challenge that was eventually decided (against Macintosh) in the United States Supreme Court. See John T. Noonan, *The Believer and the Powers That Are* (New York: Macmillan, 1987), p. 229.
[24] That slogan provided the title for Walter Rauschenbusch's most important statement of the Social Gospel program. See Rauschenbusch, *Christianizing the Social Order* (New York: Macmillan, 1912).

Barth epitomized the criticism of earlier efforts at Christian social reform in his *Epistle to the Romans*:

Asceticism and movements of reform have their place as parables and as representations, but in themselves they are of no value. In no sense can they ever be even a first step towards the Kingdom of Heaven. There is but one good and one evil, one pure and one impure. Before God everything is impure; and therefore nothing is especially impure.[25]

The Americans shared Barth's critical view of previous efforts at social reform, but they did not regard this critical attitude as a distinctively Christian message. Walter Marshall Horton, in an assessment of contemporary theology published in 1934, noted that realistic theology was part of a larger cultural force that included developments in politics, literature, and philosophy that also claimed to be "realistic."[26] What these realisms had in common, Horton thought, was a skepticism about the claims of important people and institutions. They were more inclined to uncover the greed of capitalists, the ambition of politicians, and the venality of the clergy than to romanticize their contributions to human progress.

The social criticism of the American religious realists had more in common with that of their secular counterparts than did Barth's work, and a constructive theological realism would require a similarly broad base. Barth's insistence on a realism grounded solely in the Word of God and rejecting all other points of reference had little appeal to the Americans. Horton suggested that the heirs of Calvinism were too recently emancipated to accept a theology that returned to scripture as the starting point for life in the modern world.[27] Perhaps more to the point, American theologians saw that scripture itself had been an important source of the illusions they wanted to combat. America's utopias were seldom secular, and their visions of material abundance and civic harmony drew imaginative details and persuasive power from the millennial hopes of

---

[25] Karl Barth, *The Epistle to the Romans*, trans. Edwin C. Hoskyns (New York: Oxford University Press, 1968), p. 517. This edition of Barth's *Römerbrief* was first published in Switzerland in 1921.

[26] Horton, *Realistic Theology*, pp. 10–15.   [27] *Ibid.*, pp. 36–37.

American Christianity. The notion that an earthly paradise could be built with America's people and material resources gained credence from an interpretation of scripture that said that this was, after all, God's own plan from the beginning.[28]

For too many Americans, the Bible was a key text in support of that view of history. Theological realism would have to convince Americans to rethink an optimistic faith in the light of political scandals, economic failures, and the tragedy of human conflict. The delicate task would be to separate genuine faith from cultural self-confidence without provoking the cynical response that had turned many people against both faith and culture. Reinhold Niebuhr explained this in a 1931 paper for the World's Student Christian Federation:

> In Anglo-Saxon countries the conflict between faith and reason is not insisted upon so sharply, and religious thought still expresses itself in terms less tragic than those upon which the Continent insists when it estimates the cultural and moral history of mankind . . . We may need the tragic conception of history and of the futility of moral effort, lest our religion sink into the sands of complacent moral optimism. But on the other hand we will continue to believe that we have a right to express ourselves religiously without completely sacrificing a philosophy of nature and of history which links our faith in God to the facts of common experience.[29]

For theological realism, the criterion of truth would be neither dogmatic orthodoxy nor fidelity to scripture, but coherence with *all* available sources of insight. In the effort to formulate an understanding of human experience adequate for twentieth-century life, theology cannot be ignored. That would be to accept uncritically the reductive naturalism that

---

[28] The idea that America is the focal point of a providential plan appears early in the nation's religious history. For an account of the emergence of this idea, see Ernest Lee Tuveson, *Redeemer Nation: The Idea of America's Millennial Role* (Chicago: University of Chicago Press, 1968). The early Christian Realists were perhaps more conscious of the influence of the biblical idea of the Kingdom of God on their Social Gospel predecessors at the end of the nineteenth century. H. Richard Niebuhr wrote of the significance of this idea of "the coming Kingdom" in his *The Kingdom of God in America* (New York: Harper and Row, 1959 [first published 1937]), pp. 127–63.

[29] Reinhold Niebuhr, "An American Approach to the Christian Message," in W. A. Visser 'tHooft, ed., *A Traffic in Knowledge: An International Symposium on the Christian Message* (London: Student Christian Movement Press, 1931), pp. 55–56.

sees all events in terms of material causes and the political cynicism that interprets all human aspirations as conflicting interests. Neither, however, can we assume that traditional religious ideas will remain unchanged in the encounter with modern knowledge. The point is to bring them together in a coherent understanding that discards none of the methods of inquiry by which people have located themselves in the world. Above all, the coherence must be achieved by squarely facing all the facts, including those that cast an unattractive light on our own society or on human accomplishments generally. Coherence is not a matter of wishful thinking about how things might work together, but of steady inquiry into the interactions that are really there. Walter Marshall Horton offered what is perhaps the best summary of the mood and method of theological realism when he wrote in 1934:

[The] word "realism" suggests to me, above all, a resolute determination to face all the facts of life candidly, beginning preferably with the most stubborn, perplexing, and disheartening ones, so that any lingering romantic illusions may be dispelled at the start; and then, *through* these stubborn facts and not *in spite of them*, to pierce as deep as one may into the solid structure of reality, until one finds whatever ground of courage, hope, and faith is *actually* there, independent of human preferences and desires, and so casts anchor in that ground.[30]

For many of its critics, Christian Realism is a pessimistic philosophy that holds little hope for peace or justice, and quickly yields to the requirements of power. Horton, by contrast, speaks of a methodological pessimism in service of Christian hope. Only when that hope directly confronts all the evidence of experience can it be distinguished from wishful thinking or misplaced confidence. The reality of God, unlike the illusions of self and nation, is consistent with all the evidence.

PRAGMATISM

Apart from the cultural and historical factors that made American theological realists attentive to the full range of human experience, the philosophy of pragmatism offered an

[30] Horton, *Realistic Theology*, p. 38.

alternative to the "correspondence" theory of truth, which treats true ideas simply as accurate depictions of reality. Pragmatism stresses the relationships among ideas, rather than the link between ideas and reality. As James put it, "True ideas are those that we can assimilate, validate, corroborate, and verify. False ideas are those we can not."[31]

Pragmatism in its origins is closely linked with American religious thought, although its leading exponents often had little use for conventional Christian doctrines and institutions. Peirce, the originator of pragmatism, gave considerable attention to the reconciliation of mathematical, scientific, and religious worldviews in a unified account of a single reality.[32] James, who became the best-known exponent of pragmatism, and the one whose views most influenced religious thought in the early twentieth century, produced a classic treatment of the psychology and philosophy of religious experience, but his radical pluralism tended to undermine the importance, if not the very possibility, of a monotheistic faith.[33]

In turn, American theologians in the twentieth century have given mixed responses to pragmatism. Protestants seeking to maintain a rational defense of orthodox religious truth have rejected it, and many Catholic thinkers have dismissed pragmatism as an overly simple assertion that "whatever works is right."[34] Liberal Protestants have, by contrast, endorsed elements of the pragmatic approach. If what is known of God must satisfy the rationalist critic that our idea of God corresponds to the reality of God, knowledge fails, and fideism or skepticism become the only alternatives. Douglas Clyde

[31] William James, "Pragmatism's Conception of Truth," in *The Writings of William James*, ed. John J. McDermott (New York: Random House, 1967), p. 430.

[32] For an account of Peirce's theology, see Robert S. Corrington, *An Introduction to C.S. Peirce* (Lanham, Md.: Rowman and Littlefield, 1993), pp. 68–72.

[33] See William James, *Varieties of Religious Experience* (New York: Modern Library, n.d.), pp. 514–16. On the place of pragmatism in the larger history of American philosophy and religious thought, see especially Bruce Kuklick, *Churchmen and Philosophers* (New Haven: Yale University Press, 1985), pp. 195–98.

[34] John Courtney Murray, for example, asserts: "For the pragmatist there are, properly speaking no truths; there are only results" (*We Hold These Truths* [New York: Sheed and Ward, 1960], p. ix). The Catholic philosopher Robert Johann offers a more positive appropriation of pragmatism in Catholic thought. See Robert O. Johann, *Building the Human* (New York: Herder and Herder, 1968).

Macintosh supported pragmatism against those stark alternatives, though he resisted the suggestion that religious ideas could be reduced to their implications for action.[35]

The distinctions that Macintosh sought to make between realistic theology and pragmatic philosophy are important, and we will attend to them in more detail later in this chapter.[36] Against a larger range of philosophical options, however, the differences between American Protestant theology and pragmatic philosophy must be seen in the context of agreements about how truth is known and how ideas are tested. Thus, Cornel West today places Niebuhr directly in the line of development of American pragmatism, and locates his work along with Sidney Hook and C. Wright Mills, secular philosophers who sought to apply the pragmatic perspective to the complexities of the world at mid-century.[37] By 1957, Niebuhr himself acknowledged that his work could be called a "Christian pragmatism."[38]

In contrast to those who argue that Christian political thought must begin with the certainties of Christian doctrine, Niebuhr defines Christian pragmatism as "the application of Christian freedom and a sense of responsibility to the complex issues of economics and politics, with the firm resolve that inherited dogmas and generalizations will not be accepted, no matter how revered or venerable, if they do not contribute to the establishment of justice in a given situation."[39] Niebuhr's

---

[35] Macintosh, *Religious Realism*, pp. 330–31. One evidence of Macintosh's support for theological study of pragmatism is the extensive use of William James' ideas about religion in the B.D. thesis that Reinhold Niebuhr prepared under Macintosh's supervision in 1914. See Fox, *Reinhold Niebuhr*, pp. 30, 35–36.

[36] See page 51 below.

[37] Cornel West, *The American Evasion of Philosophy* (Madison: University of Wisconsin Press, 1989), pp. 150–64.

[38] Niebuhr, "Theology and Political Thought in the Western World," in *Faith and Politics*, p. 55.

[39] *Ibid.* Niebuhr was not altogether consistent in his statement of what the "pragmatism" in "Christian pragmatism" means. In an essay published in 1963, he describes ecumenical social ethics as pragmatic "in the sense that it becomes increasingly aware of the contingent circumstances of history which determine how much or how little it is necessary to emphasize the various regulative principles of justice, equality and liberty, security of the community or freedom of the individual . . ." See Reinhold Niebuhr, "The Development of a Social Ethic in the Ecumenical Movement," in *Faith and Politics*, p. 177.

formulation suggests that religious beliefs and traditional dogmas lose their claim to validity and become literally meaningless if they are not coherent with our other ideas about the context in which we seek important human goods.

To require that doctrinal truths be coherent with the other beliefs by which we guide our choices and actions does not mean that theology cannot question scientific theories, political principles, or social scientific accounts of human action.[40] To suggest that would be to give these other systems of belief the same unquestioned status that some theologians have mistakenly given to religious dogma. Nor does it mean that we can believe anything that serves our immediate practical purposes. The point is rather that the beliefs which guide action are those by which we can coordinate all of our knowledge and experience – religious awe, scientific observation, practical wisdom, and technical skill – in pursuit of those larger aims that give direction to our life as a whole and link us in shared purposes with others.

In that practical testing and ordering of our beliefs, short-term wants are often given up because they conflict with more important goals. Particular beliefs that may be internally consistent and immediately appealing are set aside because they are inconsistent with the more comprehensive network of ideas that guides action. To assert "inherited dogmas and generalizations" without regard for their coherence with other beliefs does not honor the faith that created the dogmas. It renders the faith irrelevant to action and leaves the way open for alternative systems of belief to provide what guidance may be needed.[41]

The test of coherence cannot be applied to a theological concept in abstraction from the other beliefs that we bring to bear on our human problems. Whether a belief is coherent depends precisely on the particular beliefs that we already

---

[40] See Keith Ward, "Reinhold Niebuhr and the Christian Hope," in Harries, ed., *Reinhold Niebuhr*, pp. 65–67.

[41] Niebuhr insisted on "the relevance of the ideal of love to the moral experience of mankind on every conceivable level. It is not an ideal magically superimposed on human life by a revelation which has no relation to total human experience." Niebuhr, *An Interpretation of Christian Ethics*, p. 63.

hold, and there is always the possibility that new evidence or a different perspective on our experiences will lead us to challenge the coherence of beliefs that we have provisionally accepted. Coherence depends in important ways on social context, the community of discussion in which ideas are tested and held. James recognized that we do not simply pick ideas out of the air to inquire whether they are coherent with the rest of our beliefs. The range of possibilities, the "living options," to use James' own term, are set for us by the civilization in which we live.

> If I ask you to believe in the Mahdi, the notion makes no electric connections with your nature, – it refuses to scintillate with any credibility at all. As an hypothesis it is completely dead. To an Arab, however (even if he be not one of the Mahdi's followers), the hypothesis is among the mind's possibilities: it is alive. This shows that deadness and aliveness in an hypothesis are not intrinsic properties, but relations to the individual thinker.[42]

Carried through consistently, this idea of a "living option" implies a thoroughgoing relativism. We can say whether an idea is true in the context of the beliefs of a particular community or for people during a certain period of history, but asking whether an idea is true across those lines of time and culture seems to some pragmatists to demand an answer that cannot be given. Richard Rorty articulates the implications of this view when he stresses that we cannot impose our coherences on other ways of life or evaluate their beliefs from the perspective of our system. Our obligation is only to continue the discussion in which we are participants.[43]

---

[42] James, "The Will to Believe," in *The Writings of William James*, p. 718. James' formulation here is clearly too individualistic, even to suit his own purposes. He notes a few pages later that these relations are largely set up, not by conscious choice, but by habitual factors, including "the circumpressure of our caste and set" (*ibid.*, p. 721). Compare the idea of a "real option" in Bernard Williams, "The Truth in Relativism," in *Moral Luck* (Cambridge: Cambridge University Press, 1981), pp. 138–40.

[43] Richard Rorty, *Consequences of Pragmatism* (Minneapolis: University of Minnesota Press, 1982), p. 172.

PRAGMATIC RELATIVISM AND "BIBLICAL REALISM"

This pragmatic relativism, which has been developed more consistently by the recent work of Rorty and others, was at least implicit in James' work and helps to explain why the American theologians hesitated to call their own way of thinking "pragmatism." Macintosh centered his objections to pragmatism precisely on this point.

We need not jump to the conclusion, so characteristic of recent pragmatism, that truth means no more than the practical value of ideas, their "working in the way in which they set out to work." If that were the case, truth might contradict truth and there could be no guarantee in the nature of truth that any judgment was true universally and permanently.[44]

Clearly, however, Macintosh's formulation of the problem is not satisfactory, for it is difficult to see how any account of theological truth compatible with the realists' insistence on the importance of human experience could provide a "guarantee" that a proposition is "true universally and permanently." The solution to the problem of relativism cannot be simply to reaffirm a religious absolutism.

What the theological realists were groping for in their limited affirmations of pragmatism was a way to state their conviction that coherences tested by pragmatic methods may not exhaust the meaning of 'truth.' Contemporary pragmatists who reject the relativism in Rorty's pragmatism supply this statement in a distinction between 'truth' and 'justified belief.' Given the beliefs and purposes I now share with others in my society, I may be entirely justified in believing that a certain pattern of behavior indicates a morally culpable moral weakness of character. People once believed this about certain forms of mental illness. Today, we are justified in believing that these episodes are the result of chemical events in the brain that are not subject to voluntary control by the individual who suffers from them. We do not, however, deal with this change in

---

[44] Macintosh, "Experimental Realism in Religion," in *Religious Realism*, p. 331.

beliefs by saying that people are free to choose whichever explanation works best for them. Neither do we say that it used to be true that mental illness was a moral problem, but it isn't true anymore. Nor do we, except in a dither of philosophically induced uncertainty, mutter about "truth contradicting truth." What we say is that the older beliefs about mental illness, though they may have been justified at the time, were false. We also say that the beliefs we are presently justified in holding about mental illness are true, though experience and history warn us that we may be wrong about this. This sounds complex, but it does not require any changes in the way we ordinarily understand the meaning of 'true' and 'false.' As Jeffrey Stout puts it:

Some of the sentences, including moral ones, that we are now warranted in asserting and justified in believing are not true. We know this from observing human history and learning the facts of finitude. If we knew which ones were false, we would immediately cease believing them. But knowing that some are false isn't the same as knowing which are false. So we go on accepting each one as true until we have reason for doubting something in particular. And all the while, we also believe that something, we know not what, will need correction.[45]

Justification, in short, *is* relative to our place in history and society and the particular sets of beliefs that place offers us. A pragmatist justifies beliefs by testing their coherence with other beliefs, but a pragmatist who is also a realist understands that coherence alone does not make a justified belief *true*. True beliefs tell us how things in the world really are.[46]

The distinction between 'truth' and 'justified belief' that figures prominently in contemporary philosophy has no exact parallel in the earlier theological realism. The theological

---

[45] Stout, *Ethics After Babel*, p. 25.
[46] Compare James' account of "true beliefs" on page 47 above. Another way to express this point would be to say that understanding what a statement means depends on understanding the conditions under which it would be true, not on understanding the conditions under which we could verify that it is true. The philosophical implications of this subtle, but very important, distinction are introduced in Robert L. Arrington, *Rationalism, Realism, and Relativism: Perspectives in Contemporary Moral Epistemology* (Ithaca: Cornell University Press, 1989), pp. 119–31.

realists did, however, make a similar effort to put a pragmatic method at the service of a realist, rather than a relativist, account of knowledge in theology and ethics. Reinhold Niebuhr, especially, used that framework to interpret the narratives and symbols that present distinctive Christian claims about God. The pragmatism of the theologians thus includes what Niebuhr called a "biblical realism"[47] that employs pragmatic criteria for the assessment of particular doctrinal and moral ideas without accepting the relativism that would follow from making pragmatism the test of truth.

As Niebuhr developed this point in his later work, his appreciation of the pragmatic criteria of coherence and effectiveness was balanced by an awareness that these considerations are often least effective in responding to new evidence and new interpretations that challenge accepted patterns of thought and action. "The effort to establish simple coherence may misinterpret specific realities in order to fit them into a system."[48] Making coherence the basic test of truth limits truth to what the prevailing system of concepts can accommodate. New discoveries that undermine old categories and mysteries that stretch the limits of our comprehension become indistinguishable from mere nonsense.

By contrast, the realist acknowledges from the outset that there are realities independent of our knowledge that may be only partly grasped, or perhaps completely missed, by prevailing systems of thought. Realism thus guards against premature narrowing of our thought by the rigid application of methods that identify truth with the results of methodologically correct investigations.

Niebuhr's reasons for insisting on the limits of coherence, however, have as much to do with morals as with method. If he criticizes the coherent scientism that misinterprets the experiences of religion, he is even more concerned with the coheren-

---

[47] Reinhold Niebuhr, "Coherence, Incoherence, and Christian Faith," in *Christian Realism and Political Problems*, p. 165. Obviously, what Niebuhr intends here is a kind of epistemological realism which he finds implicit in the way the biblical writers approach the world. He does not mean that the biblical text itself provides some privileged access to reality.

[48] *Ibid.*, p. 155.

ces of religious dogmatism that yield a rigid certainty of belief and a certain eagerness to impose the system on others. Niebuhr's own understanding of the mythic element in every Christian affirmation is a way of insisting on the difference between the truth about the reality of God and the beliefs about God which a careful testing in experience allows us to hold.

Realistic theology thus rejects the interpretations that leap from the diversity of beliefs to a theory of relativism, but it must be equally critical of the moral certainty to which religious communities are susceptible. When a religious institution claims "unconditioned truth for its doctrines and unconditioned moral authority for its standards," it becomes "just another tool of human pride."[49] The consequences of this pride include not only an intensification of conflicts between religious points of view, but an erosion of the religious community's capacity to think critically about its own life.

REALISTIC RETICENCE

Up to this point, the practical conclusions of the "biblical realist" seem to come close to the judgments of Stout and other, more skeptical critics, who doubt that religious claims have any positive contribution to make to public discourse, and who fear that they may prove intractably divisive. A kind of self-constraint that draws back from absolute claims is the epistemological stance appropriate to a democratic society. Real problems are solved in terms of the interests at stake in particular cases, and local coherences may be all we need to resolve those conflicts. We want, of course, to avoid the cynical manipulation that cobbles together a "moral" argument that is nothing more than a disguise for self-interest, but when sincere and thoughtful people identify points of agreement that resolve the conflict between them and allow them to get on with their other pursuits, is that not sufficient? What makes agreement possible in a free, pluralistic society is what John

---

[49] Niebuhr, *The Nature and Destiny of Man*, I, 201–2.

Rawls has recently labeled the "overlapping consensus" between the different moral beliefs which more limited sub-communities hold, perhaps for quite different reasons.[50] Happily, most of these groups identify as basic a set of moral beliefs and practices that are widely shared, and most of them have adopted a tolerant attitude toward diversity of beliefs and practices on less important questions.

This emphasis on diversity and consensus in moral discourse provides, on its own terms, a minimal answer to Stout's question of what theistic references add to discussion in a secular, pluralistic society in which agreements about religion are generally absent. The minimal answer is that a moral and theological realism of the sort that Reinhold Niebuhr elaborates demonstrates that religious thinking need not be dogmatic or divisive, and that when it is not, it can be admitted to the public discussion along with all the other participants. To Stout, the philosopher of religion who asks what theism contributes to the public discussion, we may respond with Stout, the political philosopher, that the point is not contribution, but participation.

If the aim of public discussion is to identify elements of a consensus to which persons will agree for different reasons, rather than to offer reasons for choices one way or another, there is no reason to exclude those whose reasons may be religious, unless these religious persons, by an intolerant demand for consensus on their own terms, exclude themselves.[51] On the other hand, there are good practical reasons to invite them into the discussion, since their participation in the "overlapping consensus" may be important to its effectiveness

---

[50] John Rawls, "Justice as Fairness: Political Not Metaphysical," *Philosophy and Public Affairs* 14 (1985), 225. See also Stout, *Ethics After Babel*, pp. 227–28.

[51] The case is clearly very much different if the public discussion is understood as one in which reasons for choice are articulated rather than one in which points of consensus are identified. In that case, the question whether religious reasons can, in principle, be acceptable to those who do not share the religious premises remains an important question, even where the religious believers are clearly committed to tolerance and diversity. See the important recent discussions in Kent Greenawalt, *Religious Convictions and Political Choice* (New York: Oxford University Press, 1988); and Robert Audi, "The Separation of Church and State and the Obligations of Citizenship," *Philosophy and Public Affairs* 18 (Summer, 1989), 259–96.

as an instrument of social harmony. If that entails listening politely while they speak of God and occasionally sing a hymn or two, no harm is done and much good may accrue.

Niebuhr's understanding of public discourse sometimes claims no more than this, and his political realism leads him to suggest that asking for more definitive public choices might, in fact, be a dangerous move. It tempts us to moral absolutisms that render communities intolerant and coercive.

It is probably true that the health of a democratic society depends more upon the spirit of forbearance with which each side tolerates the irreducible ideological preferences of the other than upon some supposed scientific resolution of them, because the scientific resolution always involves the peril that one side or the other will state its preferences as if they were scientifically validated value judgments.[52]

A MEANINGFUL UNIVERSE

Reticence in pressing one's own claims and a tolerance for those of others cannot, however, provide for theological realism the only response to the problem of the diversity of beliefs. Part of our insistence on our own beliefs, no doubt, is an urge to dominate others by whatever means we have at our disposal. That must be controlled for the sake of social cooperation. Part of it, however, derives from an urge to truth. "We instinctively assume that there is only one world and that it is a cosmos, however veiled and unknown its ultimate coherences, incongruities, and contradictions in life, in history, and even in nature."[53] We stick to what seems true to us because we do not think that all beliefs are equal and that it makes no difference what people believe, as long as they do not impose their ideas on others. If we bother to communicate with others at all, it must be in part because we seek to come to an understanding with them about the world we all inhabit.[54]

---

[52] Reinhold Niebuhr, "Ideology and the Scientific Method," in *Christian Realism and Political Problems*, pp. 90–91.

[53] Niebuhr, "Coherence, Incoherence, and Christian Faith," p.155.

[54] Jürgen Habermas, in his theory of "communicative competence," has developed an extensive reply to social theories that reduce human interests to the technical control of physical or human resources. These views, Habermas suggests, ignore

The effort to establish coherence among diverse cognitive claims is matched by a human concern for a morally coherent universe. Here, too, tolerance may be a social necessity, but stopping at that point leaves out of account a basic concern to arrive at moral agreement. As Niebuhr put it in *An Interpretation of Christian Ethics*, "Moral life is possible at all only in a meaningful existence. Obligation can be felt only to some system of coherence and some ordering will. Thus moral obligation is always an obligation to promote harmony and to overcome chaos."[55]

The argument of those sentences is highly compressed, but it is crucial to the way that theological realism shapes Niebuhr's understanding of ethics. Let us try to develop the point in more detail.

Moral resolutions of conflict are possible because moral obligations override particular interests. What distinguishes a moral resolution[56] from an economic, political, or military resolution is the appeal to a principle of obligation that the parties acknowledge they are obliged to follow despite damage to their more immediate interests and desires. We must do justice, even when it is costly. We must attend to our responsibilities, even when there are other things that we would prefer to do. Moral resolutions do not represent the triumph of one interest over another. Rather, the conflict between interests has been subordinated to a higher law which both acknowledge.

Such resolutions are no doubt rare in human affairs, especially in the affairs of such large and powerful entities as nations, corporations, and political parties. Indeed, a certain sort of critical perspective, which Niebuhr would label

equally important and logically more fundamental interests in knowledge and communication. See Jürgen Habermas, *Reason and the Rationalization of Society*, trans. Thomas McCarthy (Theory of Communicative Action, I; Boston: Beacon Press, 1984), pp. 273–86.

[55] Niebuhr, *An Interpretation of Christian Ethics*, p. 63.

[56] Here I use the phrase "moral resolution" in a specific sense to refer to solutions that are based on a direct appeal to moral obligations. There is also a more general sense in which the outcome of an economic, political, or military conflict is moral if the conflict has been fairly fought, according to just rules, and in ways that did no harm to innocent third parties, etc.

"cynical," will insist that moral solutions are nothing more than frauds, perpetrated on the unwary by those who are skillful in using moral language to their own ends, or powerful enough to enforce acquiescence to their moral pieties. A different sort of challenge is posed, however, by critics who point to the limits of serious attempts at moral solutions, and it is this challenge which is more important for the present argument. What these critics remind us is that even when interests apparently yield to obligations, some of these solutions turn out in the end simply to pit a larger self-interest against the interests of some other party, perhaps even one not apparently involved in the initial conflict. Thus, when factory owners and workers come to agreement on a just wage that resolves the conflict between them, they may perpetuate the exploitation of poor laborers in another country who provide the raw materials for their industry.

Unlike the cynics, the critics who introduce this historical or contextual note into our understanding of moral resolutions do not aim to undermine our confidence in morality altogether, and there is much in their caution about the limits of the moral resolutions that a realist must affirm. The irony of attempts to do justice that end up working injustice in distant places would not be lost on Reinhold Niebuhr. Nevertheless, we must understand from the outset that if these ironies were all that our efforts to do justice come to, there would, in Niebuhr's terms, be no *moral* obligations.

To assert a moral obligation, as Niebuhr understands it, is not merely to claim that there is an "overlapping consensus" that encompasses the conflicting interests of the parties. Moral obligations rest on an imagination that transcends existing circumstances to envision conditions under which persons could live together in mutual fulfillment, instead of antagonistic rivalry. Every specific formulation of those conditions will, of course, be incomplete, but the moral obligation rests on those interests that are not contingent and opposed, nor even coincident and consensual, but universally human and in harmony with one another.

Niebuhr suggested that the teaching of Jesus is morally

compelling because it presents this demand in an uncompromising way. Drawing on the eschatological expectations of prophetic faith, Jesus' ethics presents the law of God as a demand for love which sets aside the constraints of history and the requirements of prudent planning for the future. "It does not establish a connection with the horizontal points of a political or social ethic or with the diagonals which a prudential individual ethics draws between the moral ideal and the facts of a given situation. It has only a vertical dimension between the loving will of God and the will of man."[57] The New Testament completely sets aside the requirements of self-interest and the coincidental convergences of group interests, to envision an ultimate harmony of life with life.

Niebuhr's Christian Realism is well known for insisting that Jesus' ethics of love is not a "simple possibility."[58] The distance between the absolute requirements of love and any program of action we can put into effect must not be diminished. What we must stress at present is not the Realists' familiar gap between love and practice, but the less familiar point that the distance that elevates the law of love to an impossible ideal characterizes all moral obligation. That is why people respond to the moral teaching of Jesus, despite the obvious difficulties of living up to his demands. Ordinary people understand Jesus better than theorists who are concerned to reconcile the moral obligation with the requirements of self-interest or prudence, because they know that this reconciliation is impossible. Jesus' uncompromised demands come closer to their intuitions about morality, even though they may have no idea how they could actually live by this law of love. "The real fact is that the absolute character of the ethic of Jesus conforms to the actual constitution of man and history, that is, to the transcendent freedom of man over the contingencies of nature and the necessities of time, so that only a final harmony of life with life in love can be the ultimate norm of his existence."[59]

The imaginative grasp of human unity which transcends the

---

[57] Niebuhr, *An Interpretation of Christian Ethics*, p. 24.
[58] Niebuhr, *The Nature and Destiny of Man*, I, 296.
[59] *Ibid.*, II, 50–51.

differences imposed by nature and history suggests many problems for ethics: How shall we use it as a starting point for
specific actions? How shall we reconcile it with the requirements of social life and responsible leadership? How shall we
distinguish between genuine self-transcendence and the vanity
that blows our own wishes up to the proportions of eternity?
Many of these questions will occupy our attention in subsequent chapters. For the moment, the task is to reconnect this
human unity that provides the basis for moral obligation with
the instinctive assumption that "there is only one world and
that it is a cosmos,"[60] and to relate both ideas to the theological
realism we have been explicating in this chapter.

THE LAW OF LOVE

Reinhold Niebuhr's "Christian pragmatism" sets an exacting
standard for the justification of moral claims. Niebuhr's "law
of love" cannot be compared to Kant's categorical imperative,
a single rule formulated in ways that allow all claims to be
measured against it, but the idea that moral obligation
depends on a "meaningful universe" requires that any particular moral claim find its place in a more and more extensive
system of coherent beliefs. Prevailing moral convictions, beliefs
about the facts, and the interests of the parties involved are all
included in this coherence, but the law of love requires that in
addition to being tested against one another, these beliefs should
be tested against the moral convictions of other communities,
and against claims that might be made by other groups and
interests. Because there is no single formula by which this
coherence can be established, our assertions must always be
tentative and subject to revision, but only those claims that
show substantial promise of coherence with this larger, more
inclusive set of considerations can count as establishing *moral*
obligations.

In the search for usable moral ideas, we cannot arbitrarily
stop at the boundaries of our own moral community. Once we

---

[60] See page 56 above.

have settled what morality in our local situation is, we must still ask how those moral beliefs cohere with moral beliefs in other settings. That question may arise in urgent practical forms, when business or personal relationships cross national and cultural boundaries, or when groups with different origins and expectations find themselves living together in one city or one neighborhood; but even where the question is not a "living option,"[61] the intellectual issue persists.

The Christian Realist's "law" of love is less a rule for adjudicating these conflicts than a refusal to accept a judgment of incoherence as the obvious answer in cases of moral conflict. The relativist assumes that where we cannot establish coherence, we must accept incoherence as a fact. The realist uses the distinction between truth and justified belief to give an account of moral conflicts which takes those conflicts seriously, but which does not destroy the "meaningful universe" which Reinhold Niebuhr's account of moral obligation presupposes.

Justified beliefs may conflict with one another. What we learn about human behavior from a carefully constructed psychological experiment or sociological study may not correspond to what our own experience has taught us, or to what "common sense" leads us to expect.[62] A justifiable response to physical attack in an ethic of non-violent resistance – turn the other cheek – differs from the response required by a prudent ethic of mutuality – give as good as you get – and from that justified by a norm of honor based on vengeance – impose on the aggressor more harm than has been wreaked on you. A realist must suppose that while all of these positions can be justified, they cannot all be true. The aim of inquiry is therefore to get beyond the multiplicity of justified beliefs, but we must also acknowledge the limits on our capacity to do so. The more extensive and developed our systems of coherence

---

[61] See page 50 above.

[62] Social science research usually describes such results as "counterintuitive," suggesting that the research program yields reasoned judgments, while personal experience or common sense rests on unsupported "intuitions." In point of fact, of course, our reports of personal experience and of common sense are also systems of justified beliefs, although the procedures and criteria of justification may be quite different from those of experimental social science.

become, the less likely it is that we can resolve the differences between them simply by collapsing one into the other.

> There are configurations and structures which stand athwart every rationally conceived system of meaning and cannot be appreciated in terms of the alternative efforts to bring the structure completely into one system or the other. The primary example is man himself, who is both in nature and above nature and who has been alternately misunderstood by naturalistic and idealistic philosophies.[63]

At this point, we must appreciate the importance to a way of thinking that is both pragmatic and realistic of those constructions which are at first glance quite *unrealistic*, namely those myths, symbols, and other forms of expression in which we apprehend a unity of meaning that we cannot completely formulate as a system of coherence.

Myth and symbol become especially relevant when we turn to those systems of metaphysics and theology which attempt to provide comprehensive accounts of reality, to establish a system of coherence in which all justified beliefs hold together. Like all human investigations, these metaphysical systems initially measure their successes by the coherence they achieve. Unless the limits of coherence are appreciated, however, our systematic thinking may lead to premature rationalizations that achieve intellectual coherence by eliminating important features of the world of experience. Historic Christianity, with its emphasis on "the unique, the contradictory, the paradoxical, and the unresolved mystery," seems at first primitive compared to idealistic philosophical systems and monistic religions that make an effort "to present the world and life as a unified whole and to regard all discords and incongruities as provisional or illusory."[64] These systems, however, invariably fail to grasp their object, and the coherences they define leave out important elements of the experience they seek to explain. The closest we can come to a comprehensive statement will be one that incorporates and affirms the truth of several of the ways in which the ultimate order may be understood and the

[63] Niebuhr, "Coherence, Incoherence, and Christian Faith," in *Christian Realism and Political Problems*, p. 156.
[64] *Ibid.*, p. 179.

tensions and conflicts of human experience resolved. The most coherent theological statement, that is to say, will be one that includes an element of incoherence.

To say that an appropriate effort to symbolize a ground of coherence that unites reality as a whole invariably exceeds the possibilities of complete rational systematization, and so includes discordant elements of human experience, is not to say that any symbols will do. Myths and symbols must be evaluated as other efforts to apprehend reality are, by their ability to make sense of a range of particular experiences, and especially by their ability to guide action in terms of larger goals that unify more specific human aims. "In short, the situation is that the ultrarational pinnacles of Christian truth, embodying paradox and contradiction and straining at the limits of rationality, are made plausible when understood as the keys which make the drama of human life and history comprehensible and without which it is either given a too-simple meaning or falls into meaninglessness."[65]

RADICAL MONOTHEISM

Throughout this chapter, we have been delineating a version of theological realism which makes sense of the cautious affirmation of philosophical pragmatism by the American theological realists and of the modified pragmatic method by which Reinhold Niebuhr sought to assess the relevance of "inherited dogmas and generalizations" to the "complex issues of economics and politics."[66] With this more systematic statement of the method in place, we are in a position to return to the theological affirmations themselves.

Theological realism, as Macintosh presented it, begins with the reality of God. A comprehensive account of our experience (including our religious experiences) permits us to affirm "the reality of a religious Object, such as may appropriately be called God."[67] Where Macintosh moved cautiously from experience to the reality of God, Niebuhr moved boldly from

---

[65] *Ibid.*, p. 185.   [66] See page 48 above.
[67] Macintosh, ed., *Religious Realism*, p. v.

the reality of God to experience.[68] "Biblical realism" passes the pragmatic test because the idea of one God who is the ground of all order and coherence explains the order in our experience, allows us to affirm that the order is more basic than the chaos which we also experience, and warns us that the final ordering of reality is both a fulfillment and a contradiction of the order which we know. The law of love expresses the ethical position that is coherent with this reality.

> The ethic of Jesus is the perfect fruit of prophetic religion. Its ideal of love has the same relation to the facts and necessities of human experience as the God of prophetic faith has to the world. It is drawn from, and relevant to, every moral experience. It is immanent in life as God is immanent in the world. It transcends the possibilities of human life in its final pinnacle as God transcends the world.[69]

Not every expression of prophetic faith, of course, achieves this ideal of comprehensiveness. Much of the record of historic Christianity, and of the biblical record itself, is a documentation of what H. Richard Niebuhr would later call "henotheism," belief in a single deity closely tied to the values and the fate of a particular people. "Radical monotheism," by contrast, is faith in a God who cannot be identified with any local reality. In this concept, H. Richard Niebuhr sums up much of the religious realism that had entered American theology with the Younger Theologians. That is not to say that he thought that radical monotheism had triumphed, either in American religion or in the prophetic tradition generally. Even in the most profound religious reflections, he suggested, we are acquainted with that faith "more as hope than as datum, more perhaps as a possibility than as an actuality."[70]

Nevertheless, radical monotheism provides the interpretative key that allows us to construe the coherences of experience and the connection between human lives in more than local and relative terms. Reinhold Niebuhr begins with the impulse

---

[68] For a more detailed, and somewhat different, account of the differences between the theological realism of the Niebuhr brothers and that of their mentor, see S. Mark Heim, "Prodigal Sons: D. C. Macintosh and the Brothers Niebuhr," *Journal of Religion*, 65 (July, 1985), 336–58.

[69] Niebuhr, *An Interpretation of Christian Ethics*, p. 22.

[70] H. Richard Niebuhr, *Radical Monotheism*, p. 31.

to form coherences and find order that is always part of human experience, but he interprets it in the light of a theological idea which demands that unity and order reach through the whole of reality, not just through those parts that happen to be present to our experience. Bringing order to discrepant perceptions, connecting mental experience to external reality, reinterpreting first impressions to eliminate incongruent data – all these are ways in which the mind transcends immediate experience to form an idea of a real world that also transcends the experiencing mind. The reality of God suggests further that this ordering and unifying might be extended indefinitely, insofar as all things could be ordered in relation to the One God who is the source of their reality.

We need to be clear, again, about the direction of the argument that yields this possibility. It is the idea of One God which allows us to interpret human conflict in the light of an ultimate harmony of life with life, not the proximate experiences of harmony which require or permit us to posit an ultimate unity. Not every pragmatic account of experience, not even every pragmatic account of religious experience, ends in monotheistic faith. William James, for example, regarded pluralism as the natural conclusion to be drawn from attentiveness to shifting human realities, and he treated monotheism as an exaggeration of the more limited idea of God that is supported in experience.

> Their words may have sounded monistic when they said "there is no God but God"; but the original polytheism of mankind has only imperfectly and vaguely sublimated itself into monotheism, and monotheism itself, so far as it was religious and not a scheme of classroom instruction for the metaphysicians, has always viewed God as but one helper, *primus inter pares*, in the midst of all the shapers of the great world's fate.[71]

The Niebuhrs might agree that some sort of polytheism, or perhaps more accurately henotheism, summarizes what most people have made of their religion. In contrast to this widely shared theism, which circumscribes the idea of God by what

---

[71] William James, *Pragmatism: A New Name for Some Old Ways of Thinking* (New York: Longmans, Green and Co., 1907), p. 298.

can be seen in events, monotheism is a theological realism which holds that the idea of God tells us something about the character of reality as a whole, something congruent with that part of it which we directly experience, but extending beyond that to encompass a unity that we have not experienced and cannot reduce to a completely rational formulation. Such an idea of God must be tested and refined against the world of ordinary experience, but the idea also shapes expectations and directs action in the light of hopes which are not predictable outcomes of any set of existing circumstances.

If James' pragmatism makes it rational to believe, and to act on the belief, that our values are supported by facts and that our efforts to realize them are not ultimately futile, radical monotheism requires that we construe our values and aims in such a way that their realization could be consistent with the values and aims of all other persons. In cases of conflict, James' pluralism allows a duality of good and evil in which the evil is simply to be resisted and, in the end, extirpated. We proceed toward the goal "by dropping it out altogether, throwing it overboard and getting beyond it, helping to make a universe that shall forget its very place and name."[72]

For radical monotheism, the case is more complex, as H. Richard Niebuhr indicates in his essay, "The Center of Value." Here, all values must be coherent in some way, or they could not be values at all. What makes an aim or an object "good" is its relationship not to a system of aspirations defined by reference to an individual perspective, but "by reference to a being for which other beings are good."[73] Individuals may pursue aims that set them in irreconcilable conflicts with their neighbors, but theological realism insists that these aims must be evaluated in light of a harmony of life with

---

[72] *Ibid.*, p. 297. This dualism of good and evil was not shared by all of the early American pragmatists. Peirce, for example, explicitly denies it, arguing that love must ultimately overcome and incorporate even that which appears to negate it. See John E. Smith, *Purpose and Thought* (New Haven: Yale University Press, 1978), p. 169.

[73] H. Richard Niebuhr, "The Center of Value," in *Radical Monotheism*, p. 100.

life which must be possible if all of these valuing subjects are related as objects of value to God.

Christian Realism, from its earliest formulations in the works of Macintosh, the Niebuhrs, and others of the Younger Theologians, has traced a complex relationship between the reality of God and moral obligation. The complexity precludes any simple answer to Jeffrey Stout's question about what theism adds to our understanding of human experience, but on the basis of what we have seen we can begin to provide a Christian Realist's response that moves beyond the minimal participation we have already claimed on the basis of pragmatic politics.[74]

Moral obligation is not meaningless apart from God. Specific moral obligations that transcend immediate interests can be defined without reference to divine commands or an ultimate center of value. Rather, God provides a reality in which a comprehensive unity of moral meanings is conceivable. It makes sense to seek genuine harmony between persons and groups, rather than to manage their conflicts prudently or to surrender to superior force, because human aspirations and values can be unified by the value they have in relationship to God. This unity both completes and transcends the partial resolutions of differences we anticipate in nature and history, and it impels those who apprehend it in faith to seek forms of justice that go beyond present expectations, even when that search involves considerable risk to themselves. The reality of God means that love, and not prudence, is the law of life.[75]

The claims of radical monotheism may at first seem extravagant in the light of Christian Realism's pragmatic method of assessing ideas in social and historical contexts and in relation to human purposes. The moral truth on which our obligations ultimately rest is the value that all things have in relationship

---

[74] See page 55 above.
[75] Niebuhr, *An Interpretation of Christian Ethics*, p. 65. See also Niebuhr, *The Nature and Destiny of Man*, I, 293–96; II, 68–69, 244–46.

to God and the unity of lives and aims that is possible for all persons in relation to this center of value. Is this not a "God's-eye point of view" of moral truth? Is this not the perspective precluded by the pragmatist's understanding of the relativity of all our claims and insights?

The point of Christian Realism, however, is precisely to insist that the "God's-eye point of view" can never be one's own. God, as the center of value, is necessary to make sense of the Christian Realist's distinctive understanding of moral truth, which is more complete than any of the harmonies of nature or history. What makes the Christian Realist also a moral realist is precisely the claim that this moral truth exists independently of our ideas and theories about it. What we have are only justified moral beliefs, ideas about the require- ments of love that are also products of our own culture and history, and that turn out to be sometimes closer, sometimes farther away from the moral truth.

Radical monotheism need make no absolute claims for its own moral insights. Christian Realists can engage in dialogue that may change particular moral beliefs without fear that they are thereby surrendering moral truth. Nevertheless, the concept of a reality made morally meaningful by a coherence of lives and purposes that has no ultimate limit will have little value for the thinking of persons who do not share its theo- logical premises. Whatever concept of moral obligation they may follow will necessarily be constructed on other grounds. What interest would they have in moral ideas framed in relation to a harmony of purposes that they suspect does not exist?

The answer to that question must be sought in the pragmatic method that links Niebuhr's "biblical realism" to other forms of moral realism, and to a reflective method of forming and refining moral beliefs in relation to widely shared experience. Because God relates to the moral life not with a commandment that shatters other plans of action and evaluation, but with a claim about the unity of moral obligation that clarifies and interprets ordinary moral experience, the first task of theo- logical ethics, like many other systems of ethics, is to make sense of what is going on.[76] That is a task that can be widely shared, and the results of Christian reflection should be of interest to many others, even if they want to evaluate the plausibility of the Christian perspective on other grounds.[77]

Much of this reflection is a common human task, which proceeds on the basis of assumptions, knowledge, and material constraints which will be widely shared in a given cultural and historical context. Knowledge about the natural environment, about the working of economic systems, or about the history and development of social institutions may change our assessments of moral obligations. Especially important, too, is an understanding of human nature, of what persons are likely to want and to do, and of the circumstances that enable them to live well and happily. On all these points, as moral theologies that include an idea of natural law have long insisted, an adequate Christian ethic must incorporate insights available to all reasonable and thoughtful observers.[78]

There will, of course, be points at which Christian Realism's confidence in a morally "meaningful universe" leads to an understanding of events at variance with the interpretations of those who rely on more limited coherences in nature or history. Nevertheless, because the ultimate moral truth is also a key to understanding particular events, the Christian insight should not be incomprehensible, even to those who consider it wrong. They may shake their heads over these Christians who insist on talking of love when concepts of power and interest alone would do, but from a pragmatic perspective, the Christian understanding of events is also available to be tested relative to

---

[76] Cf. H. Richard Niebuhr, *The Responsible Self: An Essay in Christian Moral Philosophy* (New York: Harper and Row, 1963), p. 63.

[77] To say that this reflective method is widely shared does not, of course, imply that it is universal, and those who flatly reject it will have little interest in the interpretations of experience that Christian Realism yields. The uninterested parties will include reductive materialists, who doubt not only the reality of God, but the possibility of any human interests that transcend individual or species survival. Also uninterested will be those whose understandings of religious ethics rest on obedience to divine commands independent of an interpretation of circumstances or on a community of faith whose understanding of the world has nothing to gain from engagement with other ways of looking at it.

[78] This point will be central to our discussion in Chapter Three.

the alternatives by its power to guide choice and action in the present.

Reinhold Niebuhr understood the importance of this pragmatic assessment of faith, both for the Christian and for society. It cannot be the final word, for the moral truth of radical monotheism transcends every particular context in which it may be partly apprehended.

Nevertheless, a limited rational validation of the truth of the Gospel is possible. It consists of a negative and a positive approach to the relation of the truth of the Gospel to other forms of truth, and of the goodness of perfect love to historic forms of virtue. Negatively, the Gospel must and can be validated by exploring the limits of historic forms of wisdom and virtue. Positively, it is validated when the truth of faith is correlated with all truths which may be known by scientific and philosophical disciplines and proves itself a resource for coordinating them into a deeper and wider system of coherence.[79]

It is faith as a resource for deeper and wider systems of coherence that made possible the insights that marked Reinhold Niebuhr as one of the leading political thinkers of his day. While we must allow more credit than he would claim for his individual genius and ceaseless effort, understanding social issues and human problems remains an important task for all people of faith, and their successes in that interpretative task remain the most persistent evidence for that morally meaningful universe in which they believe they labor.

Still, the positive validation that religious leadership in society provides does not exhaust the things that religious people do, nor does it ever secure a realization of the law of love that finally orders their doings. Love is, from the perspective of society and history, often defeated. It is perhaps even more often, from that same perspective, superfluous. Conflicts are resolved, and some justice is even done, by a rough balance of power and interest, locally established and frequently revised. It is only in relation to the more comprehensive ideal of love that these solutions begin to appear limited and inadequate, providing the negative validation of which Niebuhr wrote.

---

[79] Niebuhr, *Faith and History*, p. 152.

The law of love is not a norm of history in the sense that historical experience justifies it. Historical experience justifies more complex social strategies in which the self, individual and collective, seeks both to preserve its life and to relate it harmoniously to other lives. But such strategies of mutual love and systems of justice cannot maintain themselves without inspiration from a deeper dimension of history. A strategy of brotherhood which has no other resource but historical experience degenerates from mutuality to a prudent regard for the interests of the self; and from the impulse towards community to an acceptance of the survival impulse as ethically normative.[80]

Much of the rest of this book will be devoted to identifying the coherences which Christian Realism suggests as a basis for positive implementation of the law of love in our present circumstances. We must first, however, turn in Chapter Two to a closer consideration of the way in which this realistic understanding of moral obligation differs from other possibilities that have emerged in Christian ethics since Niebuhr's time.

[80] Niebuhr, *The Nature and Destiny of Man*, II, 96.

CHAPTER 2

Ethics

THEORY AND PRACTICE

In an important essay published in 1964, the philosopher William K. Frankena sought to clarify the normative role of "love" in Christian thought. "Love" appears in the literature both as a duty and as a goal, Frankena wrote, and if we are to understand the differences between Christian writers, we must make an effort to identify their theories as deontological or teleological, and to specify what sort of deontology or teleology, exactly, the author has in mind.[1] To make his point, Frankena analyzed and classified the ideas of most of the important Christian ethicists during the previous couple of decades, associating each with a consistent theoretical position. There was one important exception: "As for Reinhold Niebuhr, he appears to me to suggest, in one place or another, almost every one of the positions I have described; whether this spells richness or confusion of mind, I shall leave for others to judge."[2]

Whether or not Niebuhr was confused, he was certainly indifferent to the categories that Frankena made dominant in the American study of ethics.[3] A generation of students trained

---

[1] William K. Frankena, "Love and Principle in Christian Ethics," in Alvin Plantinga, ed., *Faith and Philosophy* (Grand Rapids: Eerdmans, 1964), pp. 203–25.

[2] *Ibid.*, p. 220.

[3] The influence of the terminology in Frankena's *Ethics* (Englewood Cliffs, N.J.: Prentice-Hall, 1963) on the teaching of ethics both in philosophy and in religious studies has been large. Much of that influence in religious studies was due to Paul Ramsey's appreciation for Frankena's 1964 essay and to Ramsey's subsequent insistence that Christian ethics take the philosophical categories seriously. See Paul

to recognize act- and rule-deontology and act- and rule-teleology has had no better luck than Frankena himself in locating Reinhold Niebuhr in one of those pigeonholes.[4]

Niebuhr's own inclination was not to elaborate a theory or a system, but to sketch the perspective that marks the thinking of a Christian Realist. For him, realism was a habit of asking certain questions and of questioning the answers one was likely to get in turn. One important expression of that perspective appears in his 1957 formulation of "Christian pragmatism:"[5]

We have now come to the fairly general conclusion that there is no "Christian" economic or political system. But there is a Christian attitude toward all systems and schemes of justice. It consists on the one hand of a critical attitude toward the claims of all systems and schemes, expressed in the question whether they will contribute to justice in a concrete situation; and on the other hand a responsible attitude, which will not pretend to be God nor refuse to make a decision between political answers to a problem because each answer is discovered to contain a moral ambiguity in God's sight. We are men, not God; we are responsible for making choices between greater and lesser evils, even when our Christian faith, illuminating the human scene, makes it quite apparent that there is no pure good in history; and probably no pure evil, either. The fate of civilizations may depend on these choices.[6]

With that much at stake, theoretical clarity took a back seat to normative decisiveness; but Niebuhr was not without a framework for his thought. Throughout his writings, he states definite opinions about the place of reason in ethics, the source and authority of moral obligation, and the relationship between judgments of moral truth and judgments of prudence. These are carried through consistently in his practical choices, and they point us to an ethical theory of a quite specific sort, though not one that fits neatly into Frankena's categories.

Ramsey, *Deeds and Rules in Christian Ethics* (New York: Charles Scribner's Sons, 1967), pp. 104–22.

[4] Contrast this to the work of H. Richard Niebuhr. H. Richard criticized and revised the philosophical categories, but he could and did clearly formulate their relationship to his own position. See H. Richard Niebuhr, *The Responsible Self*, pp. 47–68.

[5] See page 48 above.

[6] Niebuhr, "Theology and Political Thought in the Western World," in *Faith and Politics*, p. 56.

It will be worth the trouble to step out of Reinhold Niebuhr's orientation toward practice long enough to reconstruct
this ethical theory, and that effort will occupy our attention
throughout this chapter. Two developments in particlar
prompt this investigation. First, the analytical vocabulary
which distinguishes normative ethics from metaethics and
neatly divides normative ethics into deontological and teleological theories has itself come under criticism in recent years
from both moral theologians and philosophers, who find the
interactions in moral life more dynamic and the distinctions
less precise than the prevailing categories have allowed.[7] Upon
further consideration, Niebuhr's failure to fit those categories
neatly does indeed spell richness, and not confusion. Second,
the work of scholars in religious ethics today, while no longer
bound to the terminology of the 1960s, does appear rather
sharply divided between positions that might be labeled
"rationalism" and "narrativism." Niebuhr not only avoids the
neat categories of an earlier decade; he escapes this present
theoretical polarization as well.

The discussion in this chapter, then, has two principal parts.
First, we will consider the alternatives of *ethical rationalism* and
narrative ethics as these appear in religious ethics today, and we
will see why a Christian Realist might have reservations about
both positions. Then we will develop in more detail the ethical
theory that seems implicit in Niebuhr's realism, finding there a
form of *ethical naturalism* that is suited to the critical and
responsible attitude that Niebuhr sought to apply to the practical questions of politics and society.

RATIONALISM

The use of reason to resolve disputes and settle differences
between opposing points of view is characteristic of the
modern, scientific point of view. Some have relied on reason to
dissolve conflicts based on inherited dogmas and prejudices.

[7] See, for example, Stuart Hampshire, *Morality and Conflict* (Cambridge, Mass.:
Harvard University Press, 1983), pp. 10–17; Jeffrey Stout, *The Flight from Authority*
(Notre Dame, Ind.: University of Notre Dame Press, 1981), pp. 13–15.

Reason allows us to come to agreement on the facts and to act on a common understanding of the reality with which we have to deal. A scientific method, rigorously and objectively applied, should yield facts on which a sound decision can be based. Others, by contrast, insist that what reason allows us to see is that facts alone do not dictate actions, so that our moral agreements are not about the facts, but agreements with one another about acceptable courses of action. What we need are mutual commitments in which the interests of all parties are protected. In one version or another, reason thus contributes to the solution of controversies that custom and authority cannot untangle.

The appeal to reason in ethics is, of course, older than modern empiricism. Aristotle and Aquinas believed that reason is the distinctive human capacity that allows us to know the good at which all human activity aims, and to choose the effective means for realizing it. Because the good and the reason which knows the good are identical in all human beings, we have a common measure by which to assess different laws and customs, and by which we can create a rule for action when new situations arise that the old laws do not cover. Stoic and Christian ideas of natural law proclaimed the universality of reason and made it the basis for a universal moral community.

Contemporary *ethical rationalism* draws on these themes of the universality of reason and its superiority to tradition and authority, but it employs them in ethics in a quite specific way that marks these theories off from other ways of thinking about the place of reason in ethics. (Those who reject ethical rationalism are not, therefore, saying that reason has no place in ethics, but only that the rationalists' particular way of formulating that place is mistaken.) What contemporary ethical rationalists hold is that there is a logic that marks all legitimate claims about moral obligation, so that the truth of those claims can be settled by a formal examination of the claims themselves. To be sure, we may still need to apply some method of scientific reasoning to get the facts straight, but the moral question can be settled on its own terms, independently of other questions and other kinds of knowledge.

Philosophers disagree on exactly how to formulate this moral logic. Generally, however, their theories involve appeal to a rule that is implicit in the conscious choice of an action, together with a principle of consistency that requires the agent to apply that same rule to *every* choice, whether made by the agent or by another. The obligation to follow the basic moral rule thus rests neither on a specific choice, nor on the agent's goals, but on a logical principle such that one can act against the rule only on pain of self-contradiction.[8] Modern confidence in reason's power to clarify our thinking and make its processes explicit here combines with the ancient emphasis on the universality of reason to create a basic rule of morality which everyone is obliged to follow, and which provides a critical principle against which all specific claims and counterclaims about moral obligation can be measured.

Kant's *Groundwork of the Metaphysics of Morals* provides a paradigm case of ethical rationalism. For Kant, truly free choice must be unconstrained by fear of loss or hope of gain. Once we understand that, we will see that a moral choice cannot be dictated by any object or goal external to the action, but depends on the logic of the "maxim" or rule of choice itself. The maxim must be framed so as to require an action of us without exception, in view of our rational understanding of the rule itself, and not because we desire any of the results the action promises. The only rules that will meet this test, of course, are those that every rational being must acknowledge. Hence the "categorical imperative" is (in one of Kant's several formulations of it): "Act only on that maxim through which you can at the same time will that it should become a universal law."[9] Only if you can will that everyone should do as you are about to do can the action be called "moral."

Kant believed that only the most basic moral requirements would withstand this critical scrutiny. A strict, but limited set

---

[8] This point is most clearly formulated in Alan Gewirth, *Reason and Morality* (Chicago: University of Chicago Press, 1978). See also Derek Beyleveld, *The Dialectical Necessity of Morality* (Chicago: University of Chicago Press, 1991), including Gewirth's foreword to the Beyleveld volume.

[9] Immanuel Kant, *Groundwork of the Metaphysics of Morals*, trans. H. J. Paton (New York: Harper Torchbooks, 1964), p. 89.

of obligations would demand honesty and benevolence and forbid self-destruction and the squandering of natural talents.[10] Other customary requirements respecting social roles or religious obligations presumably would not survive, and even the requirements of prudence would be shown up as constraints observed by reasonable people who are concerned about their own self-preservation, rather than genuine moral requirements. For Kant, reason thus provides the critical principle by which we can distinguish the real requirements of morality from the demands of custom, self-interest, and authority.

Although Kant argued that reason must presuppose an idea of God to make sense of moral action in the face of the sacrifices to our own immediate interests that morality often requires,[11] ethical rationalism has often been understood as inimical to traditional religious belief and practice. In rationalism, the formulation of moral requirements proceeds by reason alone, without direct reference to God's will or divine commandments, and actions undertaken simply because they are required by God or by one's church have no moral value. The ideal which emerges is that of independent, rational individuals, legislating their own morality without benefit of tradition or ceremony.

In the two centuries since Kant, however, religious thinkers have discerned another possibility. In retrospect, it appears that Kant's purely rational religion was strongly tinged with the traditions of Lutheran piety in which he had been raised. The very idea of what is rational, universal, and human in Kant's works betrays its origins in an eighteenth-century German university town and Baltic seaport.[12]

---

[10] *Ibid.*, pp. 89–91.

[11] Immanuel Kant, *Critique of Practical Reason*, trans. Lewis White Beck (The Library of Liberal Arts; Indianapolis: Bobbs-Merrill), p. 130; also *Religion Within the Limits of Reason Alone*, trans. Theodore M. Greene and Hoyt H. Hudson (New York: Harper and Row, 1960).

[12] Because Kant deliberately avoids the use of illustrations and examples in his best-known philosophical treatises, the specific, local elements in his notions of rationality are not always seen by students whose readings are confined to the major works. A few hours spent on the *Lectures on Ethics* or the *Anthropology* may dramatically alter one's perception of Kant. See Immanuel Kant, *Lectures on Ethics*, trans.

If reason itself has a tradition, it may be that traditions – and, specifically, religious traditions – can adopt, sustain, and transmit to new generations the basic structure of moral reason. This is the case which contemporary advocates of ethical rationalism in religious ethics have argued. Ronald Green, for example, discerns a "deep structure" in all of the world's religious traditions which provides each of them with the requirements of moral reason, ways of justifying these demands, and ways of coping with humanity's persistent failure to meet them:

Religion's deep structure has three essential elements: first, a method of moral reasoning involving "the moral point of view"; second, a set of beliefs affirming the reality of moral retribution; and third, a series of "transmoral" beliefs that suspend moral judgment and retribution when this is needed to overcome moral paralysis and despair. Whatever their surface differences, religions contain these elements.[13]

Green's explorations of this "deep structure" range across cultures from traditional Africa, to classical Hinduism, to Western Christianity. John P. Reeder, Jr., confines his investigations to Judaism and Christianity, and he sees a variety of possibilities within those traditions, but he, too, points to a use of reason in religion which discerns the requirements of the moral law and justifies the possibilities of punishment and forgiveness for those who fail to keep it.[14] Instead of being unenlightened alternatives to ethical rationalism, religious traditions become pre-Enlightenment anticipations of it. The reasoned formulation of moral requirements and the rational justification of their demands are embedded in the beliefs and practices of religion as surely as they are in Kantian moral philosophy.

Louis Infield (New York: The Century Company, n.d.); *Anthropology from a Pragmatic Point of View*, trans. Victor L. Dowdell (Carbondale, Ill.: Southern Illinois University Press, 1978).

[13] Ronald M. Green, *Religion and Moral Reason: A New Method for Comparative Study* (New York: Oxford University Press, 1988), p. 3. See also his earlier *Religious Reason: The Rational and Moral Basis of Religious Belief* (New York: Oxford University Press, 1978).

[14] John P. Reeder, Jr., *Source, Sanction, and Salvation: Religion and Morality in Judaic and Christian Traditions* (Englewood Cliffs, N.J.: Prentice-Hall, 1988).

In contemporary religious ethics, rationalism has been developed principally as a method for comparative studies. In the strong, Kantian form espoused by Green, however, it also has local, practical implications. One thing that renders religion morally suspect in modern, pluralistic societies is the fear that religions will impose unique and non-negotiable moral demands on their adherents, demands that will prove irreconcilable with the smooth and peaceful operation of the political and economic institutions that make modern life possible.

The preoccupation with religious fundamentalism in recent years reflects, in part, this concern that a closed moral system may make demands on its adherents that wider social forces will be unable to moderate. If it could be shown, however, that religious ethics in all its various forms turns on the same set of rationally justified moral requirements, the threat of unique and unreasonable demands begins to recede. There may still be practical problems in relating different experiences and traditions, but there is no reason to expect ultimate conflict. If religious leaders can be held accountable to generally shared moral requirements, then we can ask them to respond to rational criticism instead of demanding blind obedience from their followers.

REALISM AND RATIONALISM

Perhaps, then, a Christian version of ethical rationalism provides the key to the critical and responsible attitude that Reinhold Niebuhr sought. There are important points of connection between Niebuhr's Christian Realism and contemporary religious versions of ethical rationalism. Both are concerned to identify ways of thinking that transcend individual and cultural differences, and despite the obvious difficulties that attend our efforts to formulate those human universals, neither Christian Realists nor moral rationalists think that those efforts are futile or that the results are without value. In both cases, too, the theoretical interest in universal, rational truth arises in part from a practical concern to get beyond the deep and sometimes bloody disagreements that make it hard for different religious groups to live together in social harmony.

From his earliest works, Niebuhr gave the critical use of reason an important place among the "rational resources" for life in a political community. The capacity to recognize and defer to the legitimate claims of others depends heavily on a sense of justice that is rooted in reason.

This sense of justice is a product of the mind and not of the heart. It is the result of reason's insistence on consistency. One of Immanuel Kant's two moral axioms: "Act in conformity with that maxim and that maxim only which you can at the same time will to be universal law" is simply the application to problems of conduct of reason's desire for consistency.[15]

While Niebuhr is more often remembered for his warnings that ideology and self-interest can distort reason than for his affirmations of Kantian consistency, one can affirm the importance of reason in ethics without claiming that it is easy to be rational in the ways that morality requires. Ronald Green, in fact, makes this point in almost Niebuhrian terms:

Of course, no one can deny that it is extremely difficult to be impartial ... Nevertheless, this serious practical problem does not lessen the value of the moral point of view as a *standard* for measuring conduct or as an ideal *reference point* for adjudicating disputes. When we try to justify an action morally, we assume it to be one that anyone looking at things impartially and objectively would approve. We may delude ourselves about this, but the need to justify even selfish conduct in this way is an inescapable accompaniment of human reasoning, the homage, as La Rochefoucauld said, that vice offers to virtue.[16]

On balance, of course, Reinhold Niebuhr could hardly be called a Kantian. The critical standard of consistency, which was for Kant the most important resource for personal and social ethics, occupies for Niebuhr a much smaller place in the moral life. It is, however, important to understand that the differences between Christian Realism and ethical rationalism are not the result of a frontal assault by Reinhold Niebuhr against the claims of reason. On the general value of reason as

---

[15] Niebuhr, *Moral Man and Immoral Society*, pp. 23–50.
[16] Green, *Religion and Moral Reason*, p. 8.

an objective standard and reference point for practical choices, Niebuhr and the rationalists are agreed. The differences turn on questions about the relationship between reason, morality, and religion.

To begin with, there is little evidence in Reinhold Niebuhr's works for a religious reason that lies beneath the surface of religious differences. Niebuhr made no serious study of the world's religions, and his approach to the differences between them seems determined by an apologetic method that sees them principally as examples of mistaken approaches to problems that Christianity has correctly solved. Particularly in his early work, Niebuhr's treatment of non-Christian religions echoes the work of liberal theologians who had accepted the historical–critical approach to Christian origins, but still believed it possible to mount a successful *historical* argument for the superiority of Christianity, in place of the *theological* argument that had failed.[17] In Niebuhr's later work, the explicit references to Schweitzer and Toynbee fade, but the approach remains the same. If Christianity is sometimes less rational than other religious alternatives, then it is less rational just at the points that give it a better grasp of the incongruities and complexities of real life.[18] Buddhism, in particular, remains a shadowy image throughout Niebuhr's work, acquiring no historical details of its own, serving only as a negative example of the "mysticism" that disavows the reasoned search for meaning within history.[19] At points, Niebuhr seems almost to argue for a negative image of Green's deep structure of religious reason. That is, Niebuhr has a concept of historical rationality that he finds *missing* from all faiths except Christianity and prophetic Judaism, whatever the surface similarities that may unite them.

The Christian Realists are not good guides to the facts about

---

[17] Reinhold Niebuhr, *Does Civilization Need Religion?* (New York: Macmillan, 1928), pp. 190–200.

[18] Niebuhr, *An Interpretation of Christian Ethics*, pp. 14–15; "Coherence, Incoherence, and Christian Faith," in *Faith and Politics*, p. 179.

[19] Niebuhr, *Does Civilization Need Religion?* pp. 190–200; *An Interpretation of Christian Ethics*, pp. 14–15; "Coherence, Incoherence, and Christian Faith," in *Christian Realism and Political Problems*, p. 179; *The Nature and Destiny of Man*, II, 13–14.

non-Christian religions, and their apologetic interests seem heavy-handed and distorting in contrast to today's comparative methods, which aim at understanding the world of experience of another faith. Niebuhr's focus on religious differences does, however, point to an important feature of his pragmatic method. Having rejected a single, foundational standard of measurement, the pragmatist must also avoid absolute judgments that extend to all possible cases. Even when comparative inquiry takes a normative turn, then, the issue is the relative adequacy of available alternatives, not the absolute superiority of one or another of them. Moreover, the standard of adequacy is a practical assessment of human needs and interests that is itself subject to revision and development. Differences must be attended to, because it is only in those differences that the specific features of any tradition or system of belief clearly emerge, but the differences are not interpreted as deviations from a single form which alone is rational. This pragmatic method which attends to both similarities and differences guides Niebuhr's work as a whole, and provides many of his most penetrating insights. Unlike either ethical rationalists, who see all moral, religious, and political systems as variations on a single theme, or relativists, who see these different ways of thought and action as largely incommensurable, the pragmatist finds them *comparable*.[20] Different traditions share enough in human purposes that their adequacy to those purposes can be compared.

Critics may argue that Niebuhr has, in effect, made his own tradition the standard of that adequacy for all cases. That is a perennial temptation for comparative studies, and one that we slip into most easily when we are not well informed about the other possibilities. Formally, however, Niebuhr's judgments about other religions nearly always retain the pragmatic method: there is a particular human practical purpose which can be formulated independently of the traditions under con-

---

[20] Todd D. Whitmore, "Christian Ethics and Pragmatic Realism: Philosophical Elements of a Response Ethic" (Unpublished Ph.D. Dissertation, University of Chicago, 1990), pp. 64–67.

sideration, and which upon examination Christianity proves to serve better than the particular alternatives in view.

Both Niebuhr's understanding of non-Christian religions, which was often incomplete, and his pragmatic method, which was often implicit, concur in a more cautious approach to claims about a common structure of religious reason than that taken by contemporary religious rationalism. Niebuhr would no doubt have been skeptical of the claim that all religions share a common structure of reason.

What is more central to the ethics of Christian Realism, however, is a different understanding of the three-way relationship between religion, reason, and ethics. For the ethical rationalist, reason can function as a critical standard for assessing moral obligations because the requirements of rational consistency are precisely what marks an obligation as moral. The requirements of prudent self-interest, the disciplines of a religious self-denial, or the ritualized practices of a community all may take on overtones of obligation, but they are not authentic *moral* obligations. Moral obligations are identified precisely by the logic that requires me to extend to all other prospective agents the same rights I claim for myself, or to impose on myself the same duties I would impose on them.[21] The ethical rationalist insists that to identify anything else as the source of a genuine moral obligation confuses the issue in ways that are apt to result in the imposition of superstition, tradition, or personal preferences in the name of moral order.

While recognizing the importance of rational consistency as a test of moral truth, Niebuhr denies that it is, in itself, the source or meaning of moral obligation. In Niebuhr's account, the dependence of rational religion on reverence for the moral law is reversed. In *An Interpretation of Christian Ethics*, Niebuhr summarizes his view of Kant's ethical rationalism:

Thus the Christian believes that the ideal of love is real in the will and nature of God, even though he knows of no place in history where the ideal has been realized in its pure form. And it is because it has this reality that he feels the pull of obligation. The sense of obligation in

[21] See, for example, Green, *Religion and Moral Reason*, pp. 13–17.

morals from which Kant tried to derive the whole structure of religion is really derived from the religion itself. The "pull" or "drive" of moral life is a part of the religious tension of life.[22]

The point is briefly stated, even cryptic, but it will be worth our while to elaborate it.

For Niebuhr, and for much of Christian ethics, moral obligation is an experience which cannot be fully represented by a logical form. There is an affective element in the experience which is itself the source of the obligation.[23] We find ourselves impelled to act on behalf of others in ways which lead us to speak of love, not reciprocity, as the ultimate standard of morality. "A rational ethic seeks to bring the needs of others into equal consideration with those of the self. The religious ethic, (the Christian ethic more particularly, though not solely) insists that the needs of the neighbor shall be met, without a careful computation of relative needs."[24]

Reciprocity demands rigorous application of moral rules. Reason identifies moral constraints that everyone can reasonably be required to obey, and reason insures that these standards are consistently applied in moral evaluations. The expectation that I will keep my promises is a moral obligation, which others may rightly claim of me, because I can reasonably impose a reciprocal obligation on them. The wish to play my trumpet each morning at 3 o'clock confers no such claims, because I cannot concede to my sleeping neighbors a right similarly to discomfort me to satisfy their musical inclinations. There are, of course, ambiguous cases. May I claim a right to play a trumpet at 3 o'clock in the afternoon? How about on the subway? How about a piccolo? The rule of reciprocity yields no automatic answers, but for reasonable people in most circumstances,[25] it is an adequate guide to recognizing the aims and interests that mark legitimate claims on other people.

---

[22] Niebuhr, *An Interpretation of Christian Ethics*, p. 5.

[23] Kant, by contrast, interprets this affection as an experience of reverence for the moral law. See Kant, *Groundwork*, pp. 68–69.

[24] Niebuhr, *Moral Man and Immoral Society*, p. 57.

[25] It is, as R. M. Hare has pointed out in a famous example, no help against the trumpet-playing fanatic, who so values the sound of the instrument that he wants everyone to play it as often as possible. Nor, more importantly, does reciprocity

Reciprocity demands strict adherence to the moral norms that survive the critical test, but it does not imply high expectations about the standards themselves. One can argue for a strict obligation to keep promises while assuming that people will make no commitments to others that put their own aims substantially at risk. One can determine whether a person has met all the requirements of reciprocity in relationships with others without asking what efforts of self-discipline or self-sacrifice might have given that person capacities to do more. In short, as the ethical rationalism is usually presented, it includes little or nothing of the aspiration to develop personal characteristics and relationships that are *better* than those we now acknowledge as moral requirements, and not just a more consistent application of those requirements.

One function of reason in ethics, as we have seen, is to keep the aspirations of moral idealists from imposing self-sacrificial requirements on those who do not share their enthusiasms. This critical, limiting power of reason, however, quickly loses its point if the complementary pull of the ideal is not present. Where the standard of moral conduct is reciprocal acknowledgment of existing aims and interests, moral reflection becomes an extension of the negotiations by which individuals seek to advance their own purposes. The question becomes: Which interests should I choose – or how should I formulate the interests that I have – in order to insure that my own aims will be protected by the sanctions of moral obligation? Without the concern for others that originates in love, the determination of moral obligations, as Niebuhr observed, quickly deteriorates into "mere calculation of advantage."[26] Without love, the reciprocity, which was supposed to lead us beyond

---

provide an argument against the Nazi fanatic, who would affirm that he himself should be persecuted if it were to turn out that he were a Jew.

[26] Niebuhr, *Faith and History*, p. 193. It may also be the case, as Niebuhr observes, that this calculation will "tend to weight the standard of justice on the side of the one who defines the standard" (*ibid.*, p. 190). However, we should not, as Niebuhr sometimes does, treat this tendency to perpetuate the distortion of moral standards by power as a defect of moral rationalism. The rational standard, consistently applied, aims to defeat special pleading concealed by ideology, as well as more obvious self-seeking exceptions.

individual interests, may prove in the end to be just another instrument for advancing them.

REASON AND HOPE

The shortcomings of rationalist theories of morality do not necessarily lead to moral failures on the part of their adherents. People who think that all moral claims rest on a logical principle of reciprocity may end up with rigorously defined rights with which they protect their freedom to pursue their own interests, but they may also be selfless advocates of a universal community of rights. The difference between those who see the claims of justice as a vindication of their own privileges and those who find an imperative to work on behalf of others lies less in their theories than in aspirations which the theories cannot completely justify. Where the theory requires a consistent rationalism, its adherents may not even acknowledge the hopes and dreams that motivate them.

In his early writings, Reinhold Niebuhr saw this most clearly in the Marxists, who believed they had the key to scientific knowledge of society, but whose revolutionary fervor linked them in fact to the religious visions of an earlier age: "The Marxian imagines that he has a philosophy or even a science of history. What he has is really an apocalyptic vision."[27] The logic of the system does not yield the commitment necessary to challenge the existing powers.

The naïve faith of the proletarian is the faith of the man of action. Rationality belongs to the cool observers. There is of course an element of illusion in the faith of the proletarian, as there is in all faith. But it is a necessary illusion, without which some truth is obscured. The inertia of society is so stubborn that no one will move against it, if he cannot believe that it can be more easily overcome than is actually the case. And no one will suffer the perils and pains involved in the process of radical social change, if he cannot believe in the possibility of a purer and fairer society than will ever be established.[28]

---

[27] Niebuhr, *Moral Man and Immoral Society*, p. 155.   [28] *Ibid.*, p. 221.

We must take care how we understand these necessary "illusions." Beliefs which do not grasp the realities of power and the risks of change may lead to reckless acts of courage, but these are usually self-destructive, with little real effect on the situation. Such beliefs are simply false. They do not enable the people who hold them to understand the constraints and possibilities of reality, and it is no part of the task of Christian Realism to glorify the suffering that results when such beliefs are taken as guides to action.

The "illusions" to which Niebuhr refers are rather those mythic, suprarational ideas which present to the imagination possibilities for which reason cannot completely account.[29] Because reality is always more complex and varied than the systems by which we render it coherent, reasonable thinking includes anticipations of more comprehensive harmonies and further developments of our understanding that a flat-footed rationalism will always reject, because they are not part of the system of coherences on which, at present, we ordinarily rely. To call these ideas "illusions" is partly ironic, but also partly accurate; for they do not depict a reality which we can understand and control, and there is no straightforward way to plot a course from today's predictable social relationships to the greater justice that we seek. Any actual changes we make will be less than the transformation for which we have hoped.

But the hopes are not false. Indeed, a system of thought from which such hopes are missing is false, because it misrepresents our present way of thinking about reality as the reality itself. When the reality under consideration is the human world of social, political, and economic relationships, the result is to restrict our thinking about social possibilities to adjustments between competing interests, and the scope of those adjustments will be limited, moreover, primarily by existing inequalities of power. Those "realistic" constraints work well for ordinary decision-making, but they hardly exhaust the possibilities for human society. Those who confine themselves within the limits this rationality suggests will always reject

[29] See p. 62 above.

hopes for radical transformation of society as "utopian" and "unrealistic," and they will be right, in part. But they will also end up settling for less than is really possible.

It was this vivid apprehension of new social possibilities that, for Niebuhr, marked the religious element in the Marxist movement and linked it to earlier, apocalyptic forms of Christian radicalism.[30] The necessary illusions are not, however, sufficient to motivate action. For those who are comfortably situated in the world as it is, a mythic grasp of new possibilities may express itself only in sentimental pity for the sufferings of the poor, or in romantic identification with the heroes of a struggle in which one is in fact not going to participate. Niebuhr suggested in the 1930s that prophetic Christianity had largely given way to that sort of sentimentalism. Marxism attracted him as a more vital alternative, but he understood that its vitality was not the result of its theories. Reason is not the cure for sentimentality, any more than sentiment is a remedy for the abstractions of theory. What seemed necessary at that point was an unyielding commitment that frightens both the sentimentalist and the rationalist.

Sentimentality and romanticism is [*sic*] the disease of observers who dream of an ideal goal without seeking its achievement. The true proletarian who nerves himself for heroic action by believing both in the purity of his goal and the possibility of its achievement is no doubt touched with sentimentality and romanticism, but he is something more than a sentimentalist. He is both more dangerous and more vital than a sentimentalist. He is a fanatic.[31]

---

[30] For Reinhold Niebuhr, it is the mythic element in Marxism – usually unacknowledged by the Marxists themselves – that marks the point of contact between the Marxist movement and Christianity. The rational accounts of economic relationships and historical change that the Marxists offer interest Niebuhr less and less as his own work develops, precisely because Marxist theory ignores the prophetic, critical ideal that makes Marxism a powerful historical movement. In this, the use of Marxism by Reinhold Niebuhr, and by his contemporary, Paul Tillich, is quite different from that of today's liberation theologians, whose chief interest in Marxism is as a theoretical tool for social analysis. See Juan Luis Segundo, *The Liberation of Theology*, trans. John Drury (Maryknoll, N.Y.: Orbis Books, 1976), pp. 13–19; Paul Tillich, *The Socialist Decision*, trans. Franklin Sherman (New York: Harper and Row, 1977), pp. 106–112.

[31] Niebuhr, *Moral Man and Immoral Society*, p. 222.

The power of historic Christianity and contemporary Marxism to unleash this fanaticism is an ambiguous feature of both movements, opening the way to real social change, but also requiring rational restraint. It is this ambiguity that has made both Christianity and Marxism historically powerful, while the purely rational accounts of social life leave their adherents unable to do more than strike a new balance of interests within the prevailing order. "The absolutist and fanatic is no doubt dangerous, but he is also necessary. If he does not judge and criticise immediate achievements, which always involve compromise, in the light of his absolute ideal, the radical force in history, whether applied to personal or to social situations, finally sinks into the sands of complete relativism."[32] Niebuhr's way of stating this point shifts with the changing times and political climate, and with the development of his own ideas. In the early works, the emphasis is on the untamed energy of the revolutionary; in later years, the accent shifts to the "degeneration" of a search for justice that is not inspired by love. Always, however, the point is that realism in ethics and politics requires both an assessment of the forces at work in the situation and a feeling for the real possibilities that exceed the limits that our analyses put on them. Perhaps, then, we should seek to explicate Niebuhr's Christian Realism in terms of those contemporary forms of Christian ethics that stress this more particular, substantive hope.

FROM PRINCIPLE TO STORY

Today, more than half a century after Niebuhr's *An Interpretation of Christian Ethics*, criticisms of ethical rationalism abound in both philosophical and theological ethics. While much of this writing is directed against the dullness and rigidity of the analytical treatments of moral language that dominated the philosophical literature for many years, recent authors frequently make the constructive point that ethics must deal with substantive questions about the good. Ethics must help people

---

[32] *Ibid.*

to know and to articulate the things they value, as well as to keep their logic straight.[33] In theology, Stanley Hauerwas and James McClendon have taken up this theme, proposing an approach to Christian ethics which concentrates on the development of character, rather than the resolution of moral dilemmas, and which stresses the role of biblical narratives in forming a personal orientation toward substantive moral goods.[34] While the intellectual questions that prompted the formulation of these recent versions of "virtue ethics" or "narrative ethics" were quite different from the issues that led to Christian Realism, it is possible that Niebuhr's objections to ethical rationalism can be understood by relating them to this more recent emphasis on substantive moral issues and the role that religious traditions play in shaping our ideas about the human good.

Niebuhr's own attention to these issues was shaped primarily by a concern to understand the sources of social, rather than personal, transformation. By identifying the religious expectation of perfect justice as a primary motivation for action against present injustice, Niebuhr joined with a number of European social theorists who had rejected the claims of "scientific socialism" and turned their attention to social ideals and utopian visions as important factors in social change. Karl Mannheim located the historical roots of revolutionary thinking in the apocalyptic expectations of Christian radicals at the beginning of the modern era.[35]

[33] One of the first important statements of this position was Iris Murdoch, *The Sovereignty of Good* (New York: Schocken, 1971). A very good recent assessment of these issues in moral philosophy is provided by Charles Taylor, *Sources of the Self*.

[34] For Hauerwas' first statement of this position, see Stanley Hauerwas, *Character and the Christian Life* (Trinity University Studies in Religion; San Antonio: Trinity University Press, 1975). See also James W. McClendon, *Systematic Theology: Ethics* (Nashville: Abingdon Press, 1986). Also to be noted in this context is the theology of George Lindbeck, although Lindbeck says little specifically about Christian ethics, and the ethics of John Howard Yoder, though Yoder's work began with a quite different set of theological and philosophical issues. See George Lindbeck, *The Nature of Doctrine* (Philadelphia: Westminster Press, 1984); John Howard Yoder, *The Politics of Jesus* (Grand Rapids: Eerdmans, 1972); *The Priestly Kingdom: Social Ethics as Gospel* (Notre Dame, Ind.: University of Notre Dame Press, 1984).

[35] Karl Mannheim, *Ideology and Utopia*, trans. Louis Wirth and Edward Shils (New York: Harcourt, Brace, and World, n.d.), pp. 211–219. Mannheim's work appeared in Germany in 1929. Niebuhr makes essentially the same point in his

The immediate source of Niebuhr's insight, however, was probably his reflection on the ethics of the Social Gospel movement in North America. The leaders of this movement – preachers, journalists, and professors of the emergent disciplines of sociology and social ethics – were appalled by the conditions of life in the new industrial centers of the late nineteenth century. They turned to direct investigations and to methods of scientific study for an accurate description of the problems, but the moral appeal of their radical alternative rested, more often than not, on the discrepancy between these blighted, wasted lives and the way of life envisioned in the New Testament.[36] Gradually, the idea emerged that the teachings of Jesus provide a social vision that differs dramatically from the individualistic constraints of traditional Christian morals, and that is incompatible with prevailing economic and social relationships.

Niebuhr, of course, challenged this easy transition from New Testament ideals to modern social applications. The high demands of the Gospel do not provide a supreme moral principle that applies directly to human affairs, but those demands are central to the "critical attitude" that Niebuhr expects Christians to bring to political life. The Christian message, grounded in the story of Jesus' universal love and radical disregard for human status and human distinctions, is more than the historical source to which all the forms of Christianity can be traced. It remains the criterion by which all Christians are judged, even though it cannot be reduced to a single principle or a rule of reason by which the Christians might, in the manner of the ethical rationalists, judge everything else.

criticism of Marxist rationalism in *Moral Man and Immoral Society*, though the earliest evidence of Niebuhr's direct acquaintance with Mannheim's work that I have noted are references to *Ideology and Utopia* in *The Nature and Destiny of Man*, I, 196–97, II, 237n.

[36] Walter Rauschenbusch presented a systematic account of the problem in his *Christianity and the Social Crisis* (Louisville: Westminster/John Knox, 1992). For a more complete account of the secularization of the Social Gospel in twentieth-century social science, see Arthur J. Vidich and Stanford M. Lyman, *American Sociology: Worldly Rejections of Religion and Their Directions* (New Haven: Yale University Press, 1985), esp. chapters 9–12.

Attentiveness to the biblical narrative and an imaginative grasp of all things in relationship to God keep our specific determinations of justice from the rigid rationalism that inevitably privileges the interests of the powerful. In contrast to his Social Gospel predecessors, Niebuhr is aware of the interpretation of Jesus' work already going on in the Gospels. The truth that transcends all systems and orders of justice is not so simply related to the story of Jesus for Niebuhr, and it is more tied to the attitude of messianic expectation.[37] Nevertheless, without the "impossible ideal" of Jesus' ethics, we have only variations on the utilitarian and prudential schemes which from the Christian critical perspective scarcely deserve to be called "ethics" at all. If the limitations of every rational system make some correction of rational justice necessary, only the morally meaningful universe apprehended by Christian faith provides a basis on which such corrections may actually be attempted.

Niebuhr thus weaves a complex relationship between Christian narrative and moral life. The uncompromising moral demands which Jesus makes in the Gospels are a necessary corrective to the shortcomings of rational ethics, which too easily becomes a justification of existing interests, rather than a motive to create new ways to resolve conflicts. But Jesus' ethics will not work for us in any simple way. If the tendency to self-justification in rational ethics gradually erodes the demands of the moral life, an uncompromised Christian ethics threatens to demolish them outright, erasing the distinction between moral concern for the neighbor's good and a blind zeal to make the will of God prevail. To achieve the Social Gospel's goal of a transformed society, it is necessary to abandon the Social Gospel's stated purpose to apply Jesus' ethics directly to the problems of inequality, poverty, and social disorder.[38]

---

[37] See *The Nature and Destiny of Man*, II, 1–34.
[38] Reinhold Niebuhr, "The Ethic of Jesus and the Social Problem," *Religion in Life*, 1 (Spring, 1932), 198.

THE CASE AGAINST RESPONSIBILITY

The impossibility of relating biblical faith directly to contemporary events and choices was a key point of agreement among American theological realists in the 1930s. In arguing that point against their Social Gospel predecessors, however, they often overlooked the need to make a case for the central point on which Christian Realists and the Social Gospel agree: the need for Christian participation in the work of social transformation. Niebuhr takes it as obvious that the Christian "critical attitude" which measures all plans against the demands of the Gospel must be balanced by a "responsible attitude" that is still prepared to make the real choices, even though all the options are less than what love requires.[39] Why is this "responsible" attitude a Christian duty? If all of the choices are evil, why not simply refuse to choose?

During Niebuhr's lifetime, this question was raised by pacifists who rejected the military defense of democracy that Reinhold Niebuhr regarded as a key expression of Christian Realism's "responsible attitude." For Guy Hershberger, a Mennonite theologian who wrote a response to Niebuhr in 1944, Christian Realism is at once an affirmation and an abandonment of the rigorous ethical demands of the Gospel. Having stated so clearly the requirements of love, no one who professes to believe them can give a good reason for setting them aside.

No doubt the most challenging anti-pacifist Christian writer today is Reinhold Niebuhr. He denies popular pacifism and the doctrine of nonviolent resistance a place in the New Testament ethic, and here he is on solid ground. He asserts that the New Testament ethic is one of uncompromising nonresistance and warns the pacifist to "leave the world of politics alone entirely ... and remind the rest of us, who fool with politics, that we are playing a dangerous game." Mennonites admire Niebuhr's sound evaluation of the Christian ethic, but they are disappointed to see him cast aside this pearl of great price in order

[39] See page 73 above.

that he might himself pursue "the dangerous game of fooling with politics."[40]

John Howard Yoder and Stanley Hauerwas have continued this line of criticism of Christian Realism in their more recent writings. Niebuhr's insistence that responsible Christianity requires a compromise of the demands of Jesus' ethics fails to ask the prior question of whether Christians should be taking responsibility for the life of society in the first place.

The differences between Niebuhr's Christian Realism and these contemporary rejections of political compromise are obvious. For the moment, however, we need to focus on the similarities, because the disagreement over the role of Christians in society takes the shape it does only because of some important ideas about Christian ethics which the parties all share.

They agree, first, that Christianity imposes moral demands which exceed, and even contradict, the requirements of ordinary prudential ethics, which is concerned to establish some sort of balance between the competing interests and powers that shape everyday life. Hershberger and Yoder trace the higher requirements in the life of a non-resistant community that lives apart from the tensions and conflicts that require prudent management. Niebuhr finds the requirements in a "dimension of depth" that religious awareness provides, enabling people to see beyond the limited interests and goals that ordinarily drive them. In both cases, therefore, Christians seek to avoid excessive identification with the surrounding culture, since that tends both to lower their moral expectations and to deprive them of the witness to alternative possibilities that is their principal contribution to a civilization that is seriously distorted by its own internal contradictions. However important the insights of sociology, psychology, and the modern physical sciences may be to an understanding of our contemporary situation, the dimension of depth must be learned pri-

---

[40] Guy F. Hershberger, *War, Peace, and Nonresistance* (Scottdale, Pa.: Herald Press, 1944), p. 298. Hershberger is quoting from an article in *Christian Century*, December 14, 1938. I have shortened Hershberger's quotation from Niebuhr.

marily from the myths and symbols – the narratives, if you will
– of the biblical tradition.[41]

The prophetic faith, articulated in the Hebrew scriptures
and fully realized in Jesus of Nazareth, has a specific, substantive understanding of the good derived from its primary image
of God as creator.

> To say that God is the creator is to use an image which transcends the
> canons of rationality, but which expresses both his organic relation to
> the world and his distinction from the world. To believe that God
> created the world is to feel that the world is a realm of meaning and
> coherence without insisting that the world is totally good or that the
> totality of things must be identified with the Sacred.[42]

A different understanding of God's relationship to the world,
or a philosophy which dismisses the theological question altogether, must necessarily have a different view of the good.
There can be no question, therefore, of a universal morality
that reduces Jesus to an example – even a very fine example –
of the human good.[43] Nor can Christians provide a rational
moral principle that would allow anyone to determine what
this prophetic ethic requires without reference to its idea of
God. The application of Christian insight to public questions
must be mediated, not by a principle, but by what Niebuhr
calls an "attitude" that is both critical and responsible.
Perhaps we could make a link with Hauerwas and McClendon
by calling that attitude a *virtue*, a settled disposition to view
situations in a certain way, and to choose and to act in ways
appropriate to that view. If so, we might expect to find a range
of characteristically Christian responses to moral challenges,
even though there would be no principle by which we might
determine in advance exactly what Christian ethics requires.

It is thus possible to offer an account of Niebuhr's ethics,
drawn particularly from the early chapters of *An Interpretation of
Christian Ethics*, which fits remarkably well with the key themes
of contemporary formulations of Christian ethics that are oriented toward ideas of virtue and narrative. To be sure, virtue

---

[41] For these themes in Niebuhr, see *An Interpretation of Christian Ethics*, pp. 1–3, 6–7,
145–46.
[42] *Ibid.*, p. 16.   [43] *Ibid.*, p. 9.

theorists in theological ethics are often sharply critical of Christian Realism, finding in its commitments to political freedom,
democracy, and justice an entanglement with cultural values
that limits from the outset the radical demands of biblical faith.
Also, both Hauerwas and Yoder seem more clearly aware than
Niebuhr of the importance of a community of faith for nurtur-
ing and sustaining the distinctive Christian vision. Upon closer
examination, however, the virtue theorists' criticism of Christian Realism often provides a curious echo of the Realists'
criticisms of their liberal predecessors.[44] Perhaps, as with Niebuhr's arguments against the Social Gospel, the continuity is
greater than the critic would at first want to admit. Successive
generations of American Protestant ethicists have been able to
carry through the twentieth century a running debate about
the appropriate participation of Christians in politics and
social issues precisely because they shared the basic idea that
biblical faith makes moral demands that transcend the possibilities of ordinary social life and call into question the terms
and conditions on which that life has been constituted.

In this broader historical perspective, one might construe
Christian Realism as an anticipation of Christian narrative
ethics. The narrative then would read that we have gradually
learned to mistrust the adjustments to modern Western liberalism that the Social Gospel made unwittingly, and that the
Christian Realists took up deliberately, as necessary compromises. As a result, so the narrative would continue, we are now
able to identify and act on a distinctive Christian ethic.
Because we no longer hold the false hope for a universal moral
reason, we are not so likely to be taken in by modern liberalism's pretensions to have attained that universality. If that
imposes on us a more critical social stance and a more marginal
political role than our Christian Realist predecessors had, that
is simply because we understand and articulate more clearly
the radical demands of the independent Christian ethic for

---

[44] Hauerwas notes this in his own criticism of Reinhold Niebuhr's christology: "In
spite of his criticism of the social gospel, much of Niebuhr's christology continued in
the vein of treating Jesus not as the redeemer but as the perfect example or teacher
of love." (*A Community of Character*, p. 234n.)

which Reinhold Niebuhr could only wish. The failure of ethical rationalism, which Christian Realism already anticipated, leaves communitarianism as the only viable alternative, however much those who wish to continue fooling with politics in a liberal democratic mode may resist the conclusion.

COMPROMISE OR COHERENCE?

The account we have just given of Protestant social ethics from Rauschenbusch, through Niebuhr, to the contemporary narrative ethics of Hauerwas and McClendon makes a number of important points. It is a useful corrective to the general impression that contemporary narrative and virtue ethics are diametrically opposed to the public ethics of the Christian Realists, and it reminds us that many of the paradigmatic conflicts in American Protestantism have taken shape against a background of more basic agreements, agreements which have provided real continuity across three or four generations of changing problems and shifting ecumenical strategies.

Nevertheless, my revisionist narrative, as it stands, is too simple, for it reduces the differences between the Christian Realists and the narrativists to a strategic question about compromise. That difference is real, but by the time Niebuhr and his colleagues had thought it through, it was more than a question of strategy. What they first conceptualized as a necessary compromise of Gospel ethics became a complex form of ethical naturalism in which the human meaning of the moral ideal only becomes available in relationship to the historical developments, political powers, and human tendencies that define specific possibilities for its application. What happens when the Christian Realist applies the requirements of love to the tasks of social transformation is not a compromise of what love requires, but rather the first clear statement of those requirements. As with other forms of human knowledge, we understand the meaning of love only when we can relate its demands to the rest of what we believe to be true about the world.

Despite the pragmatic turn of mind that characterizes all of his work, Niebuhr's earliest writings on ethics do not always develop this point clearly. In *Moral Man and Immoral Society*, the possibility of social transformation seems in the end to rest with those who deny the necessity of compromise. Their understanding of social possibilities is not true, in the pragmatic terms that Niebuhr even here understands truth. What they believe about themselves and their movements are "illusions," but they are necessary illusions. Myths and symbols provide the motivation that generates real change. The compromises that would lend stability to a new order must come from somewhere else.

In the task of that redemption, the most effective agents will be men who have substituted some new illusions for the abandoned ones. The most important of these illusions is that the collective life of mankind can achieve perfect justice. It is a very valuable illusion for the moment; for justice cannot be approximated if the hope of its realization does not generate a sublime madness in the soul. Nothing but such madness will do battle with malignant power and "spiritual wickedness in high places." The illusion is dangerous because it encourages terrible fanaticisms. It must therefore be brought under the control of reason. One can only hope that reason will not destroy it before its work is done.[45]

Moral Man and Immoral Society was by all measures a major achievement of modern religious social thought, but the idea of Christian Realism that emerges at the end of its pages lacks the synthetic perspective that Niebuhr's writing as a whole offers to the task of Christian ethics. We face a curious, lurching account of historical change in which idealists fired by fanatical energy lead us in directions that reason cannot prescribe, only to be reined in by the rationalists when the hopes for justice fail to work.

Given that statement of the problem, it is not clear where Niebuhr himself wants to stand. Rationalists have control over the real outcome of events, but their ways of thinking about the problems can at best provide a variation on the present balancing of powers and interests. Idealists have genuine alternatives and the critical insights of prophetic religion, but they

---

[45] Niebuhr, *Moral Man and Immoral Society*, p. 277.

are too unyielding in their commitments to these "illusions" to offer any guidance for the real choices. The "critical attitude" and the "responsible attitude" are here completely separated. The Christian Realist is one who understands that separation, and cherishes no illusions that it can be overcome.

The final page of *Moral Man and Immoral Society* thus presents in sharp contrasts a picture of the dynamics of change that exponents of the progressive, humanizing social effects of Christianity were understandably reluctant to accept.[46] But if we accept those contrasts, the book ends just in time, for on the next page, as it were, the Christian thinker would have to decide whether to stand with the biblical idealists or with the responsible rationalists.

Niebuhr's sensitivity to the multiplicity of ideas, ideologies, and interests that shape modern consciousness led him to hesitate before that choice. He knew that few twentieth-century Christians could rest easily with either their biblical vision of a new creation or their reasoned assessment of alternatives for very long, and the more they understood of the contrast between the positions, the more uneasy they would be with both of them. By contrast, many of the contemporary narrative theorists appear to find the choice between criticism and responsibility an easy one. It is for them a "Constantinian" distortion of Christianity's role to take responsibility for working out solutions to society's problems.[47] To take responsibility for the course of events is to suppose that we have the power to make things turn out as we think they should. Neither the biblical insistence that history is in God's hands nor the social reality of Christianity's weakness as a force in the modern world warrants that supposition for Christians. Responsibility is what they do not have – cannot have and should not want – if they understand the social implications of the Gospel.

Much of Reinhold Niebuhr's early work points us in exactly

[46] See Fox, *Reinhold Niebuhr*, pp. 136–41 for a survey of the initial critical reception of *Moral Man and Immoral Society*.

[47] See Yoder, *The Priestly Kingdom*, pp. 135–47; Stanley Hauerwas, *Against the Nations* (Minneapolis: Winston Press, 1985), especially pp. 122–30.

this direction. If we resist making this his final conclusion, as I think we should, we must make sense of Niebuhr's later claim that criticism and responsibility are not merely two independent and opposed forces, but two attitudes that can be held by one person. Since he was already clear that reasoned responsibility could not provide substantive alternatives, the key to the synthesis would have to be an account of the critical ideals that sets them in relationship to particular choices.

A theological account of responsibility thus begins with a reassessment of the ordinary social relationships that are set in contrast to the prophetic idea of relationships ordered by the law of love. These relationships are not simply an undifferentiated mass that stands inert before or in opposition to the transformative powers of love. Understanding society is largely a matter of understanding the many different forces and powers that work together or against one another to shape the course of events. Economic motives weaken traditional loyalties and permit the emergence of new social roles and new ways to organize work. Traditional loyalties reassert themselves in sentiments of nationalism, and under the conditions of modern society nationalism comes to expression in the form of a centralized state bureaucracy. A bureaucratic state functions most efficiently when it can treat all of its citizens as equals, but the power of the bureaucracy itself tends to create a new elite of administrators and officials in competition with the older aristocracies of wealth and rank. Competitive pressures from foreign powers may lead to adjustments that open new opportunities in domestic systems, or they may provoke a protective reaction that locks in existing social and economic relationships. The forces are multiple, the interactions are complex, and the variations are endless. Simply to understand them is a major intellectual challenge, and one in which Christian Realists are notoriously happy to be immersed. Reinhold Niebuhr's essays and editorials could, as his critics frequently observed, continue for paragraphs or pages with analysis of party platforms, labor disputes, and international conflicts, with hardly a mention of theological issues.

Nevertheless, the theology shapes the analysis in important

ways. If Niebuhr was able to give a coherent account of social and historical forces that other observers either ignored or overstated, the coherence and unity of his thought often derives from the power of theological concepts to illuminate elements of a situation that might otherwise be missed and to hold alternative ways of accounting for events in a creative tension. For Niebuhr, Christian narratives and symbols become a part of the system of coherences by which we order our beliefs, and they interact with other ideas in complex ways:

Niebuhr did not recommend the prophetic myth – the narrative of creation, the fall, God's judgment and redemption of history – as an object of aesthetic appreciation, a set of agreeable fictions. He maintained that it gave a true account of the human condition, superior to other accounts. Judeo-Christian prophecy, like any other myth, was prescientific, but it was also "supra-scientific."[48]

Prophetic denunciations of greed and Jesus' compassion for the poor direct our attention to specific aspects of our common life that become standards of justice and measures of the moral worth of the whole society. Attentiveness to the effects that tax, trade, or immigration policies have on the poor is not simply the result of knowing how to calculate the likely results. It depends on the conviction that these effects are morally important, that policies which neglect the poor are incoherent with significant ideas about how a society ought to function. Jewish and Christian traditions articulate this conviction in ways that coherences based on considerations of economic efficiency are apt to miss. As the National Conference of Catholic Bishops recently put it, "Central to the biblical presentation of justice is that the justice of a community is measured by its treatment of the powerless in society, most often described as the widow, the orphan, the poor, and the stranger (non-Israelite) in the land."[49] In many such ways, theological ideas identify the issues and concerns that make policy questions morally impor-

---

[48] Christopher Lasch, *The True and Only Heaven: Progress and Its Critics* (New York: W. W. Norton, 1991), p. 371.

[49] National Conference of Catholic Bishops, *Economic Justice for All: Pastoral Letter on Catholic Social Teaching and the U.S. Economy* (Washington, D.C.: United States Catholic Conference, 1986), p. 21.

tant. Where these ideas are assumed, as they often are in Niebuhr's editorials and occasional pieces, analysis can concentrate on the policies themselves. Where they are missing, as they often are in analyses shaped by narrowly defined conceptions of economic rationality, national interest, or strategic necessity, the policy proposals lack coherence with a wider set of ideas and convictions about society, however sound their internal logic may be.

Religious traditions and symbols thus identify attitudes, values, and virtues that are relevant to a more comprehensive assessment of present choices, but those present choices also give substance to the tradition. In modern society, we are aware of needs for education, self-expression, and self-respect that go far beyond the basic material needs for food, shelter, and protection from exploitation that the Bible associates with help for the poor. Even where those material needs remain the central problem, as they are for the homeless in the cities of the developed world and many workers in less developed countries, we have a better understanding of the underlying social and economic forces that create the apparent problems, and we recognize that caring for "the widow, the poor, and the stranger in the land" may involve work far more complex than relieving the immediate needs of individuals. Decisions about what ought to be done require us to relate the biblical demand for justice to investigations into social facts, theories about the economy and society, and informed assessments of the probable results of alternative courses of action. Moral choices are made when these complex and diverse elements are brought into some coherence. No single element determines the conclusion, and our thinking about all of the elements is apt to be subtly changed in the process of relating one to another.

In this moral reflection, religious concepts, myths, and symbols provide specific moral ideals, such as care for the stranger, stewardship of resources, or love for one's enemies, but they also provide what Niebuhr called the "deeper dimension of history."[50] They encourage us to believe that these

---

[50] Niebuhr, *The Nature and Destiny of Man*, II, 96; see page 71.

disparate, often conflicting elements *can* be unified, and even more important, they suggest the possibility of larger, more inclusive coherences that run beyond the solutions to immediate problems. They provide symbols and rituals through which that unity of life can be anticipated and enacted, even when it cannot be completely formulated as a system of ideas.

Ideas about God or about the end of history are always more than summaries of experience. Indeed, they are powerful precisely because they carry the conviction that *some* experiences, the real experiences of confusion, disorder, and conflict, are not the last word. But they have that power only insofar as they relate to the full range of our experiences, and do not arbitrarily exclude any of them from consideration. "An adequate religion," Niebuhr wrote in a lecture first published in 1934, "is always an ultimate optimism which has entertained all the facts that lead to pessimism."[51] Personal experiences of tragedy and physical suffering, and historical experiences of injustice, genocide, and tyranny become tests for theology. Their violence and destruction of meaning pose challenges to our symbols of unity which faith may answer, but which it cannot ignore, and our ideas about God will surely be changed in the process of finding coherences between these experiences and the others which point us in the direction of love and justice. The "meaningful universe" which Niebuhr identifies as the presupposition of moral obligation enters into our experience only as we discern these coherences between our ideas of God and the events of our lives and our history.

So it is not the case that we have a world of moral meaning that unfortunately does not exist in the real world where we live,[52] or a moral life that can be lived out in some carefully selected community setting, but not, alas, in the social and political world inhabited by other people generally. Moral ideas and systems are about choices that people have to make, about things that they can be urged or required to do. The

---

[51] Reinhold Niebuhr, *Christianity and Power Politics* (New York: Charles Scribner's Sons, 1940), p. 182.

[52] Cf. Bonhoeffer's remark that "an ethic cannot be a book in which there is set out how everything in the world ought to be but unfortunately is not ..." (Dietrich Bonhoeffer, *Ethics*, trans. Neville H. Smith [New York: Macmillan, 1965], p. 269).

meaning of moral terms is fixed as we establish coherences between what we take to be the facts about human life, the aspirations we feel as individuals or share with others in community, and the traditions of moral thought that stand in complex relationships of judgment and dependence on both the facts and our aspirations. These moral meanings take a variety of forms – virtues to be practiced, goals to be sought, principles to be followed – but they do not exist apart from the conditions of life as we presently understand them. Kant's celebrated dictum that "ought implies can" sets a limit on the use of moral terms that must be observed even by those who do not share the Kantian confidence that we can specify the transcendental conditions of that limit.

The coherentist account of moral meaning which we have sketched here is consistent with the pragmatic realism that characterizes Reinhold Niebuhr's treatment of religious ideas and symbols. But if we accept it as a theoretical formulation of Christian Realism's approach to ethics, we must then reject the language of "compromise" by which both Christian Realists and their critics have often characterized the relationship between the ethics of Jesus and social ethics. Rather, the early characterization of Christian Realism by Walter Marshall Horton seems to capture the correct relationship between Christian symbol and social fact. A realistic faith links human aspirations, social facts, and religious belief in ways that relate us to the real conditions of life, avoiding both exaggerated expectations and debilitating hopelessness.

[The] word "realism" suggests to me, above all, a resolute determination to face all the facts of life candidly, beginning preferably with the most stubborn, perplexing, and disheartening ones, so that any lingering romantic illusions may be dispelled at the start; and then, *through* these stubborn facts and not *in spite of them*, to pierce as deep as one may into the solid structure of reality, until one finds whatever ground of courage, hope, and faith is *actually* there, independent of human preferences and desires, and so casts anchor in that ground.[53]

---

[53] Horton, *Realistic Theology*, p. 38.

In this identification of the real grounds for courage, hope, and faith, the biblical resources for Christian thought – what Niebuhr calls the biblical "myths" and what Hauerwas and McClendon mean by "the Christian narrative" – play a crucial role. That role, however, is not just to represent "a political alternative to every nation,"[54] but also to represent the possibilities implicit in the immediate political realities. In a realistic Christian ethics, biblical resources help us to pick out, among a range of forces that have been clearly differentiated and accurately understood, those that move in directions that are compatible with the hope for justice, and to distinguish them from those which do not. The first task of ethical reflection is to establish the connections between human experience, social fact, and biblical symbol that make those judgments possible.

FROM NARRATIVE TO NATURALISM

The coherentist account of Christian Realism which I have presented here helps us to understand why so much Realist writing deals with labor disputes, campaign strategies, racial conflict, or international agreements, with little direct reference to theological concepts and traditions. While theological understandings are obviously subject to controversy and to revision, much of the task of ethical reflection is to connect those understandings with particular social and historical situations. The difficult part, for persons in a community with broadly shared theological ideas, is often to determine exactly what that situation is, or to persuade others to follow one's own assessment of it.

While this often leads to complaints about preachers and theologians reaching into areas beyond their competence,[55] we should not suppose that these reflections on economics, sociology, or defense strategy are amateur efforts which the ethi-

---

[54] Hauerwas, *A Community of Character*, p. 12.

[55] In 1926, British prime minister Stanley Baldwin asked how a group of bishops who were attempting to mediate a coal strike would like it if the Iron and Steel Federation attempted a revision of the Athanasian Creed. See William Temple, *Christianity and the Social Order* (New York: Penguin Books, 1942), p. 7.

cists could give up in favor of a more useful hobby. A Realist seeking a basis for action must have some explicit understanding of what the situation is in which action is to be taken, even when the elements of the situation are complex, difficult to grasp, and subject to very different interpretations. If the coherentist approach to ethics is correct, the point is not to persuade the theologians to give up fiddling with complex and technical questions, but to find ways of making those questions open to public discussion. For unless we can do that, there can be no public ethics.

Practical choices are not made by ideals alone, whether they be the biblical ideal of a justice that protects the poor and the weak, or a socialist ideal of economic equality, or simply the longings of individuals for a life that would be better, in quite specific ways, than the life they have known. What we ought to do becomes clear as we set those aspirations in relation to the workings of social institutions, the constraints of technology and natural resources, ecological requirements, and the facts of human nature – both those that we take to be stable, permanent features of human life and those that are particular to persons with our own culture and history. As we have understood it here, moral goodness is not a reality that exists independently of states of affairs, by which we might then judge that persons and institutions do or do not conform to it. Nor is moral goodness a judgment that God pronounces over situations, so that we are unable to identify the good in the situation unless we have also heard the Word. To say that a person or a state of affairs is morally good, to conclude that an action is the right thing to do, to identify a goal as better than the existing conditions – all these moral statements express our understanding that a particular constellation of facts links aspirations and limitations in that peculiarly satisfying way that we call "good." If we get the facts wrong, we will be wrong about the ethics, too; for the reality to which moral realism refers is not a separate realm of moral ideas, independent of the facts. Moral realities *are* facts about the world, properties that we judge persons, actions, and situations to have precisely because they have identifiable factual characteristics that link up in appropriate ways with other sets of facts and possibilities.

The Niebuhrian version of moral realism thus leads us in the direction of *ethical naturalism,* an account of moral facts which sees them as having a reality independent of our minds, but not independent of other, non-moral facts about the world. A description of a welfare policy or a court decision as "just," for example, is obviously quite different from an account of the same things in terms of the accounting procedures used to estimate the costs of the one or the relationship to appropriate legal precedents of the other. But the situation that is fiscally sound or legally correct is not a different situation from the situation that is just. It is the same situation, and the decision about justice turns on the facts of the case, appropriately related to other facts, as does the decision about fiscal soundness or legal correctness.

At this point, the reader may want to protest that something must have gone wrong in this effort to make a systematic distinction between Christian Realism and recent versions of Christian ethics that begin with the Christian narrative, if only because Reinhold Niebuhr himself persistently rejects what he calls "naturalism" in ethics. Nor are the objections Niebuhr's alone. Recent efforts to locate foundations for ethics in evolutionary biology or in transcendental conditions that structure all human communication have, in the end, left some philosophers more convinced that we can make no sense of ethics apart from the particular evaluative frameworks by which people structure their lived experience. The "naturalist illusion," as Charles Taylor terms it, was that moral principles could be grounded in facts in ways that would make differentiation and choice between moral goods unnecessary.[56] Niebuhr's objections to a naturalism that "vitiates the vertical tension between concrete fact and transcendent source"[57] seems, if anything, more cogent in the context of moral philosophy today than it did when it was published in the heyday of Deweyan naturalism in 1935.

[56] Taylor, *Sources of the Self,* pp. 22–23.
[57] Niebuhr, *An Interpretation of Christian Ethics,* p. 20.

Upon closer inspection, however, Niebuhr's objection proves to be against a particular form of naturalism, and not against the idea that moral judgments are about the natural properties of persons and situations. Here, as at other points in Niebuhr's thought, his penchant for sharp disagreement with specific ideas obscures a much larger area of agreement between him and his opponents.[58]

The principal alternatives to ethical naturalism are suggested by intuitionist accounts of moral knowledge and by voluntarist accounts of moral meaning.[59] For the intuitionist, the fact that so often we "just know" that an act is wrong suggests that these moral aspects of experience are unique properties of actions and situations, not discerned by examining and drawing conclusions about natural properties. Nothing we can learn by examining things with ordinary empirical tools of observation can settle whether an act is right. A voluntarist, by contrast, holds that what makes an act right is the will of an appropriate authority who pronounces it so. The moral question is a question of fact about some *will*, not the facts of the situation. For an act to be right may mean that the sovereign or the legislature has willed it so, or, in a theological voluntarism, that God has willed it.

---

[58] Niebuhr was critical of prevailing versions of ethical naturalism, not only the reductive, secular form, but also the naturalism of Roman Catholic natural law ethics. Natural law thinking, he believed, put too much trust in reason's power to discern a normative human nature amidst the conflicting facts and forces of life. Like the contemporary philosophical naturalism, treatments of natural law in moral theology emphasized the general features of human nature. For complex historical reasons, the attention of moral theologians has often been concentrated on biological determinants that all human beings presumably share, rather than the cultural diversity of their expression. This feature of traditional Roman Catholic natural law ethics has drawn a good deal of criticism from Catholic moral theologians themselves in recent years. Niebuhr regarded it as typical of the genre, and he repeatedly criticized natural law for a static, overdetermined view of human nature. Here, too, Niebuhr's complaint must be set against the background of a broad agreement that there *are* natural features of human life that are relevant to our moral choices. Those who find it worthwhile to argue about the specifics of human nature in the context of a discussion of moral choice probably already share a broad commitment to ethical naturalism. On the natural law thinking implicit in Niebuhr's own work, see Paul Ramsey, "Love and Law," in Charles W. Kegley and Robert W. Bretall, eds., *Reinhold Niebuhr: His Religious, Social, and Political Thought* (New York: Macmillan, 1956), pp. 79–123.

[59] Non-cognitivism is also an alternative, but we will not consider that here.

The appeal of these non-naturalist alternatives is that they provide a simple, single criterion by which to determine whether an act is right. If we apprehend immediately that this busy traveler, stopping to help a stranger in trouble, has done the right thing, then the matter is settled. If we acknowledge that God has commanded us to act as this traveler is doing, then we know that the action is right. No further investigation is required.

The problems begin, of course, when we disagree. Unless we have carefully constructed a system like Hobbes' *Leviathan*, in which the whole point is to have one person whose will we have agreed in advance to accept, it is difficult to know what we should do if our initial moral judgments differ. What do we investigate to decide whether this non-natural property that my neighbor intuits and I do not is really present? How do we decide what God has willed?

The appeal of coherentist ethical naturalism is not that it eliminates moral disagreements, but that it suggests a way to resolve them. Although there is no single, determinative feature of acts that identifies them as right, their rightness is constituted by natural features which we do know how to investigate, and about which we have some ideas for resolving disagreements. The rightness of an act, as some ethical naturalists put it, *supervenes* upon natural facts. An act is right because of certain natural facts.[60] Helping the stranger in distress is right because it preserves or enhances the life of the stranger, and because it involves no disproportionate risk to the well-being of the one who gives aid. Giving this particular school a portion of the money I have earned by writing is right, because this school helped me to learn those skills, and because none of the others to whom I am tied makes a weightier claim on these resources. Faced with any disagreement about these moral claims, the ethical naturalist does not appeal to intuitions or to authoritative decrees. He or she looks for misstatements of the constituent facts, or for relevant facts that have been overlooked.

[60] See Brink, *Moral Realism*, pp. 160–61. See also the discussion of ethical naturalism on pp. 13–15 above.

So far, so good. The problems that Niebuhr identifies with naturalism begin when the naturalist tries to emulate the simplicity of the non-naturalist position by reducing the range of relevant facts. The question of rightness then no longer involves weighing a variety of qualitatively different consequences and relationships, but only a single calculation of what makes for the "greatest happiness," for example.[61] The determination becomes even simpler when the reduction is made in a way that eliminates subjective measures of pleasure, satisfaction, or pain, so that the relevant natural facts are measurable in terms of economic productivity or gene pool enhancement.

Morton White labels these versions of ethical naturalism "reductive naturalism." Reductive naturalism attempts to formulate moral judgments by a simple, definitive method in which moral facts are not merely *constituted by* natural facts, but are *identical with* a specific, limited range of them.[62] Moral truth simply is whatever the facts of the case are regarding the general happiness, or the gross national product, or the gene pool.

It is this reductive naturalism that Niebuhr labels "naturalism" and then rejects, because it has no use for the law of love.[63] He is right, of course, but reductive naturalism has no use for many other things that also figure in a realistic judgment that a particular course of action is right. Non-reductive naturalism, what P. F. Strawson calls "liberal" or "catholic" naturalism,[64] by contrast treats a very broad range of facts as relevant to moral assessments. Personal satisfactions, affective responses, and the cumulative experience of individuals and communities are among the elements around which a considered moral judgment must be built, along with other considerations susceptible to more objective determination. As Morton White puts it:

---

[61] Cf. Bentham's "hedonic calculus."

[62] White, *What Is and What Ought to Be Done*, pp. 14, 104–5.

[63] Keith Ward, "Reinhold Niebuhr and the Christian Hope," in Harries, ed., *Reinhold Niebuhr*, p. 63.

[64] P. F. Strawson, *Skepticism and Naturalism: Some Varieties* (New York: Columbia University Press, 1985), pp. 1, 39–41. Obviously, there is no reference to the religious or political meanings of these terms.

The descriptive scientist, by using the linguistic structure he has built, will be able to connect some of his sensory experiences with others, and in this sense organize them; the moral judge, by using the linguistic structure *he* has built, will be able to connect his sensory experiences with his feeling of obligation. Using a mechanical metaphor rather than the biological metaphor of organization, one might say that the descriptive scientist builds conceptual bridges that allow him to move from sensory experiences to other sensory experiences whereas the moral judge builds conceptual bridges that not only get him from some sensory experiences to other sensory experiences but also from sensory experiences to moral feelings.[65]

Christian Realism is an ethical naturalism in this non-reductive, inclusive sense, although it must surely reject the reductive versions of naturalism against which Niebuhr complained in *An Interpretation of Christian Ethics*. White, Strawson, and other more recent writers provide a theoretical framework in which to understand both the feelings of faith, hope, and courage and the "stubborn and disheartening" facts that can come into play in a realistic moral judgment.

Having said that, we should not expect that the substance of the Christian Realist's moral reflection will exactly match that of the contemporary non-reductive naturalist. While the philosophers provide a clear theoretical statement about the mixed body of beliefs that supports every normative judgment, their analyses of particular normative judgments are usually limited to schematic textbook examples of moral argument in which the elements to be brought into coherence are far simpler than those involved in actual, everyday thought and speech. White speaks generally of "moral feelings" with little attention to the qualitative differences that distinguish religious awe, moral indignation, and physical disgust one from another, and sometimes set them in conflict. Strawson, in the manner of the later Wittgenstein, affirms against skepticism those "original, natural, inescapable commitments" to a world of objects in space and time, inhabited by human observers who have both an individual past and a collective history.[66]

---

[65] White, *What Is and What Ought to Be Done*, p. 37.
[66] Strawson, *Skepticism and Naturalism*, p. 28.

Ethical naturalism in contemporary philosophy focuses on the more general features of human life, the dominant tendencies that shape the purposes of each individual and the universal, or nearly universal characteristics that people share across cultural, racial, and historical boundaries. Contemporary philosophical naturalism eschews the rationalist's idea of a transcendental moral logic, but its focus on the human universal is hardly less single-minded than Kant's.

Niebuhr's work is a twentieth-century reminder that ethical naturalism does not have to work that way. Attentiveness to the full range of facts that impinge on a moral decision, when put into practice and not simply formulated as a theoretical alternative, hones the powers of observation and allows one to attend to motives and forces that others, led by their theories to concentrate on a narrower range of observations, ignore. A naturalist, unlike a narrativist, does not reject generalizations about what persons are apt to want or to do, but the naturalist also notes that these broad tendencies can be modified by culture, opportunity, and experience, so that apparently quite opposite behaviors may spring from a common source. The same anxiety that drives one person to a vaulting ambition to secure fame and power may lead another, who has fewer outlets for ambition, to a sensual lassitude that fears no loss because it finds nothing worth grasping.[67] Americans react to world events differently from Germans, Russians, and even from Britons, because of their different histories.

Niebuhr's fame as a political analyst and social critic rested on such observations, and his popularity testifies that the ethical naturalists have got something right about how people actually make their moral choices. They attempt, as Niebuhr put it in his own definition of political realism, "to take all factors in a social and political situation, which offer resistance to established norms, into account, especially factors of self-interest and power."[68] People seek credible generalizations about human nature and aspirations that frame a picture of the

---

[67] Niebuhr, *The Nature and Destiny of Man*, I, 178–79. We will consider this particular problem in much more detail in Chapter Three.

[68] Niebuhr, *Christian Realism and Political Problems*, p. 119.

good human life, but when they make particular moral choices, they also want to know what obstacles stand in the way of these aspirations and what course, under present circumstances, frustrated hopes are likely to take.

REALITY AND RELIGIOUS AFFECTIONS

In formulating the coherences on which our moral choices rest, Christian Realism's version of ethical naturalism attends to the social and religious, as well as physical and biological elements in those coherences. The person who attempts to order and integrate moral experiences is not just a biological individual, sharing characteristics common to all members of the human species. He or she is a social person, shaped by history, customs, and interests that mark each human being as a member of particular groups, as well as part of humanity in general.

It is especially important to Reinhold Niebuhr's understanding of persons that each of them has a capacity for "indefinite transcendence" of the given conditions of life. In that self-transcendence, the social artifacts with which we live provide the greatest opportunities for change. We are not bound to prevailing hairstyles, the secret ballot, or the modern state in quite the same way that we are bound to eat regularly and eventually to die. Nevertheless, where we begin is crucial for the changes we can conceive, and for whether we will greet any particular change that is urged upon us as a liberation, or mourn it as a loss.

The particularity of the social conditions in which we live also means that most of us develop quite specific loyalties and dependencies. We may speak of the human need for community in general terms, but for any one of us the communities which we need and love are quite specific. Rare individuals may be able to move freely between several cultures, or to shift the center of their lives successfully from one culture to another, though even in these cases the transitions are usually mediated by continuities in professional life, family, or ethnic ties. Contrary to what some forms of modern individualism suggest, we do not use these communities simply as instruments for personal satisfaction. They are genuine centers of loyalty, and persons can and do make sacrifices of their own good for the good of the community. At the same time, our individual need for community creates a search for approval that opens up virtually unlimited possibilities both for exploitation of the individual by the group and for megalomaniac remaking of the community in one's own image.

These social factors need to be considered when assessing a course of action, because they create possibilities and limitations far more specific than the general features common to human nature would suggest. Christian Realism, however, cannot stop with social analysis alone. Inherent in the transcendence of each particular starting point is the recognition that every loyalty we can formulate is limited.

The consequence is that it [human reason] is always capable of envisaging possibilities of order, unity, and harmony above and beyond the contingent and arbitrary realities of its physical existence; but it is not capable (because of its finiteness) of incarnating all the higher values which it discerns; nor even of adequately defining the unconditioned good which it dimly apprehends as the ground and goal of all its contingent values.[69]

The loyalties, and the distortions of loyalty, which are discerned in attentiveness to society thus lead us to a consideration of the religious elements in our self-understanding as well.

Religion is, however, more than a reflection on "the fact that man can transcend himself in infinite regression."[70] The most basic way in which religion enters into the coherences by which we assess persons and actions is through the religious affections – a sense of awe before the beauty and power of the universe, a sense of terror at the recognition of our own finitude and contingency, and perhaps, too, a sense of guilt for the disparity between the flawed and limited goods that capture our loves and the grandeur of this one worthy object which we only dimly apprehend, and to which we rarely attend. The expression, and even the experience, of these emotions is strongly

[69] Niebuhr, *An Interpretation of Christian Ethics*, p. 40.
[70] Niebuhr, *The Nature and Destiny of Man*, II, 222.

colored by the particular religious traditions through which we have learned to identify them, and yet it is hard to see the affections as *only* the artifacts of religious language.

A line of American Protestant thinkers that stretches back to Jonathan Edwards has seen the religious affections as apprehensions of a religious reality, and the Christian Realists stand squarely within that tradition.[71] If it is important to a coherent moral evaluation to build the "conceptual bridges" that link moral feelings to sense perceptions, those who see the importance of religious affections in human experience will insist that these must also be attended to and incorporated into our moral discourse.[72]

Attentiveness to these social and religious aspects of human experience results in a view of human nature that is more flexible and less predictable than some other versions of ethical naturalism. Characteristically, Reinhold Niebuhr stresses the indeterminate possibilities for good *and* evil which result from human communities and commitments. As a result, we cannot suppose that people in society will be moved only by predictable, moderate desires that can easily be satisfied in an orderly community. The community creates new wants of its own, as "natural" as the rest, but perhaps not so easily satisfied. Nor can we readily establish a normative human nature, from which what is to be done and what is to be avoided might be deduced with certainty.

The Christian Realists' account of human nature and the politics appropriate to it differs from that of their secular counterparts, but we should not suppose, as Morton White once suggested, that those differences result from the fact that

---

[71] See, recently, James M. Gustafson, *Ethics from a Theocentric Perspective* (Chicago: University of Chicago Press, 1981), I, 197–204.

[72] See Morton O. White's statement on page 111 above. One might argue that we attend to moral feelings in ethics precisely because they are *moral*, and exclude religious feelings because they are not, but this distinction between moral and non-moral feelings surely makes even less sense than the rigid distinction, which the non-reductive naturalist rejects, between moral and non-moral facts. Affections appear as "religious," "moral," or "aesthetic" primarily in terms of the kind of discourse in which they are considered. If the feeling of awe is usually regarded as a "religious" affection, while a sense of obligation is regarded as a "moral" feeling, that is because of the contexts in which we usually consider each of them. The experiences do not come so neatly labeled.

Christian Realists appeal in the end to religious knowledge that is unavailable to those who stand outside the revelation. White formulates his differences with Niebuhr this way:

> If all that Niebuhr did was to oppose simple-minded optimism of the view that men are gods, we should embrace him as a sane partisan of the empiricism and pragmatism which he assigns to wise American politicians. But surely Niebuhr wants us to learn more than that from him, since that is much too naturalistic and modest. Niebuhr believes in the doctrine of Original Sin, according to which man is necessarily evil. Yet this doctrine is just as indefensible as the theory of inevitable progress and, ironically enough, it rests on faith – a faith which has engendered even more "fanatic certainty" than that which theorists of inevitable progress assign to *their* view. The truly emancipated mind must reject both of these dogmas.[73]

White correctly identifies the idea of "original sin" as a key point of difference between himself and Niebuhr, but he ignores Niebuhr's insistence that the theological concept rests on a myth which is itself a way of representing human experience. White and Niebuhr do not disagree that our moral expectations must be formed by a broad view of human experience; they differ over what that experience is. They disagree on morals and politics precisely because they differ so sharply about experience.

Similarly, as we shall see more clearly in the next chapter, Niebuhr rejects the concept of moral principles that follow deductively from fixed facts of human nature, but this is not, as John Courtney Murray supposed, because Niebuhr held an "ambiguist" view that renders nature intractable to reason.[74] The ambiguity, too, is a product of experience, and not an *a priori* refusal to make judgments.

The Christian Realist, then, does bring distinctive Christian ideas to bear on public moral choices. Niebuhr's work would hardly have provoked the interest and the controversy that it did if he were merely offering more eloquent formulations of received opinion. The Christian tradition has attended to

[73] Morton O. White, *Pragmatism and the American Mind* (New York: Oxford University Press, 1971), pp. 226–27. (This quotation comes from White's review of Niebuhr's book *The Irony of American History*.)
[74] See Murray, *We Hold These Truths*, pp. 282–83.

features of human experience that other systems of thought, particularly those inspired by the modern search for scientific objectivity, are apt to ignore. It has found ways to symbolize those truths that preserve the ambiguity and indefinite possibilities of lived experience, and its general construal of human life in a reality that finds unity and meaning in God enables people to face the risks and confusions of more particular experiences without demanding more unity than is actually there and without placing themselves or their groups in the center of value. "Thus wisdom about our destiny is dependent upon a humble recognition of the limits of our knowledge and our power. Our most reliable understanding is the fruit of 'grace' in which faith completes our ignorance without pretending to possess its certainties as knowledge; and in which contrition mitigates our pride without destroying our hope."[75]

The reason which is able to "dimly apprehend" the "unconditioned good" which is the "ground and goal of all its contingent values" will surely make different responses to situations from one which dismisses such apprehensions in favor of more objective evidence. The concepts, symbols, and rituals which articulate that meaning and make it available for shared use along with others will play a significant role in the interpretation of situations and the choice of courses of action. The distinctive insights of Christianity must be tested against the same pragmatic criteria by which we determine other sorts of truth. If that testing leads to conclusions different from those arrived at by those who do not share the Christian insights, the question can only be settled by extending the discussion to new areas or new evidence.

The task of Christian ethics therefore is not to demonstrate universal rational principles of which the Christian traditions merely provide examples. Nor is it to use the Christian narratives to construct an alternative polity in which love prevails and violence is absent. The task of Christian ethics is to determine what the power of love and non-violence can mean for the moral life of an existing society. That determination

---

[75] Niebuhr, *The Nature and Destiny of Man*, II, 321.

takes place with varying degrees of specificity, from the Christian citizen who tries to say what justice means at a City Council meeting, to a theologian who tries to articulate the meaning of Christianity for the transformations of Western history. It also involves different balances between action and interpretation, from the organizer rallying a divided community to resist economic exploitation, to the lecturer who helps an audience locate themselves and their community within a framework of historical events. In all cases, however, what is wanted is neither the sentimental affirmation of an alternative reality that, in the end, means nothing for present choices, nor the fanatic realization of a vision that must, in the end, be corrected by a wiser reason. What is wanted is a "critical" attitude and a "responsible" attitude, an approach that joins in one person the conviction of ultimate meaning and the test of experience.

CHAPTER 3

Freedom

THE HUMAN GOOD

In Chapter Two, we interpreted Christian Realism as a version of ethical naturalism and distinguished it from Christian ethics understood as an exemplification of universal moral rationality or as the unique expression of the values of a community shaped by the Christian narrative. That theoretical clarification suggests that the Christian Realist's moral choices begin with an idea of the human good, but it may tell us less than we want to know about what that good is.

That frustration is in part characteristic of ethical naturalism. Unless naturalism takes a reductive form that treats the human good as some single thing to be observed, quantified, and compared, it must accommodate substantial differences over what the human good is and how it is to be described. A large part of the discourse of ethical naturalism is about which of the many things that persons value are actually part of the human good, whether there is a single way of life that best realizes that good, and so forth. Christian Realism, because of the expanded attention it pays to the social and religious dimensions of experience, suggests a particularly complex view of the human good. Most of us assess versions of naturalism in large part by the ideas of a good life they hold out to us. We want to know what sort of persons we would be and what kind of communities we would build if we lived as they say we should. An ethical system that tries to tell us that we will be better persons by living in ways that are unrecognizable or repugnant to us will have a difficult case to make. In this chapter, we must begin to make Christian Realism a persuasive and plausible version of ethical naturalism, by showing that the life of freedom guided by love is not only consistent with the requirements of human nature, but also, recognizably, a human good. That will require at least the rest of this book, but in this chapter we will make a beginning, by understanding both the centrality of freedom and the characteristic forms of its denial.

NATURE

To speak of human nature as a norm for human choices suggests that there may be discrepancies between the morally correct choice and the course of action that individuals find most desirable, or even the course they would describe as most "natural" for themselves. What we call "human nature" is not simply an account of what persons are biologically determined to do or how they are statistically likely to behave. The idea of human nature which shapes the norms of ethical naturalism is, in Aristotelian terms, an idea of human excellence or perfection, or, to use the more contemporary terminology, an idea of "human flourishing." It may require us to do things we find difficult or unappealing, such as spending long hours in libraries reading theological texts, in order to achieve the good of knowledge. It may require us to postpone immediate gratifications in order to achieve greater goods at a later date, or to subordinate goods that are attractive and immediately available to other goods that are harder to achieve and further into an uncertain future. Nature thus provides moral standards by picking out from among the things that persons are able to do or may be inclined to do those which are commended because they contribute to human flourishing and those which are prohibited or discouraged because they work against it.

Ethical naturalists who have comprehensive and determinate ideas of the human good may arrive at a deductive system of morality, in which moral imperatives follow from known facts about human goods and principles that specify the sorts of acts we are to choose or reject with respect to those goods.

Roman Catholic moral theology, based on Aristotle's logic as well as Aristotle's ethics, long provided the best example of such a deductive system in Western ethics. Recent philosophical formulations have sought to make it even more rigorous, explicating and defending the "intermediate moral principles" that were previously accepted as theological truths not in need of philosophical justification.[1] While proponents of these deductive systems have long acknowledged that the risks of error and the possibilities for legitimate disagreement become larger as the moral conclusion becomes more "remote" from the first premises, the goal nonetheless remains a definitive moral system derived with the certainty of deductive logic from a knowledge of human nature.

For some modern critics, the universality and rigor of these claims leads to a rejection of ethical naturalism. The flaw in all arguments that proceed with such certainty from human nature to norms of action is that human beings do not have a fixed, determinate nature like rocks, ants, oak trees, and internal combustion engines. Human beings are what they make of themselves, the products of their own freedom. The critics differ over whether this self-creative freedom belongs chiefly to the species as a whole, to some organic community of race or nation, or – in the manner of twentieth-century existentialism – to the individual alone. For all who follow this line of criticism, however, the point is to set the claims of freedom against the claims of nature, and so to deny that what we ought to do follows deductively from certain truths about who we are by nature.[2]

In this particular controversy, it is sometimes difficult to decide where the Christian Realists stand. While we have interpreted Christian Realism as a version of ethical naturalism, Reinhold Niebuhr repeatedly criticizes traditional natural

[1] John Finnis, *Fundamentals of Ethics* (Washington, D.C.: Georgetown University Press, 1983), pp. 69–70.
[2] For the important role of this tension between freedom and nature in modern thought, see Paul Ricoeur, "Nature and Freedom," in *Political and Social Essays*, ed. David Stewart and Joseph Bien (Athens, Ohio: Ohio University Press, 1974), pp. 23–45. See also Charles Taylor, *Hegel and Modern Society* (Cambridge: Cambridge University Press, 1979), pp. 1–14.

law thinking because, as he sees it, it reduces human cultures to determinate products of nature and ignores the large element of freedom and creativity in every social arrangement. On the other hand, the realistic assessment of the forces that work against the realization of human ideals, and the sober realization that those ideals themselves may be fatally flawed and limited, warn against unlimited confidence in freedom. Those who like to cite texts will find sufficient resources in Reinhold Niebuhr to make a case for either side.

Perhaps the clearest systematic statement comes in Niebuhr's Gifford Lectures, delivered in 1939 and subsequently published as *The Nature and Destiny of Man*. While the Gifford endowment's assignment of a series of lectures on "natural theology" is loosely laid on the lecturers, it seems to have pressed Niebuhr to develop the theological presuppositions behind his observations on history and politics, and explicitly to compare the understanding of human nature held by Christian Realism with alternative formulations in Christian thought and Western philosophy. For present purposes, we will take the discussion of "original righteousness" which closes the chapters on "Human Nature" in *The Nature and Destiny of Man* as the starting point for a resolution of the problem of freedom and nature.[3]

Niebuhr suggests that any adequate account of human nature must treat freedom not in opposition to a fixed human nature, but precisely as part of that nature. Human nature includes the capacity to stand outside given conditions, to see them as contingent facts, and to imagine how they might have been or might yet be otherwise.

The essential nature of man contains two elements; and there are correspondingly two elements in the original perfection of man. To the essential nature of man belong, on the one hand, all his natural endowments, and determinations, his physical and social impulses,

---

[3] The chapters on "human nature" are derived from the first series of Niebuhr's Gifford Lectures, delivered in April and May of 1939, just before the start of World War II. Niebuhr returned to Edinburgh to complete the assignment after the war had begun. For further biographical details concerning the development of Niebuhr's theology and the delivery of the Gifford Lectures, see Fox, *Reinhold Niebuhr*, pp. 146–47, 178–92.

his sexual and racial differentiations, in short his character as a creature imbedded in the natural order. On the other hand, his essential nature also includes the freedom of his spirit, his transcendence over natural process and finally his self-transcendence.[4]

The characteristic problem with theories of natural law, Niebuhr suggests, is that they deal with the human as creature, but not the human as spirit.

FREEDOM

The relationship of freedom to the various determinations that Niebuhr lumps together under the heading "the natural order" appears at once in the fact that freedom is defined in relation to those determinations. There is here no simple dualism between "nature" and "spirit."[5] Freedom is precisely the natural capacity that persons embedded in the given circumstances of nature and history have to imagine and to create a new reality in relationship to the limitations from which they started. Other animals may use tools, perhaps even rudimentary signs, to achieve their aims in a given environment. Only humans, so far as we know, can manipulate signs and symbols to imagine a different world, and direct their efforts toward making it real. That "transcendence over natural process" is freedom, but it bears emphasizing that it is only in relation to natural and historical starting points that we recognize it as free.[6]

Freedom begins with the capacity to project oneself imaginatively into a situation in which the constraints of present experience no longer hold. A hungry primate that sees a cluster of fruit as its next meal still operates within the processes of nature. A tribe of desert-dwelling nomads who begin to live in expectation of a land flowing with milk and honey have

---

[4] Niebuhr, *The Nature and Destiny of Man*, I, 270.   [5] *Ibid.*, I, 74–76.

[6] We must, for the purposes of this chapter, set aside complex theological questions about God's freedom of action, and about whether the freedom of God can be in any way understood as analogous to human freedom. Some theologians will insist that analogies between human freedom and divine freedom are apt and illuminating. I do not mean to imply that the analogy is unworthy of pursuit, but I emphasize that we will not be pursuing it here.

achieved a degree of freedom. So, too, has a homeless alcoholic who begins to imagine a life beyond the streets and the shelters or a young student in a one-party state who begins to question the party's truth, though in these cases the constraints that freedom transcends are more the making of human choice and history than of nature.

Freedom that transcends given circumstances must soon include transcendence of the self, for I cannot get very far toward imagining a different world to live in without imagining myself as in some sense a different person. This is true for the teenage drug addict trying to imagine herself finishing school, getting a job, and being a good mother; but it is also true for the successful academic, seated before a blank piece of paper and trying to imagine something she has not already written. In either case, freedom means knowing that I am not just the record of what I have already done, or failed to do, as the case may be.

Freedom as self-transcendence suggests, further, the possibility of critical questions about the goals themselves. Had I not been so frightened as a child by those unexpected changes in my family, would I still see predictability and control as the most important achievements in my life? If our people did not have such bitter memories of poverty and unemployment, would we still regard security as a higher economic priority than productivity? If we had ever known real hardship, would we be so enthusiastic for the competitive melee of a free-market economy?

There are no clear limits to the questions freedom poses or permits. Scientists and engineers must ask whether the most basic material conditions of life can be altered or circumvented. Legislators and political theorists may imagine a polity ordered by a totally new constitution. Historians, humanists, and theologians may speculate on how our lives would be different if certain quite specific, contingent events had worked out differently. Or we may, with great difficulty, contemplate what our lives and commitments would be like if we had to live in quite different circumstances – as members of a different race, or social class, marked by different handicaps and abilities, shaped by a different culture.

What marks these primary experiences of freedom is that they involve possible ways of life for ourselves. We may imagine what it would be like to be a knight in armor or a Confucian sage, or a highly developed extraterrestrial being with a silicon-based metabolism, but those are exercises in fantasy, not freedom. Freedom imagines circumstances different from our own in the context of goods toward which our lives and efforts might be directed. In that context, of course, there may be freedom in fantasy. Good writers of fiction certainly know how to use fantasy in that way. In that context, too, freedom may seek human good through an awareness of great evil or suffering. A vivid sense of the horror of genocide or famine may be a way to begin reordering our own lives and values in ways that help to prevent those evils in the future. Imaginative identification with those who have suffered illness or personal tragedy may help us to cultivate virtues of patience and hope that will make us better persons in our own easier situations.

While freedom is, as Niebuhr puts it, "indefinite transcendence"[7] of our circumstances and ourselves, it is freedom precisely because it is situated. Freedom is not the "view from nowhere"[8] that provides an objective picture of everything as it is. Freedom starts from somewhere, and views that starting point in relation to other possibilities. For a single mother struggling against poverty to care for her children and protect them from the consequences of bad housing and urban social decay, the tedium of the suburban housewife who wields her mop against the backdrop of a well-stocked refrigerator and spends the afternoon driving her children to well-planned recreational activities may be the picture of freedom. Freedom for the suburbanite may require a little more dirt and disorder.

In the Christian Realist's ethical naturalism, then, freedom occupies a place not unlike that of reason in Aristotle's ethics. Freedom, like reason, is a basic human good. Life without freedom is not something we would choose, no matter how

---

[7] Niebuhr, *The Nature and Destiny of Man*, I, 3–4.

[8] Thomas Nagel employs this phrase to characterize the Enlightenment view of reason, to which his own more pragmatic approach offers an alternative. See Thomas Nagel, *The View from Nowhere* (New York: Oxford University Press, 1986).

comfortable the material circumstances might be. Those persons who choose comfort at the expense of freedom elicit pity or contempt, but not envy. Those crushed by circumstances that destroy this freedom we regard as the most wretched of our fellow human beings. "The reduction ... to a mere biological existence, in which an independent human spirit has been extinguished" rings in our ears as a description of a life not worth living.[9]

But freedom is more than a good. It is also the capacity by which we know the good and identify the things that are good. For Aristotle, reason knows an objective good that is the same for everyone, but freedom is more akin to the insights in myth, which capture coherences larger than we can explicitly formulate. Freedom grasps good from a distinctive angle of vision, based on its own starting point. It is no accident that Reinhold Niebuhr rejects the Aristotelian claim that reason is the defining feature of the human person, relying instead on an Augustinian formulation that encompasses reason, memory, and imagination.[10] Any definition of humanity must include the particularity of individual experience as well as a capacity to grasp the universal.

HUMAN DIGNITY

In ethical naturalism, the essential role that freedom plays in a good human life has normative implications. Because we can hardly be human at all without being free, we must use our own freedom. Because we can hardly be said to deal realistically with others unless we treat them as persons with freedom, we must not act in ways that violate the freedom of others. Indeed, some traditions, notably Catholic moral thought in recent decades, prefer to use the term 'human dignity' for this fundamental freedom, precisely to distinguish it from particular political freedoms which may be given or

---

[9] The phrase comes from an account of centuries of oppression of the Romanian peasantry in Robert D. Kaplan, "Bloody Romania," *New Republic* (July 30, 1990), p. 12.

[10] Niebuhr, *The Nature and Destiny of Man*, I, 153–66. See also "Freedom," in *Faith and Politics*, p. 79.

withheld by a government.[11] The basis for freedom is not political choice, or the requirements of a specific political order, but the nature of human consciousness itself.

Some of the implications of freedom or human dignity are chiefly personal. Freedom requires of us a delicate balance between humility and self-assertion. We must refuse to be completely identified with either our successes or our failures, acknowledging that, in our freedom, we may yet fall below the achievements that others have come to associate with us, or we may live out potentials that even we have not yet recognized. Freedom requires the inner-city youth who has failed every conventional test of economic and social success to shout, "I am somebody!" Freedom also requires successful men and women to repeat softly, "I am *not* the Chief Executive Officer, the Most Valuable Player, the prize-winning author, the life-saving surgeon, the favorite teacher ..." Against the determinisms that threaten to reduce us to whatever we just happen to be, and the fantasies that tempt us to think we already are everything we can imagine, freedom is the capacity to see ourselves in relation to both reality and possibility. Because such freedom is essential to our well-being, there is in ethical naturalism a moral obligation to maintain that capacity in ourselves.

Freedom imposes other requirements that are more clearly social and political. As Niebuhr put it:

The social and political freedoms which modern democratic communities accord the person express the belated convictions of modern communities, gained after desperate struggles, that the community must give the person a social freedom which corresponds to the essential freedom of his nature, and which enables him to express hopes and ambitions and to engage in interests and vitalities which are not immediately relevant to the collective purposes of the community, but which in the long run enrich the culture and leaven the lump of the community's collective will and purpose.[12]

[11] See especially "*Dignitatis humanae*," the Second Vatican Council's declaration on religious liberty, in *The Documents of Vatican II*, ed. Walter M. Abbott (New York: Guild Press, 1966), pp. 675–77. See also John Courtney Murray, *The Problem of Religious Freedom* (Westminster, Md.: The Newman Press, 1965).

[12] Niebuhr, "Freedom," in *Faith and Politics*, p. 81.

Against the tendency of institutions and governments to limit dissent and to allocate all resources to projects that match prevailing ideas of what is useful, freedom gives us a perspective on the limitations of the present order and sparks the play of imagination and experiment from which new possibilities emerge. In ethical naturalism, there are also moral obligations to respect those capacities in others.[13]

DENIALS OF FREEDOM

The importance of freedom or human dignity to a realistic account of human nature should now be clear. Unfortunately, it is rather less clear how this freedom is to be maintained and respected. What people seek is not freedom as an abstraction, but the particular hopes, dreams, and goals that mark the exercise of their own freedom. Other accounts of human nature may yield determinate goods toward which all persons ought to strive, but the aims of freedom clearly are not all the same. Some could easily be realized, given a little more cooperation by other persons. Others are beyond the reach of present-day technology or the resources of today's economy. Some hopes and goals contradict others, so that we cannot further the freedom of environmentalists who dream of unspoiled wilderness habitats without at least temporarily frustrating the freedom of loggers in search of economic security and developers who dream of new communities in which to work and live.

Modern thought has usually dealt with this troublesome diversity of aims by suggesting that there is value in the achievement of any human aim. None of the goals and plans of life that people have is, in itself, better or worse than another. The moral and political problem is to arrange things so that as many of them may be realized as possible. William James articulated the basic premise behind this radical pluralism of

---

[13] This suggests, though we cannot take the time to argue it here, that the lines between "negative" freedoms, by which we are protected from interference by others, and "positive" freedoms, by which we are assured of their cooperation and assistance, should not be so sharply drawn as they sometimes are. The distinction is analytically useful, but in practice the effective exercise of any freedom will require resources, counsel, and cooperation from others, as well as their non-interference.

human values: "Take any demand, however slight, which any creature, however weak, may make. Ought it not, for its own sole sake, to be satisfied? If not, prove why not. The only possible kind of proof you could adduce would be the exhibition of another creature who should make a demand that ran the other way."[14]

The human sympathy which enables us to understand the aims of others and to feel their joys and frustrations is real enough, but a Christian Realist will note that these insights give us at least as much reason to be wary of others' successes as to rejoice in them. Their purposes, after all, may conflict with our own, not only in practical terms of competition for opportunities and resources, but in more fundamental ways. We may find the aims they pursue abhorrent, so that our sympathy with their success is in immediate conflict with our hatred of the result. More important, freedom can envision goals that are exploitative, that expand the freedom of the self by limiting the freedom of others.

Freedom, then, is both a key human good and the capacity that makes our identification and pursuit of other goods possible, but little follows morally from the claim that a particular aim, plan, or action is an exercise of freedom. Because the broad tradition of moral and political liberalism tends to regard all expressions of freedom as of equal value, it concentrates on removing obstacles to those expressions. Liberalism imposes restrictions only where an individual's exercise of freedom begins to limit the freedom of another.[15]

Realism, by contrast, calls attention not to the inevitable conflicts between one individual's freedom and another's, but to internal contradictions that mark some exercises of freedom as a denial of the basic realities of freedom itself. Recall that freedom begins with human beings in particular, contingent circumstances imagining possibilities different from the reali-

---

[14] William James, "The Moral Philosopher and the Moral Life," in *Essays on Faith and Morals* (New York: Longmans, Green and Co., 1943), p. 194.

[15] Cf. John Stuart Mill's principle: "the only purpose for which power can rightfully be exercised over any member of a civilized community, against his will, is to prevent harm to others." See Mill, "On Liberty," in *Selected Writings of John Stuart Mill*, ed. Maurice Cowling (New York: New American Library, 1968), p. 129.

ties they now experience.[16] Being realistic about humanity means treating them – ourselves and others – in ways that respect that capacity and acknowledge its fundamental place in any way of life that human beings could find acceptable. But realism also requires that freedom does not attempt to deny or defeat the conditions that make freedom possible. To suppose that we could create a good that was no longer particular and contingent, but somehow universal, permanent, and itself unsusceptible to further change and development would be to suppose that freedom could achieve its aims by destroying itself. Doubtless, the freedom of many people would be trampled in the attempt to create and maintain such a system, but from the viewpoint of ethical naturalism the fundamental moral problem with such efforts is not that they infringe on the freedom of others, but that they ignore the basic realities within which freedom functions. Freedom is a capacity of finite, limited persons whose capacities for change are also limited, and who can only bring about new situations that are also themselves particular, local, and contingent. Exercises of freedom which attempt to deny or alter this reality are wrong from the start, even if they do not get to a point of real conflict with the freedom of other persons.

For Reinhold Niebuhr, *sin* was the most adequate theo-logical term for this denial of finitude, and the biblical myth of the Fall and the doctrine of original sin provided the most telling formulations of the pervasive self-contradiction in the exercises of human freedom. The terminology became closely associated with Niebuhr's version of Christian Realism, and for many it is a shorthand way of saying what Christian Realism is all about. By the end of his career, Niebuhr somewhat regret-ted the terminology, since his readers tended to evaluate his political thought rather quickly in terms of their own ideas about what 'sin' means. Because modern secular thinkers often associate the concept of sin with a religious denial of human worth and an authoritarian suppression of human needs, the evaluation was often negative, and the real point of Niebuhr's

[16] See page 123 above.

analysis was obscured.[17] The point, however, is important, and it may be as relevant to today's limited political expectations as it was when Niebuhr first defined it against the extravagant hopes of liberal democracy and Social Gospel theology. It will repay our efforts to understand clearly what Niebuhr meant by interpreting sin as the denial of human freedom and to see the variety of forms that this denial can take.

SIN?

There is a tendency in Western religions, particularly apparent in Christianity at certain points in history, to associate sin with finitude, change, and limitation. Truth, beauty, and goodness exist in a world of unchanging Forms or in the mind of God. The material world, where things develop and decay, is necessarily imperfect and less good than the ideal one. The human powers which grasp the eternal truths are superior to the powers of perception and the mechanical skills that deal with illusive and unwieldy matter. This approach also leads to gender stereotypes. The male, who is concerned with reason and order, is necessarily superior to the female, who deals with generation, nurture, illness, and death.[18] From this point of view, sin is the set of desires and actions that involve us with this realm of finitude and decay, and the doctrine of original sin is witness to the fact that we are all initially involved in it through the very material realities of birth and sexuality.

While that is surely an incomplete picture of the Christian understanding of sin, it represents a way of thinking which is an especially vulnerable target for modern critics of Christianity. For them, these ideas are evidence that Christianity – or perhaps religion in general – denies life and misinterprets natural human limitations in order to deprive people of joy and freedom, or to browbeat them into submission to religious authority. In this century, the criticism has taken from Freud-

---

[17] See Niebuhr's 1964 introduction to *The Nature and Destiny of Man*, p. viii, also *Man's Nature and His Communities*, p. 24.

[18] For an interesting recent study of these themes, see Margaret R. Miles, *Carnal Knowing: Female Nakedness and Religious Meaning in the Christian West* (Boston: Beacon Press, 1989).

ian psychology the ironic twist that it is *themselves* that religious people deprive and oppress most, repressing their humanity with a stern superego informed by what they take to be the eternal laws of God.

It is important to Reinhold Niebuhr to reject this under-standing of sin. Its place in historic Christian thought cannot be denied, but it flies in the face of a more fundamental affirmation of the goodness of Creation. "The whole Biblical interpretation of life and history rests upon the assumption that the created world, the world of finite, dependent and con-tingent existence, is not evil by reason of its finiteness."[19] The sense that worldly existence and biological life are evil is an alien idea, pressed on biblical faith by the "dualistic and acosmic" religions of the Hellenistic world.[20] It is more at home in the "non-historical cultures of the oriental world," Taoism, Hinduism, and Buddhism, with their mystical disavo-wals of meaningful history.[21] Niebuhr's understanding of Asian religion in this passage can hardly be defended, and recent scholarship has shown that the relationship between Christian and classical sources in the denial of the body and sexuality was more complex than Niebuhr supposed.[22] Nonetheless, his con-structive point is surely correct: only as contemporary Chris-tians find resources in their traditions to address the problems of contingent, historical existence can Christianity speak to the modern age which finds its questions there.

Instead of regarding our involvement in history and finitude as evil, therefore, Niebuhr identifies sin as the *denial* of that involvement:

[Humanity's] partial involvement in, and partial transcendence over, the process of nature and the flux of time . . . is not regarded as the evil from which man must be redeemed. The evil in the human situation arises, rather, from the fact that men seek to deny or to escape prematurely from the uncertainties of history and to claim a freedom, a transcendence and an eternal and universal perspective which is not possible for finite creatures. The problem of sin rather

---

[19] Niebuhr, *The Nature and Destiny of Man*, I, 167.   [20] *Ibid.*   [21] *Ibid.*, II, 13.
[22] Peter Brown, *The Body and Society: Men, Women, and Sexual Renunciation in Early Christianity* (New York: Columbia University Press, 1988).

than finiteness is, in other words, either implicitly or explicitly the basic problem of life.[23]

By connecting freedom and finitude, Niebuhr offers the critics of Christianity a more subtle answer than a simple reaffirmation of the human life and powers that some religious traditions have denied. If it were only a matter of declaring good what some have thought bad, the way would be open for unqualified endorsement of human wants and wishes, and for an ethics which takes the satisfaction of human wants as the main business of the moral life. By contrast, Niebuhr regards the constraints of finitude as morally important. A large part of the task of a realistic ethics is identifying those constraints and settling the questions of how the limits they set on our aspirations shall be handled and how the burdens they impose shall be distributed. Working within the conditions of a real but limited freedom, human goodness is achieved by a clear-sighted recognition of the limits on our knowledge and power, and by just and caring responsiveness to the tragic conflicts which sometimes arise.

In the half-century since Niebuhr wrote *The Nature and Destiny of Man*, the consensus on this point has, if anything, grown. His work, particularly before World War II, was directed against the still-popular belief that modern industry could provide expanding prosperity and material comfort for everyone, and against the Social Gospel creed that took this realm of endless plenty to be God's will for human history, as well as the aim of Christian action. The urgent message of Christian Realism was that this reading of social ethics, Christian or secular, was badly mistaken.[24]

The late twentieth century seems to agree. Social critics have not only all but forgotten the more extravagant hopes of the Social Gospel; they find in secular affirmations of unlimited prosperity both the roots of totalitarian schemes that force people to create their own happiness and the origins of an ecological crisis that results from the effort to make unlimited

---

[23] Niebuhr, *The Nature and Destiny of Man*, II, 3.
[24] Bennett, *Christian Realism*, pp. 46–49.

use of finite resources. In philosophy, the Enlightenment effort to build a structure of knowledge on a foundation of certainty gives way to a modest pragmatism that claims only that we know how to do what we clearly can do, and to a rediscovery of Aristotle's practical reason, which demands no more certainty than the nature of changing, contingent things will admit. Others carry the criticism even further. Martha Nussbaum finds at the heart of the Western philosophical tradition an impulse to control events that cannot, in fact, be controlled. She directs us to the Greek poets, rather than the Greek philosophers, for an appropriate recognition of "the tragic power of circumstances over human goodness."[25] Bernard Williams argues that effective moral arguments, far from depending on universal moral truths, can only be made from within the acknowledged confines of a particular historical situation.[26] The hope is that within those limits clear thinking and open discussion will enable us to set aside past mistakes and illusions and to solve the immediate problems we face, including the problems created by our previous solutions.

While there are important differences between these writers, they share a broadly humanistic affirmation of the natural needs and powers that give shape to our lives. The revulsion from earthy, generative realities, the suspicion of the senses, and the fear of pleasure that marked the thought of earlier periods in Western history has become for these contemporary thinkers almost incomprehensible, but unlike their more optimistic counterparts from, say, the middle of the nineteenth century to the middle of the twentieth, these contemporary thinkers do not suppose that human freedom and creativity, loosed from superstition, will be able to create utopia or an earthly paradise. They seem, at least initially, to share with Reinhold Niebuhr a critical assessment of the optimistic liberalism against which his realism was first directed. They, like him, are less concerned with the goal of perfect justice than

---

[25] Martha C. Nussbaum, *The Fragility of Goodness: Luck and Ethics in Greek Tragedy and Philosophy* (Cambridge: Cambridge University Press, 1986), p. 50.

[26] Bernard Williams, *Ethics and the Limits of Philosophy* (Cambridge, Mass.: Harvard University Press, 1985).

with the daily choices that make for a little more human happiness, or a little less misery, and so make a real difference in specific human lives.

The profound antipathy of many of these authors toward sin as a concept for interpreting political and social reality[27] suggests, however, that there may still be important differences between their acceptance of human finitude and Niebuhr's Christian Realism. One could attempt to smooth out these differences by emphasizing, as Niebuhr did himself, that his idea of sin is apt to be misunderstood by secular thinkers who associate it with older notions of an inherited corruption.[28] The theologian, in effect, apologizes for employing a particularly difficult religious symbol to present an important public idea, and the secular philosophers acknowledge that they have read too much of their own idea of what 'sin' means into Niebuhr's use of the term.

That reconciliation, however, would be too easy. The differences between Niebuhr's understanding of freedom and finitude and the more recent affirmations of human limits remain profound. What divides Niebuhr's recent interpreters is the question of exactly what those differences are.

ORDER

One interpretation of Christian Realism stresses the new threats to freedom which emerge when people organize themselves into political societies. All agree that the temptations to deny finitude and fallibility and to make absolute claims fall heavily on those who hold political power. The differences appear when we ask just which ideas are apt to lead us into that temptation.

Those who reject the Christian claim that sin is an inescapable human reality object to more than the low estimate of human moral powers this doctrine seems to imply.

---

[27] See, for example, Martha Nussbaum, "Our Pasts, Ourselves," *The New Republic* 202 (April 9, 1990), 34. Nussbaum's essay is a review of Charles Taylor's *Sources of the Self*.

[28] See page 130 above.

They also reject the political consequences of the doctrine. According to these critics, when those who believe that human aims are inevitably flawed come into power, they are likely to exercise a tight control over their subjects to keep the human error from getting out of hand. Moreover, because they believe that sinful human beings are flawed in reason as well as in purpose, they will not be very susceptible to argument or persuasion by those they seek to control. The political result of a belief in original sin is, in short, authoritarianism.[29] The best assurance of political freedom, by contrast, is a confidence that people can select limited and achievable goals, discipline themselves to achieve them, and respond competently to the unknown challenges that will arise in the course of the effort.

Those with less trust in human capability will, of course, insist on stronger social and political constraints. More important, they also argue that a realistic response to the genuine need for authority is our best protection against the authoritarianism. Glenn Tinder articulates this view of political power, and he relates it explicitly to Christian ideas of sin: "Christianity is nearer to Machiavellism than to idealism. Machiavelli maintained that the pride and selfishness of human beings naturally give rise to disorder and that disorder requires the remedy of power; since civilization depends on order, and order on power, there can be no civilization without power. Such views are fully in accord with Christian principles."[30] Given that power will always be used in holding together a political community, Tinder suggests that the real danger of authoritarianism lies with those who do not understand the link between political power and human evil. Augustinian Christians, or, to use Tinder's terminology, "Reformation" Christians will not hesitate to use power to secure the minimum conditions of a civilized order, but they will not be tempted to think that they can move beyond order to some sort of social ideal. By contrast, those who see the evil

[29] Here again, Nussbaum provides an articulate recent formulation of these ideas. See Martha Nussbaum, "Recoiling from Reason," *New York Review of Books*, 36 (December 7, 1989), 40–41.

[30] Glenn Tinder, *The Political Meaning of Christianity* (Baton Rouge: Louisiana State University Press, 1989), p. 133.

as incidental and eradicable will eventually be led to try for a greater good. Their aspirations at that point blind them to their own participation in sin, and their readiness to impose their own vision on a reluctant public knows no limits. The best protection against this kind of tyranny, Tinder suggests, is a Christian community that is clear about its own understanding of politics:

Secular theories of the state consistently obscure the evil inherent in the twofold fact that the state always serves ends more or less particular rather than universal and imposes these ends coercively on unconsenting members. These theories give rise to a concept that Christianity enables us to recognize as profoundly false – the good state, a concept not only self-contradictory, but implying that human beings can organize morally pure spheres of life in the world and in history. Admittedly, Christians have sometimes accepted this concept. In doing so, however, they have allowed themselves to accept a view that is distinctly Hellenic and pagan in its origins, secular and humanistic in its modern development, and contrary to the deepest Christian principles – at least as these principles are understood in the "Reformation" tradition.[31]

For critics of the concept of sin, then, the doctrine poses a threat to human freedom because it limits the scope of competent political action. For Tinder, the concept protects freedom by warning us against large political aims that crush the freedom of individuals and groups. On those terms, history suggests that Tinder has an important point. Christian thinkers who have lived close to the utopian horrors of National Socialism and Soviet communism often stress the inherent limits on the creative competence of the state.[32]

Even more pertinent, perhaps, is the resonance of Tinder's themes with a strand of American Catholic thought. Although the natural law tradition has a generally more positive evaluation of the moral uses of state power and legal authority than

---

[31] *Ibid.*, p. 142.
[32] See, for example, Bonhoeffer, *Ethics*, p. 210: "The divine mandate of government presupposes the divine mandates of labour and marriage. In the world which it rules, the governing authority finds already present the two mandates through which God the Creator exercises his creative power. Government cannot itself produce life or values. It is not creative."

the Reformation sources on which Tinder relies, American Catholics who have reflected on pressures toward social and religious assimilation exerted by Protestant power in local and national governments have insisted on similar constraints on the state's role as a creator of social goods.[33] We are perhaps unlikely to confuse Hitler's Reich with a responsible affirmation of human freedom. Can we, however, say definitively that the efforts to cultivate Protestant values in the public schools and instill Protestant habits in the settlement houses were the result of an insistence on order, rather than the work of people who were confident in their human capacities and seeking only to free them for a competent response to the new problems of urban industrial life?

The need to restrain the moral fervor of the powerful and the unruly impulses of the masses is an important theme in the literature of Christian Realism. Indeed, for many it is the key point of Christian Realism, the vital truth that liberal activists with their aspirations for social transformation are apt to overlook.

If we stop at this point, we will have no doubt framed an important issue that divides Niebuhr, Tinder, and other Christian Realists from the confidence in human finitude articulated by contemporary secular philosophers. To stop here, however, also leaves the connection between human sin and human freedom to be resolved by apparently endless historical argument about whether, in any given case, a belief in the pervasive reality of sin has either suppressed creative freedom or preserved freedom by checking the impulse to totalitarian utopianism.

A survey of Reinhold Niebuhr's writing leaves little doubt which side he would take, particularly if we concentrate on his defense of democracy during World War II, and then, later, on his attacks on the "moral pretension" of Soviet communism.[34] There are, however, other indications in his work which suggest that the argument should be moved to another level.

---

[33] Cf. Murray, *We Hold These Truths*, pp. 144–45.

[34] Niebuhr, *The Children of Light and the Children of Darkness*; "Why Is Communism So Evil?," in *Christian Realism and Political Problems*, pp. 33–42.

The "Augustinian" or "Reformation" interpretation, with its emphasis on the inherent limits to political creativity, provides a realistic counterpoint to the unlimited optimism of earlier American defenses of democracy, but Niebuhr could also acknowledge that Augustine's realism was "excessive" in its failure to recognize the sense of justice that animates real political communities, and that Luther's pessimism was "too consistent" in its failure to recognize that the creative powers of government, though often distorted and always subject to abuse, are nonetheless real.[35] The concept of sin is important for understanding the human situation and human action, but it has no simple, univocal relationship to the loss of political freedom. Either the Christian pessimist or the liberal optimist may be right about a particular historical situation, but neither has a comprehensive understanding of the possibilities and limits inherent in all situations. For that, we must turn to a different understanding of the good to be sought and its relationship to the persons who seek it. Only then will we be able to see what is really wrong with the unqualified acceptance of human finitude and the rejection of original sin.

ANXIETY

There is yet another way to understand, respect, and live within the limitations that human nature imposes on our social projects. It is less developed in the literature, but it is, I think, the most adequate contemporary interpretation of Christian Realism. From this point of view, the problem with the contemporary affirmation of human finitude is not that it expects too much, but that it demands too little. Freedom, which is the primary human good that our social institutions must protect and promote, depends on a critical self-awareness of the limitations of our perspective on events *and* on a creative effort to go beyond those limits, to imagine, and then to realize, new forms of social life that open new possibilities for freedom. If sin consists in denying this balance between limits and possibilities

---

[35] See Niebuhr, *The Children of Light and the Children of Darkness*, p. 44; "Augustine's Political Realism," in *Christian Realism and Political Problems*, p. 127.

and so denying the morally meaningful reality that is known in relationship to God, then many affirmations of human finitude risk sin not by claiming too much for our intellectual and political powers, but by binding them too exclusively to an existing system of social values and meanings. A moral realism which acknowledges the difference in principle between our ideas *about* what is good and what really *is* good provides an intellectual framework for the necessary conditions for freedom in moral judgment and political arrangements. By contrast, to accept finitude in a way that implies that our moral terms have meaning only in the reality defined by our own culture and language risks the loss of that self-transcendence on which freedom depends.

Sin here is not a certain theory of moral meaning – as if an ethical theory could be evil, and not just mistaken – but the limitation of the moral meaning to which the theory gives expression. To insist that whatever can be meaningfully said must be expressible in moral terms which my own language and culture have taught me to use is to reject the idea of a center of value in which genuinely conflicting values can be brought into harmony. It is to dismiss the idea of a morally meaningful universe, if not to find it unthinkable, and so to turn one's back on God.

Reinhold Niebuhr's most extensive treatment of the idea of sin, at the end of the first part of *The Nature and Destiny of Man*, identifies the motive behind these denials as anxiety.

In short, man, being both free and bound, both limited and limitless, is anxious. Anxiety is the inevitable concomitant of the paradox of freedom and finiteness in which man is involved. Anxiety is the internal precondition of sin. It is the inevitable spiritual state of man, standing in the paradoxical situation of freedom and finiteness. Anxiety is the internal description of the state of temptation.[36]

Many things provoke this anxiety: our vulnerability to the powers of nature and history; the inevitabilities of aging and death; the fragility of the material possessions and social successes on which we depend; and our own weakness, not only in

---

[36] Niebuhr, *The Nature and Destiny of Man*, I, 182.

the face of external threats, but also before the internal forces of fear, self-contempt, and rage against others that prompt us to bring down on ourselves the evils we most wish to avoid.

Anxiety before these vulnerabilities is not itself sin. Indeed, without anxiety, we could not recognize the points at which life demands our careful attention to insure that possibilities for freedom are not prematurely crushed or needlessly wasted. The reckless driver who apparently knows no fear or the manager who risks safety to improve the "bottom line" is not more free than the defensive driver who is always on the alert for someone else's moves or the shop foreman who is constantly checking the safety regulations. Heedless people more often fall short of the care for life that anxiety elicits than they rise above the fears anxiety evokes.[37] The problem is that the response anxiety requires is both a recognition of our own limits and a trust in meanings that lie beyond us that few, if any, can grasp.

The ideal possibility is that faith in the ultimate security of God's love would overcome all immediate insecurities of nature and history ... It is significant that Jesus justifies his injunction, "Be not anxious" with the observation, "For your heavenly Father knoweth that ye have need of these things." The freedom from anxiety which he enjoins is a possibility only if perfect trust in divine security has been achieved.[38]

The Christian theologian will want to explore further this ideal possibility of perfect trust in God and the claim that it is realized and exemplified in the life of Jesus of Nazareth. The Christian Realist, mindful of the obstacles to such ideals, will focus critical attention on the responses that fall short of the ideal in characteristic ways. Since few, if any, are capable of complete trust, most persons will either deny the fragility of their own efforts and give their own achievements an importance and a permanence that they cannot have, or they will find a more proximate system of values that they can understand

---

[37] Niebuhr, following Martin Heidegger, notes that the watchful care and seriousness about life implied in the German *Sorge* is an important part of the capacity for freedom. That positive element of concern appropriate to the vulnerability and contingency of human life is often missing from the connotation of "anxiety" in English. See *The Nature and Destiny of Man*, I, 183–84n.

[38] *Ibid.*, I, 183.

and devote themselves entirely to its demands. The characteristic forms of human sin appear in these efforts to overcome anxiety by denying the freedom which elicits the anxiety.

Prominent among these responses is the denial of vulnerability itself, the insistence that whatever may be the case with other people's lives and dreams, ours are secure. This may take the form of a personal confidence that with the right diet, regular exercise, and a certain vigilance against other persons' degradation of the environment, I am protected from the threat of ill health that I have seen break the lives of others. Or it may assume the grander form of false confidence in political programs that promise economic prosperity, military security, and cultural stability. These programs assure their adherents that the historic cycles of growth and decline are herewith superseded, so that the present greatness – and the present regime – will continue forever.

These attempts to overcome the anxiety that our human vulnerability elicits through an assertion of invulnerability are what Niebuhr and the Christian Realists call "pride." Despite the uneasiness which this religious terminology often elicits, the phenomenon is one which other observers who are concerned about a realistic account of human limitations readily recognize. We have strong motives to deny that the finitude that marks every insight and achievement applies to us as well. We readily generate theories to explain our own exceptions, just as we seek followers who will confirm our ideas and power to enforce their acceptance by the uneasy and the unconvinced. The claim to a competence that is able not only to manage within the limits of the human condition but to transcend them is widely recognized as a source of evil, both by those who locate our ultimate security in God and by those who do not.

There is, however, another response to anxiety of which Niebuhr also takes note. It, too, is a response to the "paradox of freedom and finiteness," but it does not seek escape by creating a refuge too strong to be shaken by the forces that threaten the lives of others. Rather, it hopes to align itself with those powerful forces so completely that it seeks nothing beyond what they have to give. Instead of asserting a freedom which cannot be destroyed by the limitations of human finitude, anxiety in this form yields its freedom to some power it can grasp and follow. It seeks the security that comes from trust in God, but it cannot trust a center of value that both affirms and negates its aspirations, so it transfers its trust to some center in which what is to be done is always already clear.

Niebuhr calls this form of sin "sensuality," in contrast to pride. "Sometimes man seeks to solve the problem of the contradiction of finiteness and freedom, not by seeking to hide his finiteness and comprehending the world into himself, but by losing himself in some aspect of the world's vitalities. In that case his sin may be defined as sensuality rather than pride."[39] In sensuality, the risks and demands of freedom are evaded, because both the choices that freedom requires and the awareness of our own limitations that make those choices anxious are suppressed. We are drawn into an experience in which what we should do seems immediately, urgently clear, quite apart from any deliberation about it. And as long as we are doing exactly what it seems we should, we have no fear that we have done the wrong thing.

On the whole, Niebuhr gives less attention to sin as sensuality than to sin as pride. Biblical religion, he says, regards sin primarily as pride and self-love, and that must always be remembered as a caution against the Hellenism that creeps into Christian thought as a rejection of finite, bodily existence. No doubt, Niebuhr here has in mind not just some of the early Greek Fathers, but also the stern moral rectitude of more recent Protestants, who quickly condemn sins of self-indulgence with no awareness whatever of the pride and self-love that elevated them to the position of rulers and judges of other persons' lives.[40]

Niebuhr's own presentation, however, contributes to the trivialization of sensuality that he wants to avoid. Sensuality seems to be the sin of little people, rather than important ones, a sin for those who cannot afford the luxury of pride. Sensuality seems confined to individual lives and personal relationships,

---

[39] *Ibid.*, I, 179.   [40] *Ibid.*, I, 228.

with little hint that it might take institutional forms as well. A balanced understanding of Christian Realism requires a further exploration of this idea, and a fully developed concept of sensuality will illuminate some forms of sin characteristic of our own times that prove curiously resistant to Niebuhrian denunciations of pride. Taken by itself, a warning against pride may only increase the temptation of those whose characteristic sin is to avoid anxiety by immersing themselves in activities that require minimal creativity and stick close to basic organic needs. There are ambiguities in creativity, which result both in new expressions of freedom and in inordinate self-assertion, but there are other, and perhaps more subtle, ambiguities in humility. The cry of the Psalmist:

> O Lord, my heart is not proud,
>   nor are my eyes haughty;
>   I do not busy myself with great matters
>   or things too marvelous for me.
>
> (Psalm 131:1–2 *NEB*)

finds its place in the canon of scripture as a poetic expression of the humility of the contingent creature before the eternal God. The same thoughts, however, may be motivated by a desire to measure our contingent achievements by a standard easier to grasp and more to our own liking.

A more complete understanding of this form of sin begins with recognition that the sensual evasion never involves escape into purely natural forces and processes. As Niebuhr himself observes, "Human passions are always characterized by unlimited and demonic potencies of which animal life is innocent."[41] Even the most basic sensuality is shaped by cultural creativity. Cultural forms of eroticism direct desire and heighten anticipation. Social rituals prolong the enjoyment of food and drink and add new aesthetic dimensions to the experience. Animals mate and eat; they do not make love or dine.

Once the role of cultural forms in these obviously sensual enjoyments is noted, we can see more clearly an element of what Niebuhr would call sensuality even in activities that seem

[41] *Ibid.*, I, 179.

rather far removed from the vitalities and processes of nature. Anything serves the purpose which gives us a well-regulated set of activities that seems to justify itself. We can then lose ourselves in doing what the system requires. Alasdair MacIntyre has developed the idea of such a well-regulated set of activities in his idea of a "practice."[42] The point of such practices is that there are goods internal to the practice itself. Playing chess well, or football, perhaps, has its own rewards. So, too, does music or dance, solving mathematical puzzles, reading a poem, or, perhaps, writing a book about ethics. Practices demand an engagement with their internal critical standards. We have to work hard at understanding what it is to play a Mozart sonata well, and even then we may argue long over whether someone has really done it. It is these internal goods that allow a practice to absorb our energy and attention. Doubtless they are rooted in basic natural activities that satisfy some demand of our human nature – responsiveness to rhythm, for example, or the enjoyment of order and symmetry, but the internal goods and the criteria by which they are measured are developed far beyond any simple conformity to natural satisfactions.

Practices do not exist in isolation. Each of us may participate in several of them, and a well-ordered society will manage its political affairs and the distribution of external goods in ways that allow the greatest possible enjoyment of goods internal to a wide variety of practices. The way of life which emerges, MacIntyre suggests, will be one in which understandings of excellence are widely shared and the standards for critical evaluation of one's own performance and the works of others will be clear and specific.

These highly developed practices and the community of evaluation in which they are cultivated seem far removed from what we ordinarily imply by calling something "sensual," but they provide exactly the sort of opportunity for escape "by finding a god in a person or process outside the self"[43] that Reinhold Niebuhr had in mind. What marks sensuality is that

---

[42] Alasdair MacIntyre, *Whose Justice? Which Rationality?* (Notre Dame, Ind.: University of Notre Dame Press, 1988), pp. 30–46.

[43] Niebuhr, *The Nature and Destiny of Man*, I, 240.

it holds anxiety at bay by total absorption in an activity that raises no questions beyond itself. If our constitution as physical, sexual, pleasure-seeking beings suggests some obvious opportunities for that absorption, we create many more by the elaboration of cultural practices on top of the basic natural vitalities. Frequently, the theologian's critical eye cast on these more developed activities sees them as works of pride, but the relationship between pride and sensuality in practices such as making music, playing tennis, or preaching sermons is very complex. The creative effort to establish or transform a practice often requires an assertion of self against established standards and a stubborn confidence in one's own achievements that verges upon, where it does not actually enter into, pride. Once the practice is in place, however, it demands the dedication, attention to detail, and total commitment to performance that characterizes the sensual escape from anxiety. It takes pride to create these cultural practices, but sensuality uses them for its own purposes.

To the prevailing images of sensuality as a life of softness and luxury that eventually loses all structure and discipline, we must now add the unexpected image of the dedicated amateur athlete whose quest for her "personal best" determines all her choices and relationships, and even the image of the ascetic scholar whose burning need for the precise facts and the perfect footnote has crowded out all other questions and desires. There are many differences between the varieties of sensuality in this wide view of the subject. There are often good prudential reasons to prefer one form of sensuality over another for oneself, just as there are more dubious motives that lead us to urge one form of sensuality instead of another on other people. Like pride, sensuality often accompanies real accomplishments, and, again like pride, a measure of sensuality is so much a part of ordinary human life that we would at first glance think that something was missing in the life of anyone who actually achieved the simple trust that would make both pride and sensuality unnecessary. It takes the more extreme forms of both pride and sensuality to remind us of the fundamental condition of sin that unites them. Each marks a failed

effort to secure freedom by denying the tension between finitude and transcendence that makes freedom possible.

SENSUALITY AND POLITICS

Sensuality thus appears as a far more prominent feature of the
condition of human sin than the term itself calls to mind.
Perhaps Karl Barth has a better name for the problem. He calls
it the sin of "sloth," though even this has a suggestion of
laziness and inertia that obscures what Barth clearly recognizes: this sin is an active flight from God.

> At every point, as we shall see, this is the strange inactive action of the
> slothful man. It may be that this action often assumes the disguise of a
> tolerant indifference in relation to God. But in fact it is the action of
> the hate which wants to be free of God, which would prefer that there
> were no God, that God were not the One He is – at least for him, the
> slothful man.[44]

Barth notes that Western Christianity, and Protestantism in
particular, underemphasizes this aspect of sin.[45] Niebuhr, with
his probing of the pride that shakes nations and subjects the
lives of others to its demands, is typically Protestant in this
respect, and the fact that his American audience had roots in
Protestantism that went even deeper than their secular faith in
progress may partly explain their receptiveness to his sobering
message. Yet the complementary theme is also there. Sin is
present not merely in the ambition that remakes the world to
suit its own plans, but in the sensuality that loses itself in
immediate possibilities, in the sloth that absorbs itself in petty
concerns and excuses its mediocre performance, and even in
the disciplined pursuit of excellences that have been carefully
defined by someone else.

It would be interesting to pursue the historical and systematic questions that would enable us to establish a definitive
relationship between these two faces of sin, the denial of finitude in pride and the escape from freedom in sensuality or

---

[44] Karl Barth, *Church Dogmatics*, trans. G. W. Bromiley (Edinburgh: T. & T. Clark,
1958), IV/2, 405.
[45] *Ibid.*, p. 403.

sloth. Perhaps it is true, as Niebuhr suggests, that pride is the primary form of sin in the biblical texts and in the Augustinian tradition. Perhaps, as Barth has it, the sin of pride is revealed in the rejection of God's action as reconciler, while the sin of sloth becomes apparent in the rejection of God "wholly and utterly sanctifying and awakening and establishing grace."[46] For the practical concerns of Christian Realism, however, systematic and historical studies of this question are an auxiliary enterprise. The presentation of the theological point must be dialectical, and the exposition will be controlled not only by the structure of the theology, but also and primarily by the assessment of the cultural situation. When pride predominates and threatens, Niebuhr's attentiveness to the transcendent power that turns our solemn boasts to wry irony is most important. But when we are fascinated by the discovery of our own limits, when we count ourselves happy if we have done exactly everything that those limits tell us we may and must do, then a Niebuhrian message may sound very different from Reinhold Niebuhr's words. For we will then have to say that unless persons and nations are straining toward a good that stands in judgment on every concrete form of excellence they know and have achieved, they have yielded to the temptations of sensuality and of sloth. In their anxiety, they have sought to achieve freedom by denying that they are free, and this is true even for those heirs of Puritanism who compound the contradiction by working very hard at being slothful.

It is this latter situation, I think, which faces us today in the cultures of the developed Western democracies. This is apparent not only in the self-indulgent consumer society that clerics and professors tend to deprecate, but also in the obsessive rituals of diet and health, exercise, safety, and ecology in which many of us participate. It is present too, and not least evident, in the forms of philosophy and theology that assure us that learning to use the languages and narratives of these limited and well-defined systems is what morality is really all

[46] *Ibid.*

about. A little more attention to our expanded understanding of sensuality and sloth will show what I mean.

Alongside the temptations to pride that we identify so readily in the lives of the powerful, there is a temptation to sensuality or sloth that must not be ignored in the lives of those who are confined to a more limited sphere of influence. Feminist writers were among the first to notice that Niebuhr's warnings against pride may undermine the assertiveness that women need to escape the subordinate roles in which they have been locked in the family and in society. It is not just a matter of not having enough pride. Women are actually tempted with sensuality. They are encouraged to believe that by attending more or less exclusively to organic, basic needs for nurture, they are respecting the order of nature and the finitude of human life. Theirs is not to worry about the transcendence of self and situation that occupies the energy and creativity of others. They express themselves in good food and a loving home.[47]

Some do, of course. It is impossible to identify any particular activity as invariably proud or sensual. An appreciation of the full range of ways that anxious persons deny their freedom makes us aware that what is for one person a meaningful expression of creativity is for another a temptation to pride or to sloth. Women have, however, discovered that many activities that have been held up to them as models of virtue, or at least represented as innocent enjoyments, are in fact profound temptations to surrender their freedom for the security of a place in someone else's system of achievement. Their insights should lead other persons, especially male intellectuals of the sort who are apt to write books on ethics and politics, to reconsider the part they have played in these systems of subordination.

Another lesson which everyone should take, however, is the re-examination of one's own life for those points at which the

---

[47] See Judith Plaskow, *Sex, Sin and Grace: Women's Experience and the Theologies of Reinhold Niebuhr and Paul Tillich* (Washington, D.C.: University Press of America, 1980), p. 151; Catherine Keller, *From a Broken Web* (Boston: Beacon Press, 1986), pp. 39–43; and Daphne Hampson, "Reinhold Niebuhr on Sin: A Critique," in Harries, ed., *Reinhold Niebuhr and the Issues of Our Time*, pp. 46–60.

appearance of choice and control is actually an illusion, result-
ing from a sensual acquiescence in limited options which have
actually been defined to suit the purposes of others. Those who
find their work meaningless and who lack significant personal
relationships will find much encouragement in a consumer-
oriented society to devote themselves to new forms of gadgetry
and to establish a firm decorative control over their limited
personal environment. These evasions of freedom, along with
the forms of indulgence more usually associated with the term
'sensuality', must be seen as genuine forms of sin.

Perhaps the most important point at which Niebuhr's
account of sin needs to be supplemented, however, is in the
delineation of institutional sources of sensuality. In addition to
the pride and collective egotism of groups that is expressed in
totalitarian politics or imperialistic foreign policies, we must
also identify a form of institutional sin that elicits sensuality or
sloth from persons by demanding commitments that preclude
responsible attention to the range of choices and responsibilities that they ought to be attending to for themselves. The "up
or out," "publish or perish" career trajectories imposed by
businesses, law firms, and academic institutions provide familiar examples of this sort of pressure. The pressure may originate in institutional pride, which subtly reduces persons to
instruments for the aggrandizement of the institution. It may
even originate in the identifiable pride of quite specific deans,
vice-presidents, or senior partners. Those who yield to these
pressures are often pictured as ambitious, "fast-track,"
achievers whose chief temptation would seem to be to emulate
the pride of their seniors and superiors. In fact, however, their
achievements are often expressions of sensuality and sloth. The
rising executive or scholar abandons the difficult balancing of
obligations that marks a life of freedom constrained by human
finitude, and substitutes a single set of goals defined by outside
authorities. This does not obviate the anxiety of achievement,
but it does eliminate the deeper anxiety of choice. The over-
achiever stills anxiety in precisely the way that Niebuhr
describes the sensual evasion, "by finding a god in a person
or process outside the self."

There is, moreover, the possibility of a kind of sensuality that directly involves institutions themselves. Like the sensuality of individuals, it is a temptation that may become more attractive if the dangers of pride are too vividly presented. Institutions, we are told, become proud when they take themselves too seriously and define their goals too broadly. A corporation that thinks its purpose is to make life better, and regards its employees as participants in that noble aim, is in fact more apt to constrict freedom than one which believes that its purpose is to make gadgets, and pays its employees to secure their cooperation in a venture that would otherwise be quite indifferent to them. That problem of institutional pride is obvious enough, but it should not obscure the fact that an opposite institutional sensuality threatens those who see their collective aims too narrowly. It may result in corporate executives who give up any appropriate concern for the social effects of their work and surrender themselves to a corporate process that, far from maximizing freedom, draws more and more persons into the service of its singular objective.

INSTITUTIONAL SLOTH

As a counterpoint to the emphasis on pride in Reinhold Niebuhr's theological criticism of social and political life, I have offered a brief survey of the forms of sensuality that seem more evident in the chastened pride and diminished expectations that characterize society and politics today. The examples could be multiplied, but the main features of sensuality in this extended use of the Niebuhrian concept should now be clear.

Sensuality evades the anxiety of human freedom by entering into a pattern of activity that draws attention away from the self and focuses it on the activity. Whether in indulgences that overwhelm anxiety by immediate gratification of the senses, or in demanding forms of excellence that require concentration so intense as to shut out other questions, one simply becomes the lover, the athlete, or the chess master, the futures trader, vote-getter, or vocalist. True humanity, which must both choose these excellences *and* know their limits, both struggle to master them *and* constantly question their worth, is traded for the exhilaration of an activity which raises none of these questions and asks only that we pay attention to the rules of the game.

The elaborate patterns of activity that mark sensuality cannot, of course, promise success in those tasks or security from the misfortunes that may befall us while we are concentrating on something else. Indeed, it is characteristic of the forms of sensuality that they constantly remind us of this limitation. Pride usually asserts its own invulnerability. Sensuality playfully reminds us that "it's only a game," even when the game is politics or high finance. Or it warns us, more soberly, that goodness is fragile and our excellences may easily fall victim to circumstance. In either case, sensuality provides, alongside the patterns of competitive activity, roles for the good sport and the cheerful loser, and appropriate rituals of grief for those stricken by tragedy. We have practices to master, even in defeat.

Christian Realists, always alert for signs of institutional pride and the arrogance of power, may overlook the problems that arise when contemporary affirmations of finitude identify the moral life with the mastery of these practices. The closer linking of moral goodness to specific forms of virtue recognized by tradition may provide more concrete guidance, but it may also lose the consciousness of freedom out of which we are able to make moral choices. Morality becomes a problem of mastering yet another set of tasks.

Niebuhr's moral criticism of the sin of pride focuses on the destructive effects that pride has on those who find themselves in the way of its aims and pretensions. Those who relieve the anxiety of their human condition by asserting themselves in pride require an inordinate share of life's resources to sustain their illusions of immortality and invulnerability. Their demands deprive other persons of what they need to satisfy more moderate aims. Indeed, the demands of pride actually use persons themselves as resources, reducing them merely to instruments of the plans of others. "The ego which falsely makes itself the centre of existence in its pride and will-to-power inevitably subordinates other life to its will and thus does injustice to other life."[48]

Set against the ambitions of the Southern planters who built cotton fortunes on the labor of African American slaves, or the horrors of Hitler's Reich, or even the petty brutalities of today's speculators in futures markets, real estate, or the hotel business, the sins of sensuality and sloth seem rather innocuous. Indeed, in the expanded definition we have given to those concepts, they may seem truly beneficial in comparison to the ravages of pride. Socially defined practices, after all, may lead us to concentrate on the internal goods that are their own reward, and to think less of the external goods of wealth and power that are the tools of pride. Those who concentrate on developing their own excellences are perhaps less likely to impose their pride on their neighbors, and less susceptible to the lures of wealth and power that might turn them into instruments of the pride of others. Excellences in art and music, literature and sports are no doubt good things, and even modest accomplishments in the virtues to which everyone may aspire can make social life more harmonious. We could all do with better manners. Even where the excellence achieved provides nothing more than a distraction from the tensions and anxieties of daily life – ethics professors trying to improve their times for a ten-kilometer run, for example – the activity may be a healthy alternative to the brooding self-absorption that too readily yields to the temptations of pride.

Christian Realism need not neglect these excellences or deny the important exercise of human freedom that is involved in combining them in a coherent way of life. To that extent, MacIntyre's ethics of virtue and other contemporary versions of Aristotelian eudaimonism are compatible with the Realist's emphasis on freedom. Eudaimonism, too, recognizes the element of human creativity involved in all pursuits of human good, and rejects the more reductive forms of naturalism that try to find the whole of human good determined by human nature. Christian Realism insists, however, that whatever *moral*

---

[48] Niebuhr, *The Nature and Destiny of Man*, I, 179.

meaning human excellences may have cannot be derived from their place in a single way of life. Moral goodness, for Christian Realism, is primarily the ordering of lives and cultures toward an ultimate harmony of life with life.

The concrete requirements of that harmony are not available to us with the same specificity with which we can know the excellences and virtues of our own way of life. Excellences and virtues can be observed and emulated in concrete examples. Love, *agape*, however, is known only in an imaginative grasp of possibilities beyond present conflicts. Its requirements are communicated in myth and symbol, rather than by example. The idea of an ultimate harmony of life with life that transcends particular ways of life is not something that we can enact in the present in the way that we can be courageous, truthful, or compassionate according to the virtues of our own community. But the idea of ultimate harmony opens up the possibility of a different kind of moral choice. If moral meaning is not dependent on the particular community and tradition in which I have learned to make my choices, then it is possible to be moral not only by choosing among the alternatives offered by that way of life, but also by choosing against them. It is possible to be a good person not just by emulating one or another of the forms of the good life offered, but also by risking those goods and perhaps losing them for myself, in an effort to create a new form of community that achieves harmonies between lives hopelessly divided and alien to one another in our present ways of living.

Few will achieve that creativity in important and lasting forms. Gandhi's dream of a unified India, the efforts of Martin Luther King, Jr. and Nelson Mandela to replace segregation with racial equality, or the transformation of totalitarian states by the work of dissidents in Eastern Europe and the Soviet Union stand out as rare achievements. The people who initiate these changes become historic figures precisely because the changes they envision and enact go beyond ordinary political transitions and policy changes within a social framework to mark the beginning of a new society.

But these same people also become heroes, even to some who

originally regarded them as criminals. They become heroes precisely because people see in their achievements a possibility that exists in relation to all conflicts, even the perfectly ordinary ones that are settled by prevailing mechanisms of compromise or coercion. In addition to the resolutions that involve the victory, partial or complete, of one set of interests over another, the idea of a moral resolution to conflict presumes that there is a solution through which the interests of the parties, though transformed, can be brought into a harmony which each can recognize as good. To believe in a morally meaningful universe is to believe that such a resolution is always possible, even in the historic conflicts of religions, classes, and nations in which the opposing forces seem to have at present nothing in common. But it is also to believe that that possibility structures even the more limited conflicts within cultures and societies, for unless one enters into moral problem solving with a commitment to these possibilities for the transformation, as well as the vindication, of one's commitments, the moral claims quickly deteriorate into another instrument for gaining an advantage over the opposition. The possibilities that are realized in historic moral transformations are thus implicitly present in every situation of conflict. Niebuhr formulates this claim in his repeated insistence that "the heedlessness of perfect love is the source and end of all reciprocal relations in human existence, preventing them from degenerating into mere calculation of advantage."[49]

The morally meaningful universe of the Christian Realist thus has a complex, dialectical relationship to the competences and excellence that mark the human good in an ethics of virtue. "If the *Agape* of New Testament morality is the negation as well as the fulfillment of every private virtue, it is also the negation and the fulfillment of all structures and schemes of justice."[50]

Contrary to what the critics of the idea of sin appear to believe, Christian Realism is not a simple negation of the possibilities and achievements of ordinary human life. The

[49] Niebuhr, *Faith and History*, p. 193.   [50] *Ibid.*

negations of Christian Realism are more complex. They are directed, obviously, against the claims of pride which identify a perfect society already in sight, or at least on the drawing boards. In that, the negation is also an affirmation of the achievements of ordinary morality and the possibilities for concrete, limited improvements in our society. Those everyday approximations of justice find fulfillment in the idea of a love that unites persons despite the reality of their differences, and the sacrifices of proximate concerns that justice sometimes requires are justified by commitment to the possibilities that love envisions, even when they are not compensated by a society's approximations of reciprocity.

If Christian Realism thus conceives love as in some ways the fulfillment of human finitude, it must negate the achievements of those virtues and excellences, though hardly in the ways that contemporary critics suppose. For Christian Realism negates "every private virtue" and "all structures and schemes of justice" primarily by insisting that the possibilities of human freedom find their fulfillment only in love. The negation is a revelation of the sensuality that leads us to limit moral aspirations to the prevailing forms of virtue and excellence. "The vision of universal love . . . is relevant to all social relationships. For the freedom of man makes it impossible to set any limits of race, sex, or social condition upon the brotherhood that may be achieved in history."[51]

Those words of Reinhold Niebuhr ring somewhat dissonantly in our ears, and not only because of the exclusive language in which he expresses his gender-inclusive vision. They do not "sound" like Christian Realism because both the critics and the friends of Christian Realism have become too familiar with Niebuhr's denunciations of pride and his emphasis on the moral significance of finite humanity. However, when our social beliefs change from the simple assertion of national, religious, or technological pride to the simple acceptance that our own community and culture provides the largest moral universe we can fathom, then the more complex, dialectical

---

[51] Niebuhr, *The Nature and Destiny of Man*, II, 85.

message of Christian Realism must change to an insistence that there are larger possibilities, and that those possibilities are relevant even to our most limited choices. Freedom, we must reiterate, makes it impossible to set any limits on moral achievements within history.

There is always the danger, of course, that this announcement will itself be heard in a simple, undialectical way, and thus become an invitation to pride, instead of a call to eschew sensuality and sloth. That danger is inescapable, given the complexity of Christian Realism and the ambiguity of history. The misinterpretation cannot be prevented, but it can be discouraged. Christian Realists should pursue the unlimited possibilities for moral achievement not in a single, grand scheme that purports to indicate the one better way beyond our present divisions and conflict, but in a multiplicity of experiments that test the limits of existing social virtues and give specificity and clarity to possibilities that are at present only dimly glimpsed in the languages of myth. Properly understood, the Christian Realist claim that there are no limits to our moral achievements within history is not an invitation to pride, but to politics.

CHAPTER 4

Politics

THE OTHERS

Christians have always been somewhat at a loss when confronted with people who share their world, but not their faith. They tend to suffer from what W. H. Auden called "the conceit of the social worker: 'We are all here on earth to help others; what on earth the others are here for, I don't know.'"[1]

The puzzle becomes acute in politics. Here, the others tend to stick to their own opinions and to demand a voice in the choice, rather than passively submitting to "help" administered according to Christian insights. They insist on squabbling over details, rather than attending to the main point with meek heart and due reverence.

What are we to make of this intransigent otherness, which will not even submit to become the Other with a capital "O" – a conceptual otherness that can be located within my own horizon of meanings – but insists on being some particular other, a different point of view, or a different set of interests? In politics, I must respond to this other in some concrete way, modifying my practices and maybe even my beliefs in ways that take this specific otherness into account.

Politics seems not so much a field in which Christianity can be applied as one in which it is inevitably lost. The compromises and the preoccupation with mundane details that inevitably mark political solutions often seem poor soil for

---

[1] W. H. Auden, *The Dyer's Hand and Other Essays* (New York: Random House, 1962), p. 14.

spiritual growth. Politics, like the theater, has been an occupation that Christians are counseled to avoid.

Reinhold Niebuhr, the pre-eminent Christian Realist, was also, however, eminently political. He was active in political organizations, civic commissions, and partisan politics. He reveled in the ironies and ambiguities that lead many intellectuals to shrink from political controversy. Most important, he understood that the conflicts and oppositions that make Christians uneasy about politics may also be the most effective instruments of social transformation. The Christian Realist is one who understands that social ethics depends at least as much on the seriousness with which we take our conflicts as it does on the quality of our ideals.

The church would do more for the cause of reconciliation if, instead of producing moral idealists who think that they can establish justice, it would create religious and Christian realists who know that justice will require that some men shall contend against them ... This kind of Christian realism would understand the perennial necessity of political relationships in society, no matter how ethical ideals rise.[2]

From this point of view, the others are there neither to be served nor to be defeated. They are there to supplement, from their own partial perspectives, the necessarily incomplete understanding of reality with which we begin. Insofar as Christianity has something to say about how life ought to be lived in society, it must subject that point of view to the scrutiny and supplementation of others who do not share the same faith. Far from merely tolerating the others in a political community, Christian Realists recognize their own need for difference, and indeed, for opposition. Without it, the Realist does not even know for certain what his or her *own* truth is.

Niebuhr's relation to the assessment of politics in Christian tradition is not a simple one. He believed that this tradition, particularly in its Augustinian and Lutheran forms, offered the only understanding of human nature realistic enough to make good politics possible. But Niebuhr also believed that the

---

[2] Reinhold Niebuhr, "When Will Christians Stop Fooling Themselves," in D. B. Robertson, ed., *Love and Justice: Selections from the Shorter Writings of Reinhold Niebuhr* (Louisville: Westminster/John Knox, 1992), p. 43.

actual political thinking of these great historic realists was flawed. It fell short of its possibilities, precisely because it was so consistently realistic about self-interest and power. As a consequence, Augustine, for example, was unable to make the important distinctions between degrees of injustice on which practical Christian judgments about real political choices must rest. "On the basis of his principles he could not distinguish between government and slavery, both of which were supposedly the rule over man by man and were both a consequence of, and remedy for, sin; nor could he distinguish between a commonwealth and a robber band, for both were bound together by collective interest."[3]

Modern thinkers, by contrast, are more ready from the outset to make discriminating political choices, but their overly optimistic view of human nature leads them too easily to the assumption that people are creatures of moderate desires which can easily be brought under the control of reason. No one with such a circumscribed view of human motivations can understand the tenacity of political commitments or the intractability of political conflicts.

Yet Niebuhr, who made his reputation as a political thinker by dissenting from the hopeful consensus of progressive liberal optimism, remained in some ways a liberal in his own mature politics. Politics was for him an instrument of proximate goals, rather than ultimate commitments. He was interested in compromise and pragmatic choices, rather than in theological or ideological purity. Though he often said and did the right thing, he probably would not abide our contemporary obsession with "political correctness." For all his complaints about liberalism, especially in its post-Enlightenment forms, what he wanted, as he acknowledged late in his career, was a "realistic liberalism" that would combine an appreciation of incremental gains in justice with a realistic assessment of the limits of reason and the power of tradition.[4]

---

[3] Niebuhr, "Augustine's Political Realism," in *Christian Realism and Political Problems*, p. 127.
[4] Reinhold Niebuhr, "Liberalism: Illusions and Realities," *New Republic* 133 (July 4, 1955), 13.

Whether such a combination is plausible depends on how the Christian Realist reads the complex relationship between Christian thought and modern politics. Our aim in this chapter will be to study that problem, though we will not exactly duplicate Niebuhr's reading of the history. We will, however, arrive with him at a more positive assessment of the possibilities of politics than other Christian thinkers have held, and that, in turn, will serve as a starting point for an exploration of the problem of justice in Chapter Five.

THE LIMITS OF POLITICS

It is in the nature of political units – cities, provinces, and nations – that they gather up all people within a given geographical area, and so must create a workable community from those who have not come together sharing a set of beliefs or commitments. These persons may have a government that meets their needs, keeps them secure, and allows them to live the lives to which they aspire, but that is an achievement, not a given. Politics is the process through which that comprehensive community is created.

Near the beginning of Western political thought, Aristotle identified politics as the search for the highest human good, precisely because it takes place in these most comprehensive communities. The good which a political community seeks "embraces all the rest, aims at good in a greater degree than any other, and at the highest good."[5] Politics is the culmination of ethics as the search for practical truths about the human good.

Later, in Roman times, Stoic philosophers confronted a far different political reality, but they, too, held that the greatest good is the most comprehensive. The right person to ask about the human good is the *kosmopolites*, the citizen whose city is the whole cosmos. Both Greek and Roman philosophers, then, linked politics to a cosmic order, and to a universal reason which could comprehend that order. Such a politics excludes

[5] Aristotle, *The Politics*, trans. Benjamin Jowett (Cambridge: Cambridge University Press, 1988), p. 1.

those whose concerns are more local or more bound to their immediate needs. Traders, housekeepers, aliens, and unfree laborers have no stake in politics, and whatever human good may be available to them will be the portion determined by those who do participate in the political process.

From Greek and Roman sources, Christian political thought inherited the belief that political communities, because they are the most comprehensive, are also the places in which human good can be sought and known in the most general terms, even though few persons may have the material and intellectual resources adequate to that task. The Hebrew prophet's image of a divine creator who had made from the formless void a world for human habitation connected with the philosophers' idea of universal reason. "The Stoic idea of Natural Law, which the Apologists regarded as identical with the Christian moral law,"[6] became the rule of political, as well as moral, life.

Christians, however, also inherited memories of a people who came together to build a tower that would reach to the heavens, in defiance of the created order. They recalled the people of Israel, who against the advice of their prophet insisted on having a king like the other nations around them. They also found themselves living in communities of fellow Christians who shared equally in the grace of God, which wiped out the distinctions of citizen and alien, male and female, slave and free that elsewhere set the limits of participation.[7] The immediate community of faith provided a region of freedom and equality, while the larger world where cosmopolites supposedly sought the highest good seemed to be corrupted by its wealth and power. Christians were sure about the underlying moral structure of reality. They were far less certain that politics provides the environment in which that moral reality can best be known.

Little wonder, then, that for many Christian writers the most powerful image of political reality has been the image of

---

[6] Ernst Troeltsch, *The Social Teaching of the Christian Churches*, trans. Olive Wyon (Louisville: Wesminster/John Knox Press, 1992), I, 150.

[7] Cf. Genesis 11, I Samuel 8, Galatians 3:27–29.

Babylon – the center of power which exists, temporarily, in defiance of God's order. Augustine's *City of God* introduced a dualism into Christian thinking about human communities. The true commonwealth is the church, whose people are united by a love of God. Political communities, by contrast, are part of the human city, whose people are united merely by their own momentarily shared interests. That is what makes the state indistinguishable from a band of robbers.[8] Although these earthly cities are places of exile where Christians for the moment have to dwell, they can never be a place where Christians are at home.

One response to this sense of exile and alienation has been to avoid political involvements entirely. These Christians suffer the impositions of politics when necessary, but they do not voluntarily join in its self-interested pursuits. Early Christian monasticism, which sought to create a community of faith outside of the decaying framework of Roman society, and the sects of the sixteenth-century "radical Reformation," who carried the reform of the church to the point of attempting to create a whole new way of life, have become paradigm examples of this Christian rejection of politics.

Withdrawal from government and political activities has been stressed down to the present by those who find the promises of social transformation through Christian action illusory, and who see the non-violent witness to one's faith as the only possible response to intractable evils. Guy Hershberger offers a modern statement of this rejection of politics:

The mission of nonresistant Christians is not a political one. It is rather a curative mission. It is to bring healing to human society; to prevent its further decay through a consistent witness to the truth . . . A people who provide this witness are not parasites living at the expense of organized society. They are its greatest benefactors. Let those who aspire to nothing higher perform the task of the magistracy, the police, and the military. There will always be more than enough people ready to fill these positions; but candidates for the

---

[8] Augustine, *City of God*, ed. David Knowles (Harmondsworth: Penguin Books, 1976), pp. 866–67, 885.

higher place, which the nonresistant Christian alone can fill, are altogether too few.[9]

Contemporary rejections of politics do not always take the form of withdrawal from society. Those who are skeptical about the value of political activity may nonetheless take an active role in helping the victims of natural disasters, wars, and social problems. They may even engage in intense and highly focused political activity to secure support for these programs or to oppose policies they regard as based on the use of force or disrespect for human life. What they share with Hershberger's rejection of politics is the conviction that politics, as presently constituted, is a poor forum for the articulation of Christian truth. Stanley Hauerwas puts it this way:

[T]he church's social task is first of all its willingness to be a community formed by a language that the world does not share. I do not deny the importance for the church from time to time to speak to the world in statements and policies, but that is not the church's primary task. The widespread attention given to the Catholic Bishops' recent Pastoral on nuclear war can be misleading in this respect, since it looks as if they have had an impact on the public debate if not policy. Thus the churches are tempted to think they will serve the world well by drafting more and more radical statements. Yet the church's social ethic is not first of all to be found in the statements by which it tries to influence the ethos of those in power, but rather the church's social ethic is first and foremost found in its ability to sustain a people who are not at home in the liberal presuppositions of our civilization and society.[10]

Given the widespread disillusionment with politics in American life today, Christians of any tradition may be attracted to this rejection of politics and the suggestion that political tasks might better be given over to those who are less scrupulous about their own integrity. There is, as Hershberger observed, never any shortage of them.

There is, however, another possible response. Augustine, whose sharp differentiation between the City of God and the

---

[9] Hershberger, *War, Peace, and Nonresistance*, p. 301.

[10] Stanley Hauerwas, *Against the Nations: War and Survival in a Liberal Society* (Minneapolis: Winston Press, 1985), pp. 11–12.

human commonwealth made withdrawal from politics an attractive possibility, nevertheless cautioned against leaving the human city to its own devices. Despite Niebuhr's complaint, Augustine was not altogether indifferent to degrees of good and evil in the human city.[11] The peace of Babylon is no true peace, but Babylon at peace is better than Babylon at war, and this is as true for the Christians who live there in exile as it is for the people for whom Babylon is home.

Meanwhile, however, it is important for us also that this people should possess this peace in this life, since so long as the two cities are intermingled we also make use of the peace of Babylon – although the People of God is by faith set free from Babylon, so that in the meantime they are only pilgrims in the midst of her. That is why the Apostle instructs the Church to pray for the kings of that city and those in high positions, adding these words: "that we may lead a quiet and peaceful life with all devotion and love."[12]

This provides a starting point for participation in politics on a quite different basis from the Aristotelian pursuit of the human good in common. Not the pursuit of good, but the restraint of evil is the reason why the Christian enters politics. At a time when the civil order was collapsing, that was reason enough, for there was no one else to whom Christians could leave the task while they pursued their higher aims.

Luther, living in the formative period of modern politics, offered similar reasons. He mistrusted the secular officials and princes that he saw around him, but he also saw the importance of a strong civil power in restraining persons whose avarice and rebellion would otherwise work great harm on unprotected, innocent people. It will not do simply to say that Christians should be generous and loving and not use force against their enemies. The question is: what would then become of all those who would be subjected to the depredations of those who are not Christian?

Hence a man who would venture to govern an entire country or the world with the Gospel would be like a shepherd who should place in one fold wolves, lions, eagles, and sheep together and let them freely mingle with one another and say, Help yourselves, and be good and

[11] See Niebuhr's comment on page 160 above.   [12] Augustine, *City of God*, p. 892.

peaceful among yourselves; the fold is open, there is plenty of food; have no fear of dogs and clubs. The sheep, forsooth, would keep the peace and would allow themselves to be fed and governed in peace, but they would not live long; nor would any beast keep from molesting another.[13]

So Luther, like Augustine before him, encouraged Christians to set aside the requirements of love and take up the use of force, where force serves the public good and restrains evil. "Therefore, should you see that there is a lack of hangmen, beadles, judges, lords, or princes, and find that you are qualified, you should offer your services and seek the place, that necessary government may by no means be despised and become inefficient or perish. For the world cannot and dare not dispense with it."[14] Luther's realistic assessment of the secular realm led him to caution Christians against expecting very much from this political activity, but he did anticipate at least one good result. There would be order. Good might not be achieved, but evil would be restrained.

The Christian way of thinking about politics which Reinhold Niebuhr inherits from Augustine and Luther bears this suspicion of politics into modern times. Government represents a center of power that is necessary for order, but alien to faith. Augustine and Luther recognize an obligation to obey the secular ruler, and even an obligation to serve as a ruler, judge, or executioner, should the opportunity present itself. Conduct in that service, however, bears little relationship to the standards that govern relations between Christians, and is no service at all to the faith. For their own part, Luther insists, Christians should prefer to suffer evil than to wield coercive power to correct it.[15] Only the needs of the neighbor drive them to the point of public service.

---

[13] Martin Luther, "Secular Authority: To What Extent It Should Be Obeyed," in John Dillenberger, ed., *Martin Luther: Selections from His Writings* (Garden City, N.Y.: Anchor Books, 1961), p. 371.

[14] *Ibid.*, pp. 374–75. See also Augustine on Christians taking up public office in *City of God*, p. 878.

[15] Martin Luther, "Secular Authority: To What Extent It Should Be Obeyed," p. 388. On a more positive note, Calvin regarded the support of politics as essential to our human nature, and Thomas Aquinas conceived of a human law which could be framed and enforced in accordance with the requirements of the natural law. See

Modern democracy makes no essential change in this grim reality. In place of the arbitrary prince, we have an elected legislature and an accountable executive, but this merely places more effective checks on a morally dubious power. It does not make the power itself more moral. Government and politics remain an unavoidable evil, for which the Christian's only praise is to remind us that a world without government would be even worse. Glenn Tinder makes a faithful presentation of these views in contemporary terms:

> Christians do not deny that governments ordinarily are evil – deceptive, selfish, arrogant – and often are atrocious; but they are indispensable. We should keep them within constitutional limits and subject them to popular consent; it would be futile, however, to try to do without them or even to try to substitute for the centralized power of government the voluntary agreement of citizens. The necessity of living under centralized power is one of the most tragic conditions of historical existence. It is inherent, however, in our fallen state.[16]

One prominent tendency in Christian thought, then, has linked *moral* realism regarding a permanent order and pattern for human life to a very different, skeptical *political* realism, which insists that we must face up to the fact that people acting in groups, people striving for power and forming governments are going to act in ways contrary to the requirements of the moral life. The tempting prospect of using power to secure the good must be rejected, because that is not how real politics works. What we can do is to enter into politics as an act of service, risking our own inner peace to spare our neighbors the loss of outward peace.

This Augustinian–Lutheran tradition provides a significant warrant for political activity by Christians. Those who accept it will by no means sit on the sidelines, and when their opposition to injustice is linked to a prophetic sense of urgency, it will be unrelenting. Tinder, again, articulates the position in contemporary terms: "The prophetic stance, accordingly, pre-

John Calvin, *Institutes of the Christian Religion*, ed. John T. McNeill (Philadelphia: Westminster Press, 1960), II, 1487; Thomas Aquinas, *Summa Theologica*, I-II, Q. 95, a. 2.

[16] Tinder, *The Political Meaning of Christianity*, p. 134.

supposes a disposition to attack concrete, visible injustices. To pursue the ideal of a perfect justice is to ignore our fallenness; but to attack injustices in the world around us – injustices we must either attack or tacitly accept – is essential to the integrity of prophetic hope."[17]

In the literature on Christianity and politics, Tinder's "prophetic stance" is probably a minority report, lodged as it is between the more radical criticism of politics articulated by Hershberger and the more enthusiastic pursuit of justice represented by, say, the National Conference of Catholic Bishops. In the lives of persons who understand themselves as Christians, however, Tinder's severely realistic opposition to injustice is no doubt better represented. Those who work in law, law enforcement, and social services usually have few illusions about the effects of their work, and they certainly do not expect to create perfect justice. Their work is difficult and poorly paid relative to their counterparts in business or academic positions, and often it is physically dangerous. Their commitment, though they might hesitate to say it this way, is to serve their neighbors by keeping their circumstances from becoming worse. What they do often leads them into politics, because that is where evil can be effectively restrained, even if it cannot be eliminated.

Niebuhr took the Augustinian–Lutheran insistence on the limitations of politics and the service of one's neighbor very seriously. His aspiration for a "realistic" liberalism was essentially directed toward a politics that would affirm human freedom without neglecting the realities of power and self-interest in the formation of communities.

His critical insights, however, led him beyond Luther on at least one important point. It is not only those who have evil intentions who need to be restrained if order is to be preserved. Those who intend only good, who want a society more just and more abundant than the one they know, may also have to be kept in check, lest they destroy what order does exist and then prove unable to replace it. Even those whose intentions are good may inflict tremendous suffering on others in their zeal to

[17] *Ibid.*, p. 66.

achieve their utopian visions. Human life is a fragile thing, and those who die in revolutionary violence, or in reactionary violence, or in famine and disease brought on by a breakdown in the regular organization of agriculture and health care will not benefit from the justice of the new order. People may well judge the evils of the present system more tolerable than the suffering they would endure in a transition to the new, especially in situations where attentiveness to human finitude makes us aware that in the end there are no guarantees that a new regime will achieve the justice it seeks. A realistic skepticism about the human capacity to achieve perfect justice always argues against undertaking means that only the end of perfect justice could justify. To that extent, there will be a preference for whatever order exists over the prospect of a revolutionary change that may result in no order at all, and Christians contemplating political action will probably be counseled, as they were by Augustine and Luther, to take up the distasteful tasks that have some realistic expectations of maintaining order, rather than the revolutionary endeavors that merely hope to obtain justice.

THE POLITICS OF FREEDOM

Reinhold Niebuhr lived his own intense involvements with public issues in some tension with this Augustinian–Lutheran perspective that shaped his theological assessment of politics. Richard Fox, in his biography, catches the irony of Niebuhr's popularity in the early 1940s. "Niebuhr's popular reputation was taking on a life of its own. 'Niebuhrian' was coming to mean 'pessimistic,' even 'resigned.' Meanwhile, Niebuhr was working beyond endurance in one cause after another to help mold the fate that was supposedly beyond molding."[18]

Niebuhr was not, however, simply living at odds with his ideas. The cold light of Luther's pessimistic realism is needed whenever people begin to link goodness too closely to any center of power, established or revolutionary, but Luther and

---

[18] Fox, *Reinhold Niebuhr*, p. 202.

Augustine do not have the last word. Their realism is either inconsistent, because it does not recognize that the rulers who maintain order need to be held in check too;[19] or it is too consistent, failing in the end to distinguish the coercions of tyranny and slavery from the incomplete, but still quite real, achievements of rulers who do justice.[20] What is needed is not the rigid consistency of a single line of explanation, but an assessment of politics "qualified to accord with the real and complex facts of human nature and history."[21]

To understand the intellectual balance behind Niebuhr's combination of realism and activism, we must move beyond the consistently negative judgments of Augustine and Luther to incorporate the more positive valuation of politics in modern thought. Niebuhr criticized the optimism and universalism of political liberalism, defects which he believed liberalism acquired primarily under the influence of the continental Enlightenment and the French Revolution. His role, as he saw it, was not to purge Christian political thinking of these alien elements altogether, but precisely to reconnect liberalism to its origins in the political traditions of Christianity, so that its important contribution would not be lost in the collapse of its Enlightenment illusions.[22]

The key to that contribution is the modern idea of political freedom, or liberty. Liberty, unlike the freedom of consciousness that is central in Christian Realism's account of human nature, is a political achievement. Ask what makes the risk and effort of politics worthwhile, and the answer is clear: liberty. In nature, human beings live constrained by needs and natural forces. Life is at best a perilous struggle to do what one must to survive another day, and at worst it is, in Hobbes' memorable phrase "solitary, poore, nasty, brutish, and short."[23] To be truly human is to break free of these restraints into a realm of

---

[19] Niebuhr, *The Children of Light and the Children of Darkness*, p. xiii; *Christian Realism and Political Problems*, p. 127.

[20] Niebuhr, *Christian Realism and Political Problems*, p. 127.

[21] Niebuhr, *The Children of Light and the Children of Darkness*, p. xiv.

[22] Niebuhr, "Liberalism: Illusions and Realities," pp. 11–12. We will have more to say about this project of a "realistic liberalism" in Chapter Five.

[23] Hobbes, *Leviathan*, p. 186.

action that is governed by choice. By creating stable rules and expectations, under which property is secure and wealth can accumulate, people free themselves from the brutal necessities that drive those who do not live in political communities.

In this characteristically modern way of thinking, politics again becomes, as it was for Aristotle, the most significant realm of human achievement, but for quite different reasons. For Aristotle, the *polis* was a place in which free men used their freedom to create human good on a larger scale. The aim was to make a difference in the life of the community, and personal freedom was the ticket of admission to this opportunity for lasting honor. Women, slaves, and other dependents were excluded. Early modern democracies imposed similar limits on the franchise, but their aims were more individualistic. Liberty is the goal of politics, not its premise. We enter into politics to secure for ourselves a freedom of action that would be inconceivable if we had to defend our person and our goods continuously. It is our mutual agreement to avoid doing one another harm that makes us free.[24]

For liberalism, then, it is not the freedom we have by nature that is politically important. What is politically important is the freedom we create by consent. We are free to do whatever we can agree with others to permit. Consent, of course, is different from arbitrary desire; but it is a choice that knows no natural constraints. The only rule of choice is that we must not defeat ourselves by choosing something that will make us individually worse off than we were before. It is likely, then, that we will choose to make all of our desires moderate ones, and trade off our wants with one another until we arrive at a balance in which everyone is satisfied. If these market mechanisms should fail, or if someone should be so imprudent as to violate them, we will want a government at hand to set things right and to restrain the offender. Mostly, however, we will depend on the self-regulating actions of individuals who

---

[24] See Locke's account of "the beginning of political societies," in John Locke, *Two Treatises of Government*, ed. Peter Laslett (New York: New American Library, 1965), pp. 374–75.

know what they want, and who do not want anything exces-
sively.[25]

Where the Augustinian–Lutheran understanding of politics
required a powerful authority to insure that the weak were not
oppressed by the strong, liberal democracy creates a system of
rights based on mutual consent. Luther reminded Christians
that their well-being depended on having a good ruler, and
then he realistically warned them that the ruler was likely to be
bad. Liberal democracy not only disperses many of the powers
of the ruler among the ruled. It also provides constitutional
limits which insure that the powers of the government serve the
purposes of liberty for which they were brought into being.
Democracy, as Niebuhr puts it at the very beginning of *The
Children of Light and the Children of Darkness*, is a "form of social
organization in which freedom and order are made to support,
and not to contradict, each other."[26]

To be sure, modern liberal democracy is susceptible to
corruption and failure, degenerating into tyranny as bad as
Luther's princes. The forms that democratic rights typically
have taken bear marks of the interests of the bourgeois
gentlemen who first proclaimed them, and those of other
gender or lesser resources have often found their own access to
liberty denied and their interests insufficiently protected by the
particular constitutions under which they have had to live.
Nevertheless, the idea that political communities exist to secure
the liberty of those who constitute them, and that their powers
can be limited and their actions judged by reference to that
purpose, is a major human achievement.

Although the freedoms promised by liberal democracy were
sometimes formulated specifically in opposition to religious,
rather than civil, authority, Western Christianity has generally
assimilated the liberties of democratic politics into its own
accounts of the human good, and systematically related the
freedom that is the goal of politics to both the freedom of
consciousness that is essential to human nature and the spiritual freedom which is the gift of God. As human rights have

[25] Cf. Niebuhr, *The Children of Light and the Children of Darkness*, pp. 42–43.
[26] *Ibid.*, p. 1.

become a global concern, other religious traditions have experienced similar developments.[27] The freedom that politics promises has become a religious goal, as well as a political one.

THE TRIUMPH OF POLITICS?

Niebuhr wrote his major works on liberal democracy at a time when it was threatened by ideological alternatives that have now largely disappeared. The dramatic collapse of Soviet communism has been followed by the nearly universal affirmation of the principles of liberal democracy, which now receive lip service even from the various forms of authoritarian nationalism that are its most important remaining rivals.

The resounding affirmation of democratic principles has, however, been accompanied by a growing sense of the deterioration of democratic practice. People interviewed on the street explain the failures of government by saying that "there's just too much politics in it." Their frustrations are echoed in more nuanced terms by experienced administrators and legislators who complain about the obstruction of comprehensive programs by groups that represent small, but well-organized constituencies. Most important, the concern grows that the problem is not just corruption or a failure of leadership, but a weakness in the system of liberal democracy itself.

The liberty that is the goal of modern political life is an instrumental good. Citizens are presumed to aim at liberty not for its own sake, but for the security it provides them in their pursuit of various other ends. Initially, that is supposed to be part of the genius of liberalism. Persons who cannot agree on what the true good is need neither submit the question to an authority who will tell them what good to pursue, nor come to blows with one another in an unresolvable conflict about what the aim of their common life ought to be. They cannot agree on the good, but they can agree on a system of order that leaves them free to pursue the good they identify for themselves.

---

[27] See, for example, Robert Traer, *Faith in Human Rights: Support in Religious Traditions for a Global Struggle* (Washington, D.C.: Georgetown University Press, 1991).

Government and politics is instrumental to whatever their own highest good may be.

An Aristotelian, asked why a person should want to engage in politics, might plausibly reply that because politics is about the highest human good, the exercise of leadership and political choice is a human excellence that should be pursued for its own sake. A Lutheran or Augustinian, as we have seen, would respond that it is a way to meet the Christian's obligation to serve one's neighbors, even if this service must unfortunately take the form of hanging some of them.[28] A liberal, who appears to have a higher assessment of the goals of government, must nonetheless reply that one engages in politics because it serves one's own purposes.

A political realist, assessing these three responses, might well judge that liberalism is the most secure political system, because it has harnessed the power of self-interest to the work of politics, and need not rely on moral or religious motivations to insure that the necessary tasks are done. In a modern, secular society in which people are often divided over very different goals and distracted by many tasks, liberal democracy, which can serve all goals and thus engage everyone's interest, may seem to have the best chance of success.

A politics which confines its aims to instrumental goods and restricts its motives to self-interest must, however, severely restrict the scope of political discourse. If politics avoids the potentially divisive question of what our humanity requires of us, it cannot discuss truth and excellence. It cannot try to persuade us to want something different from what we already want, cannot tell us that we would be better people if we did. It can only try to reassure the maximum number of individuals that this program, party, or candidate has the same interests as they do. It does not take long to do that.

There is a tendency to blame the erosion of political discourse on the thirty-second "sound bite," but we might also consider the possibility that the "sound bite" exists because it is an appropriate expression of what politics, reduced to instru-

---

[28] See page 166 above.

mental goods, is all about. The sound bite is too short a space in which to persuade you of anything, but it is a very efficient way to find out whether a candidate agrees with what you already believe to be in your own interest. If that is, politically speaking, all you need to know, you can get your answer quickly and get back to the conversations that really matter.

In that environment, many groups will act on fierce commitments to one cause, or to a small number of closely related causes. Political leadership becomes a matter not so much of envisioning comprehensive programs as of convincing the maximum number of quite specific interests that your administration offers the best prospect for attention to their particular goals. Uneasy coalitions of libertarian conservatives and fundamentalist Protestants, or blue-collar ethnic groups and patrician Republicans, spring up across the landscape, win their unexpected victories, and quickly fragment when the more wide-ranging work of government begins.

David Stockman described this phenomenon of single-issue interest groups that have virtually eliminated the power of government to undertake necessary, comprehensive reforms, and he called it, ironically, "the triumph of politics."[29] One need not share Stockman's program to share his concern. However, the clash of groups, each defending a tightly focused interest against modification by others, is hardly the activity of persons who see their life in a community as an important achievement in itself and an essential expression of their humanity. Measured against that classical Western understanding of politics, the prevailing conditions of American public life bespeak the near disappearance of politics, not its triumph.

The perennial rejection of politics by "nonresistant Christians" like Guy Hershberger, who confine their public life to bearing witness to another possibility, thus finds a peculiar contemporary echo in the sullen rejection of disillusioned liberals, who have no alternative but the cynical pursuit of their own interests. The danger from utopians who expect too

[29] David Stockman, *The Triumph of Politics* (New York: Harper and Row, 1986).

much of politics appears considerably less than that posed by apocalyptic sectarians who have given up on it entirely. In our present situation, we do not need Reinhold Niebuhr to remind us not to expect too much of politics. We do need a Niebuhrian Realism that will reconnect politics with the vital center of human activity.

Man requires freedom in his social organization because he is "essentially" free, which is to say that he has the capacity for indeterminate transcendence over the processes and limitations of nature. This freedom enables him to make history and to elaborate communal organizations in boundless variety and in endless depth and extent. But he also requires community because he is by nature social. He cannot fulfill his life within himself but only in responsible and mutual relations with his fellows.[30]

Both the consistent pessimism of Augustinian–Lutheran theology and the consistent self-interest of liberal democratic philosophy prove in the end to be too consistent to grasp the incoherencies and vitalities that make up real human life. For a politics adequate to that, we must turn from liberty, the freedom that politics creates, back to the essential human freedom that is the starting point for Christian Realism's ethics.

REALISM AND FREEDOM

For Christian Realism, the freedom which politics secures is possible only because of the capacity for self-transcendence that is itself a part of nature. Once that is understood, the characteristically modern opposition between freedom and nature is no longer possible, but it is also true that freedom is no longer absolute. To speak of an "indefinite transcendence" of the existing conditions of life implies that our imaginative grasp of other possibilities cannot be restricted by *a priori* limits. But that freedom does not look down on all realities from an equal distance. It is in the nature of human freedom, as we noted in Chapter Three, that it starts from *somewhere*, that it

---

[30] Niebuhr, *The Children of Light and the Children of Darkness*, p. 5.

envisions possibilities out of quite specific discontents and deprivations.[31]

The result is not only that we are unable to formulate a universal definition of freedom; there is also no certain way to identify an experience of it. That is what makes us prey to the appeals of demagogues and car salesmen, religious charlatans and hairdressers, all of whom in their own ways promise to set us free from our problems, though the result most likely proves in the end to be just another kind of bondage. This uncertainty about something as important to us as freedom also makes us prey to our own anxieties, leading us to forms of pride that deny our vulnerabilities, or to a timidity that takes no chances for fear that it might be wrong.

When the limits of freedom are understood in this realistic way, the possibilities of politics take on a different shape than they have in political liberalism. In liberalism, political communities are instrumental goods which all of us create together in order to secure for each of us the enjoyment of the more particular goods we happen to want. If, however, our freedom is limited in the ways that Christian Realism suggests, politics is at once more integral and more dangerous to human life than liberalism has made it out to be.

The dangers are obvious. Much of twentieth-century history has shown us how fragile our aspirations are in the face of massive power. The good we seek for ourselves and the people we know most intimately can easily be overwhelmed by military or economic forces that treat us merely as obstacles to be overcome, or as instruments of someone else's purposes. Those who are destroyed in this way are not in any direct sense participants in politics. They are victims. Our solidarity with them should seek to empower them in ways that end their victimization and makes politics possible for them, too.

True political danger, however, does not begin with victimization, when someone else mobilizes forces to destroy us. It begins when politics makes us co-conspirators in our own oppression. Raw power can destroy us despite our best efforts

---

[31] See Chapter Three, especially pp. 123–31, for a more extended treatment of Niebuhr's understanding of human freedom.

to fight or to flee. Only politics can secure our consent to the destruction of our freedom.

It is for that reason that people in the twentieth century have elaborated the concept of human rights that protect the freedom of the individual from absorption into the aspirations of the leader, or the party, or the people. Persons in their freedom deserve protection from what politics can do to them. Just because we know that our freedom is contingent, limited, and embodied – because we know that freedom itself is not absolute – we will be inclined to make the protections of freedom as nearly absolute as we can.

A bill of rights alone is not enough, of course. Protecting freedom from politics requires active voices, and organizations to amplify those voices and spread their words through print and broadcast media. It also requires organizations like churches and universities, in which those voices can be educated to their task, and supported when it becomes difficult or dangerous. Without communities that nurture persons who undertake these difficult tasks of advocacy, even the freedom to organize is a hollow commitment. If you have a little time, you can stifle dissent by creating a narcissistic culture, in which people do not care what happens to their neighbors, even more effectively than you can control dissent by forbidding it.

Much of twentieth-century political thought has concentrated on these dangers in politics from which freedom seeks protection. There is, however, also a participation in politics that freedom positively needs if it is to be fully realized. This is less well recognized, but it also follows from the nature of freedom. Freedom cannot be carried to completion as an individual, personal act. A prisoner who survives solitary confinement and psychological intimidation has created a certain space of freedom, as has the welfare mother who dreams of starting afresh with a decent job and a clean apartment. Even the harassed scholar who mentally escapes the demands of lectures, appointments, and mortgage payments to a cabin in the woods well stocked with books and writing paper expresses freedom in that imagining, but such expressions are obviously incomplete.

Individual expressions of freedom are incomplete not only because the dreamers individually lack the power to realize their visions, but because most often the alternatives individuals envision are mirror images of their present problems, rather than fully developed views of human fulfillment. The employee harassed by the petty tyrannies of an office supervisor may imagine what revenge she would exact if *she* were seated at the head desk, or even in milder moments picture her own reign as a benevolent despotism. That is consciousness's minimal transcendence of present injustices, but it is hardly the full scope of freedom. For that, she requires some understanding of the needs of other workers, including the overbearing supervisor, and some awareness of the larger purposes of the work.

As freedom realizes its aims, those goals are also changed. In the long run, freedom achieves its goals not by imposing them on recalcitrant facts and resistant people, but by a process of adjustment in which visions are reshaped to conform to material limitations and, above all, renegotiated to secure the willing and sustained cooperation of other persons.

Achievements that endure are the work of communities. That does not imply that they result only from cooperative efforts. As Niebuhr notes in speaking of the achievement of justice, community is sometimes the union of adversaries. We must, more often than we might like, accept these adversaries as important participants in the achievement of durable versions of our own visions. The entrepreneur may need the union organizer and the government regulator to turn his business into an institution that can maintain a loyal workforce and live alongside its neighbors, even though wage demands and pollution controls for the moment reshape his plans in ways that he does not like. The city planner may feel defeated when the geometrical regularities of his master plan are sacrificed to purely local interests, but the chances are that his vision will be more intact a hundred years later than the plans of a rival who demands the whole plan or nothing.

Plans are sometimes dramatically changed in the political process, and other factors may ironically reverse the intentions of the planners, as Niebuhr loved to remind his readers.[32] Few are thoroughly satisfied with what the community makes of their visions, and probably none would want to claim the effects in their entirety. Such, however, are the achievements of finite human beings. They are inevitably transformed by the people who participate in them, and they endure, if they endure at all, only by becoming political.

That is where politics relates integrally, rather than adventitiously, to the self-transcendence that is the key to human freedom. In its divided and sometimes chaotic reality, politics is the best approximation we have of a community of discourse in which our ideas about the human good could be tested against all the real human beings that the ideas are about. To free oneself from one's starting point is not merely to imagine the same self in a different situation, but to understand the possibility of a quite different human self. If I understand a situation only in terms of how it might be altered better to suit my needs or the needs of persons very much like me, I am not yet free of it. But the only practical way to know that I have grasped a different set of possibilities is to have my perceptions confirmed, transformed, or challenged by others with quite different experiences. Only when we understand politics in those terms can we avoid reducing it to an instrument by which we gain our ends at the expense of others who are less skilled in manipulating the system.

STATE AND NATION

We might begin by rethinking the relationships between the government, on which much of our disillusionment with politics centers, and the other institutions, which are also political, that make up our common life. The liberal, instrumental understanding of politics tends, as we have seen, to divide experience into two spheres, public and private.[33] In the public sphere, our activities are designed to serve as means to

---

[32] Reinhold Niebuhr, *The Irony of American History* (New York: Charles Scribner's Sons, 1952).
[33] See page 173 above.

everyone's ends. What we do is regulated by bureaucratic norms and established procedures, and the possibilities for individual choice are strictly limited. Each person's work must fit into a larger pattern of productivity and meet widely shared expectations, so that every banker, dentist, stockbroker and editor – even the solitary scholar, the creative artist, and the personal counselor – must be very much like every other one of that ilk. The emphasis on personal "style" which dominates consumer marketing reveals in the end that personal expression is today largely confined to superficialities. Institutions impress themselves on personalities long before there is a chance to work the effects the other way around. In this highly organized economic system, the distinction between what is truly public, i.e. governmental, and what is nominally private, i.e. the "private sector" not under government control, is blurred by interlocking systems of regulation and common patterns of bureaucratic organization.

By contrast, the private sphere is increasingly equated with the *personal*, the realm outside the productive system, where choice is limited only by the imagination and, of course, by the amount of money one can earn in the public sphere to support one's private aspirations.

A Niebuhrian Realist may share this uneasy sense that private satisfactions now are stressed at the expense of public life, but Niebuhr drew the lines of demarcation somewhat differently from the usual distinction between public and private. For him, the important difference was between "state" and "nation," between the institutions of government "through which the life of nations is organized and their wills articulated," and the nation itself, which is this organized community in all its parts. The organization of national life and the articulation of the will of a people is a high moral task for the state, but it by no means encompasses the whole of national life, nor does it escape a critical scrutiny that asks whether those who have power in the state really speak for the nation, or only for their own more limited interests.[34] Nie-

[34] Niebuhr, "Do State and Nation Belong to God or the Devil?", in *Faith and Politics*, pp. 83–87.

buhr's distinction between state and nation, though it is not very clearly drawn, recurs throughout his work, and largely corresponds to the more systematic distinction in Catholic social thought between "state" and "society," or to Ernst Troeltsch's idea of the social sphere outside the specific concerns of government which is the subject of the "social" teachings of the churches.[35]

The point, then, is not simply to press the moral claims of public, as opposed to private life, but to identify within the public sphere a range of institutions distinct from the state which nonetheless engage our public concerns and require of us something like those civic virtues that the republican tradition assigns to government service.[36] In Athens or other ancient city-states, it may have been possible to assign all choices beyond the necessities of economic life to an undifferentiated public realm. By the time that Christian political thought emerges in the context of large territorial kingdoms, however, it is necessary to distinguish the powers and tasks of government from other essential elements of public life – the church first, but also the schools, and then those emergent forms of economic organization that encompass more than the extended household. The classical ideal of civic virtue focuses attention on the importance of public life, but it also distracts from the inevitable tensions between the various institutions of the modern public sphere, and leads to the easy identification of the nation or the society with the state.

For those whose interest in public life extends to society as a whole, the state poses special political problems. The modern state reaches into all aspects of life and cannot be narrowly confined to issues concerned directly with the limited functions of minimal government. It is, moreover, part of the very definition of a modern state that it has a monopoly on coercive

---

[35] For a recent statement of this distinction in Catholic thought, see Richard P. McBrien, *Caesar's Coin: Religion and Politics in America* (New York: Macmillan, 1987), pp. 123–25. For Troeltsch's distinction, see Troeltsch, *The Social Teaching of the Christian Churches*, I, 27–30.

[36] On civic virtue and its role in contemporary public life, see William Sullivan, *Reconstructing Public Philosophy* (Berkeley: University of California Press, 1986), pp. 163–65.

power. Other social institutions may exercise strong influences on behavior, either by moral persuasion and the pressure of the opinions of others or by their control of economic incentives, but the state alone has authority to compel compliance by force and punish disobedience by loss of liberty. So while we must insist that the state is not the whole of society, nor government the whole of politics, the state is the one unavoidable reality in most political calculations. The decisions made in this politics can reach everyone in the society.

As a result, both detractors and supporters of any government will tend to exaggerate the power of the state and over-state its importance in the lives of individuals. Detractors will talk about "getting government off our backs" and ridicule the costs and complexity of bureaucratic regulations. They will, especially if their opponents happen to be in power, point to the failure of programs that were supposed to meet human needs, and they will warn that the reach of the state is about to abolish individual choice and personal privacy. Supporters, by contrast, will cite statistics to show that private charity is not solving the problems of homelessness and hunger, or that voluntary programs do not really eliminate discrimination against women and minorities in the workplace. They may, with practice, become as vigorous as the detractors in their denunciations of waste and fraud in government, but they will also point out that the very scope of those costs reminds us that government alone is large enough and powerful enough to bring adequate resources to bear on the social problems that we all have to face together.

While others debate the extent and limits of state power, each successive administration, whether it comes to office as a supporter or a detractor of that power, will closely identify its own authority with the power of the state. This is not always for the venal ends of securing the fortunes of the office-holders or providing them with lucrative second careers as political "consultants," though that may be a factor. The key point is that even for those who think that the state has become too big and too powerful, the power of the state is the only effective tool they can use to attempt to reduce its size and scope. Some

of that power depends on effective use of legislation and regulation, but, as Niebuhr noted, it also depends on using the
majesty of the state to lend authority to one's plans, transforming them from the election platform of a political faction into
an expression of national purpose.[37]

So administrations or governments tend to identify themselves with the state, of which they have temporary custody,
and states tend to identify themselves with the majesty and the
will of the nation or the society of which they are but a part.
Nations, finally, have an idolatrous tendency to identify themselves with universal virtues which, at best, they only partly
realize. There is here a pyramid of hypocrisy and self-
deception which, if it is not recognized, can create a state
which overwhelms other centers of creativity and invests the
state and its leader with pretensions to virtue that no actual
person or institution can sustain. This has happened often
enough in the twentieth century to keep us wary, but it is also
true that these deceptions are plausible because states and
nations may very well represent more inclusive values than the
aims of the individuals and groups within them. As usual,
Christian Realism precludes blanket judgments about the
power of the state and requires us to evaluate specific cases
with the full range of possibilities, positive and negative, before
us.

This realistic approach to politics and government may be
contrasted to other ideas, which seek to avoid the excesses to
which the state is susceptible by limiting our reliance on its
powers. In Catholic social thought, these limitations are
summed up in the idea of *subsidiarity*. Under the influence of
Aquinas' teaching that politics is a natural human activity,
and not just a way of restraining sinful aggressions against the
innocent, Catholic writers since the Reformation have tended
toward a higher evaluation of the moral possibilities of political
activity than their Protestant counterparts. The rise of the
modern state, and, more particularly, nineteenth-century
European conflicts between the church and newly powerful

[37] Reinhold Niebuhr, *The Structure of Nations and Empires* (New York: Charles Scribner's Sons, 1959), pp. 34–35.

secular states led, however, to a doctrine that governments should be restricted to a rather narrow range of powers necessary to secure order and justice. Police power, law courts, taxation, and defense are unquestioned prerogatives of government, but when its activities impinge on other areas of life, on the family, education, or religion, for example, the role of government must be strictly subsidiary. That is, it must aid these institutions in achieving their proper purposes, but it must not seek to replace them or to do for them what they can, with subsidiary assistance, achieve for themselves.[38] John Courtney Murray summarized the import of this idea for the role of the state in a way which virtually deprives governmental politics of any creative role in social life. In an interpretation of the major social encyclical of Pope Leo XIII, Murray wrote:

> *Rerum novarum*, adhering to the Western Christian political tradition, makes it clear that government, strictly speaking, creates nothing; that its function is to order, not to create. Perhaps more exactly, its function is to create the conditions under which original vitalities and forces, present in society, may have full scope to create the values by which society lives. Perhaps still more exactly, the only value which government is called upon to create is the value of order. But the value of order resides primarily in the fact that it furnishes *opportunitates, facilitates* ... for the exercise of freedoms which are the rightful prerogative of other social magnitudes and forces. These freedoms, rightly ordered, are the true creative sources of all manner of social values.[39]

Others have interpreted Niebuhrian Realism about self-interest and power to mean that we should avoid the pretense of excessive virtue by minimizing the role of government in the making and enforcing of moral choices. Robert Benne praises

---

[38] What has come to be called the doctrine of subsidiarity can be traced back to the relations between the state and other social institutions prescribed in the encyclical *Rerum novarum*, issued by Pope Leo XIII in 1891. The term itself was introduced into discussions in moral theology somewhat later, but appears in Pius XI's encyclical *Quadragesimo anno*, a fortieth-anniversary restatement of the principles of *Rerum novarum*.

[39] John Courtney Murray, "Leo XIII and Pius XII: Government and the Order of Religion," in *Religious Liberty: Catholic Struggles with Pluralism*, ed. J. Leon Hooper (Louisville: Westminster/John Knox Press, 1993), p. 78.

market mechanisms which remove problems of choice from the arena of explicit political decisions and disperse them among the individual economic choices of the populace, because this dispersal reduces the need for divisive choices about goals and values in the politics of government: "Market systems, by relying on voluntary exchange relationships based on self-interest, decrease the need for consensus on the moral, ideological, and social level. They contribute to the decentralization of power by making it unnecessary to have cultural and moral agreement."[40]

Efforts to be realistic about the dangerous powers of the modern state have thus shown a tendency to circumscribe its powers and to isolate its politics from the creative and moral aspects of social life. They show a preference for the decentralized choices made, in Benne's Protestant model, by individuals in the marketplace, or in Murray's understanding of the Catholic doctrine of subsidiarity, by families, local communities, and religious groups. The message seems to be that we can risk creativity and moral judgment on a smaller scale, where the results can be evaluated more directly and are less likely to be thrust upon unwilling participants or unmotivated recipients.

There is an important practical lesson in these reservations. Leo XIII framed the doctrine of subsidiarity in response to the disruptions of church and family by militant policies of secularization. American Catholics experienced no such militant secularism, but they readily accepted the doctrine because of their own experiences with a militant Protestant culture in American public schools, and because they understood the important role that ethnic community, religious organizations, and their own institutions for health care and social services played in maintaining the fabric of social life. Benne's high estimation of the marketplace as a forum for evaluating social experiments arises in part from the recognition that innovations sponsored by government are often extensive, costly, and hard to terminate, even when they fail to meet their objectives.

---

[40] Robert Benne, *The Ethic of Democratic Capitalism* (Philadelphia: Fortress Press, 1981), p. 143.

In addition, as Benne points out, adoption of an explicit policy toward a problem requires a far higher level of public consensus than a plurality of local and private experiments, which require only the looser agreement that something ought to be done.

When the practical lesson about restraint is raised to a principle, however, it becomes unrealistic. It substitutes the idea that government is at best the agency of last resort for the solution of society's problems for a realistic evaluation of the possibilities and limitations of the state as a center of resources, to be deployed in specified ways for the solution of particular problems. A realism that tempers our tendency to assume that government can solve all our problems becomes instead the "too consistent" pessimism of Augustinian–Lutheran realism, which sees all forms of government as inherently limited by the need to bring under control forces of evil which cannot be dealt with according to the norms of Christian morality.[41]

A more balanced realism, by contrast, stresses the indeterminacy of human vitalities in both their individual and their collective forms. "Actually human vitalities express themselves from both individual and collective centers in many directions, and both are capable of unpredictable creative and destructive consequences."[42] This does not mean that we cannot learn from experience, but it does imply that we must wait for experience to tell us what government can and cannot do. Its functions cannot be limited in advance by a restrictive doctrine.

Though it is true that government must have the power to subdue recalcitrance, it also has a more positive function. It must guide, direct, deflect, and rechannel conflicting and competing forces in a community in the interest of a higher order. It must provide instruments for the expression of the individual's sense of obligation to the

[41] Benne, in fact, evinces a strongly Lutheran reading of Reinhold Niebuhr in the early chapters of *The Ethic of Democratic Capitalism*, pp. 27–47. Murray, and Catholic writers generally, would presumably want to remain closer to the affirmation of politics in Thomas Aquinas, but it is hard to see how the doctrine of subsidiarity as Murray applies it can avoid the implication that government is a special area in which moral possibilities are more limited than they are in other spheres of social life.

[42] Niebuhr, *The Children of Light and the Children of Darkness*, p. 47.

community as well as weapons against the individual's anti-social lusts and ambitions.[43]

This affirmation of the positive functions of government is an important qualification of Niebuhr's otherwise strong insistence on government's role as the keeper of order. He was convinced that the political liberalism which animated many of the leaders of his time led them to overstate the role of consent in keeping people within the limits of law and social cooperation, and to underestimate the importance of sheer force as the foundation of social order. That problem is real, and the leadership which ignores it runs the danger of slipping into anarchy, just as those who worry too much about order may end up imposing a tyranny instead. But the delicate balance between anarchy and tyranny, important as it is in Niebuhr's political thought, is not for him the sum of governmental politics.

Politics is about a more fundamental freedom than the set of liberties which a government grants or the constraints which it must impose to insure that persons can exercise their freedom under conditions of reasonable security. Politics begins with the capacity for indefinite transcendence of present circumstances. Politics is involved in every aspect of human life because it is only in political activity that the freedom that characterizes human beings can be realized in forms that are more substantial and permanent than flights of imagination or intellectual abstractions.

Real politics, of course, seldom sustains the consistency and purity of the original vision of freedom, and politics as practiced in real communities may lack the critical rigor that intellectual scrutiny can bring to visions and values. People pursuing their goals in a political process at any level, from office politics to international politics, are apt to deceive themselves about the universality of their values and to be deceived by others about the extent of the agreement they share. The ideal circumstances of communication are likely to be more nearly approximated in careful, critical reflection than in the

[43] *Ibid.*, p. 44.

mixture of self-interest and social concern that characterizes real politics.

So there is always a danger that politics will miscarry and result in the imposition of some new form of domination, rather than a genuine increase of freedom. The risks of this deception, and its costs, rise as the political community grows larger and more powerful. Although the problems of "idolatry" are exhibited in units as small as exclusive suburbs and academic departments, they are less likely to be perceived by the idol- aters and more likely to wreak havoc on their neighbors when it is a nation that confuses its goals and virtues with universal values. We cannot solve this problem, however, by attempting to remove the state from politics or by reducing the politics of government to some truncated version in which moral choice and social creativity are systematically eliminated. Freedom is not preserved by restricting its range to institutions in which it is unlikely to be abused, and we must understand that solving human problems with resources that only the state can command is as much an exercise of freedom as the use of individual liberties.

The aim of Christian Realism is more than the check on evil and disorder that marked the limit of what Augustine and Luther expected from government. It is also more than the relentless criticism of the ideological self-deceptions of the powerful that Niebuhr regarded as a necessary complement to the power of the state. The aim is to make government fully political, to allow individuals to give their visions institutional reality by enlisting the support of others, but also to transform those visions in the light of a more inclusive idea of freedom that emerges when persons are free to challenge, persuade, and criticize one another. Public order is an indispensable means to politics on this scale, but if it becomes the only purpose of government, then politics is excluded from precisely the com- prehensive community in which it might make the most difference.

There is, however, an important truth in the principle of subsidiarity. That truth is that a fully political government is unlikely to exist without a healthy political life in other institutions in society. The failure of politics on a smaller scale leads to a situation in which people perceive other groups and other visions only as threats to their purposes. As a result, they begin to feel powerless to effect changes that would give their visions institutional form, and they hold those visions tightly among small groups of like-minded persons. The others are to be shunned or defeated, and there is no confidence that they could be persuaded, or that we might even create new possibilities out of the confrontation.

Those who have not learned that confidence in schools, churches, offices, and community organizations are unlikely to learn it from government. However, there is no reason why those who have learned it cannot use government to advance political purposes as creatively as they use the other institutions of society. Both the popular belief that "you can't legislate morality" and the more nuanced claim that government provides only the *opportunitates, facilitates* for social creativity are mistaken. Government can lead society, but it cannot substitute the mass politics of government for a full range of developed political institutions throughout society.

Christian Realists, who understand that their own freedom is bound up with these political possibilities, have an important stake in politics in all those institutions. It is not just a means of service to others. It is also a way of grasping that truth which they have and do not have.[44] People of faith who reject politics or ignore it not only leave the way open for the idolatries propagated by those of more limited vision. They also cut themselves off from a place in which they might meet the One true God.

[44] See Niebuhr, *The Nature and Destiny of Man*, II, 213–20.

CHAPTER 5

Justice

THE PROBLEM OF JUSTICE

John Rawls, at the beginning of *A Theory of Justice*, relates justice and truth by saying that "Justice is the first virtue of social institutions, as truth is of systems of thought."[1] Some thirty years earlier, Reinhold Niebuhr had drawn a similar connection, but with a distinctly Niebuhrian twist: "The struggle for justice is as profound a revelation of the possibilities and limits of historical existence as the quest for truth."[2] Where Rawls characterizes the searches for truth and justice as the most important achievements of thought and action, Niebuhr sees both quests as also revealing characteristic human limitations.

The contrasts suggested by these aphorisms are borne out in each author's treatment of the problems of justice. Rawls regards justice as a social achievement that has value for any society of persons with diverse goals and interests, whatever other things those persons may seek and value. Niebuhr understands justice in relation to love, which is for him the ultimate value that all persons share. Precisely because complete justice is identical with a human good in which everyone would participate, however, it is impossible to achieve; and it is when we try to create human good on the scale of nations and empires that we become most acutely aware of our limitations.

---

[1] John Rawls, *A Theory of Justice* (Cambridge, Mass.: Harvard University Press, 1971), p. 3.
[2] Niebuhr, *The Nature and Destiny of Man*, II, 244.

REALISTIC LIBERALISM?

Niebuhr and Rawls understand justice differently, and some of these differences can be traced to changes in the historical context in which they wrote. Though each man was attuned to the nuances of liberal political thought in the mid-twentieth century, changing social problems led to significant changes in the role that an idea of justice was expected to play in public life.

From the 1940s onward, Niebuhr thought of himself as a critic who stood within the traditions of liberal democracy, calling liberalism to a more realistic view of human limitations and a more profound appreciation of human aspirations.[3] His editorial fulminations against "liberalism" were directed far more at religious liberals and reductive naturalists than at the commentators and theorists whose own accounts of political liberalism often showed great appreciation for Niebuhr's corrective insights.

The role in which Niebuhr cast himself as a Christian social ethicist[4] was to provide a dimension of depth, making clear the assumptions on which liberalism's moral power rests. Like Paul Tillich during the same period, Niebuhr understood the theological task not as distinguishing faith from politics, but as supplying an element that was often missing in purely political discussions.[5] Tillich, more than Niebuhr, spoke of this as an "ontological" grounding of the political discussion. The basic idea, however, is much the same: politics requires an understanding of the more fundamental human realities on which it rests if it is to deal successfully with the forces of totalitarianism that threaten liberal democracy.

Niebuhr articulated these realities for a generation preoccupied with threats posed by alien political systems in Nazi Germany and the Soviet Union. The issue, as he framed it in *The Children of Light and the Children of Darkness*, was to formu-

---

[3] See Niebuhr, "Liberalism: Illusions and Realities." Also, see Chapter Four, page 160.

[4] Niebuhr persistently refused to describe himself as a "theologian." See Reinhold Niebuhr, "Intellectual Autobiography," in Kegley and Bretall, eds., *Reinhold Niebuhr*, p. 3.

[5] Paul Tillich, *Love, Power, and Justice* (New York: Oxford University Press, 1954).

late a more realistic version of liberal democratic values that would make their defense more plausible and compelling.

Domestic problems, such as racial segregation, were typically interpreted as failures to put these democratic values into practice. Myrdal's *The American Dilemma* provided the classic formulation of this point. Niebuhr's own analysis of the Civil Rights Movement in the South as a conflict between national standards and local practices is another example. At the level where national authority prevails, there is a consensus that would allow us to live together in a reasonable approximation of justice. What must be done is to make that consensus effective everywhere.[6] Niebuhr suggested that when the liberal consensus and the political systems it supports are challenged by totalitarian or materialist alternatives, it falls to the voices that speak from the biblical tradition to articulate the premises on which the consensus rests, correcting its tendencies toward secularism and relativism and recalling it to the meaningful moral universe on which it depends.[7]

Niebuhr's position on these matters was echoed by other writers at mid-century. Despite significant differences over pragmatism and natural law between Niebuhr and his leading Roman Catholic counterpart, the Jesuit theologian John Courtney Murray, the two men have an ecumenical approach to liberal democracy: The biblical faith provides the ideas about human good and moral responsibility on which the liberal democratic consensus rests. When that consensus is confused or threatened, recourse to the faith that sets its fundamental terms is a necessary part of its self-defense and self-renewal.[8]

[6] Niebuhr, *The Children of Light and the Children of Darkness*, pp. xiii–xv. See also Gunnar Myrdal, *An American Dilemma: The Negro Problem and Modern Democracy* (New York: Harper and Brothers, 1944), p. xlvii; and Reinhold Niebuhr, "The Supreme Court on Segregation in the Schools," *Christianity and Crisis* (June 14, 1954), 75–77. The contrast between national and local standards, which is a commonplace in Niebuhr's writings on civil rights, can be seen in his foreword to Mississippi Education Foundation, Inc., *Mississippi Black Paper* (New York: Random House, 1965), and in Reinhold Niebuhr, "The Effect of the Supreme Court Decision," *Christianity and Crisis* 17 (February 4, 1957), 3.

[7] See Niebuhr, *An Interpretation of Christian Ethics*, pp. 62–63.

[8] See, for example, the discussion of "the American consensus" in Murray, *We Hold These Truths*, pp. 79–123.

Changing times gave rise to a different political liberalism, with a quite different understanding of a democracy's relationship to the moral and religious beliefs of its citizens. Niebuhr's generation believed there was a national moral consensus. When Niebuhr died in 1971, however, the United States was in the midst of upheavals in which vast cultural disagreements over values had become apparent. Racial justice proved to require far more than an equal opportunity for African Americans to become like their white middle-class counterparts. Demands for the recognition of alternative traditions and values became prominent, first among African Americans and then among many other groups united by ethnic identity, social status, or physical or mental challenges. The role of the United States as a global military and economic power came into question, and a counter-culture emerged that defined itself precisely by its opposition to the values and goods that Niebuhr's generation might have identified as the American consensus.

In the same year that Niebuhr died, John Rawls published *A Theory of Justice*, beginning with his memorable claim that "justice is the first virtue of social institutions." He might also have said that it is the last hope of a pluralistic society. In place of a political system based on a value consensus that everyone could share, it seemed necessary to specify the claims which individuals have on society's goods and to provide rights that would protect the use of those goods in pursuit of self-chosen aims. By settling on one or another of those criteria, we could determine the minimal requirements of social justice, even if we continued to disagree on almost everything else.

As Niebuhr differs from other Protestant Christian Realists and from his Catholic contemporaries, so too there are significant differences between Rawls and other late-century liberals, primarily over the constraints that justice imposes on individual freedom of choice. What the liberal theorists agree upon, however, is that justice can be determined by rules that do not depend on a shared idea of human fulfillment. When liberal democracies are divided on questions of policy or threatened by totalitarianism, it is primarily because someone claims to have discovered the true way of life or a comprehensive good. Strife and tyranny follow when those who agree seek to impose that good on those who do not. The solution is not a more articulate rendition of the underlying consensus, but clearer thinking that demonstrates that such a consensus is unnecessary. Liberal democracy is about the new human possibility that we can live together in reasonable harmony without agreeing on God or the good.

A Theory of Justice achieved its status as a contemporary classic not only for the intellectual power of Rawls' system, but also for the clarity with which he provided the sharply defined, minimal version of justice that the times seemed to require.[9] It is instructive to compare his explicit premises at a couple of points with Niebuhr's unspoken assumptions.

A Theory of Justice asks us to conceive of persons trying to settle the basic rules of justice in a hypothetical situation in which they do not know the specific interests, resources, and roles that they will have in the society for which they are making the rules. If we can figure out what rules people in this "original position" would plausibly choose, we will have principles of justice that distribute society's burdens and benefits fairly, rather than reflecting the interests of one group that is prestigious and powerful.[10]

One thing we must assume about persons in the original position is that they are, as Rawls puts it, "mutually disinterested."[11] That is, they are in general neither altruistic nor egoistic in their relations with other persons. Egoists, who consistently seek their own advantage without regard to the interests and welfare of others, cannot make a commitment to justice, because that would require them to limit their selfish pursuits. Altruists, who consistently put the good of others

---

[9] *A Theory of Justice* remains the most important systematic statement of the liberal theory of justice, and one in relation to which all other versions of liberalism frame their positions. Rawls has subsequently clarified and expanded his theory, most importantly by acknowledging that the premises of "justice as fairness" are not dictated by reason alone, but articulate the values shared by citizens of modern liberal democracies. See especially John Rawls, *Political Liberalism* (New York: Columbia University Press, 1993).

[10] Rawls, *A Theory of Justice*, pp. 12, 17–22.   [11] *Ibid.*, pp. 13, 127–28.

ahead of their own welfare, create the same problem in a different way. Persons who have no interests they seek to defend cannot make a commitment to justice because they are already willing to sacrifice everything for the good of their neighbors. There is nothing they seek to withhold, so they cannot make rules governing what they must be willing to surrender.[12]

Persons capable of determining what justice requires, then, are primarily conceived as those who go about their business pursuing their own ends. They do not need to defeat their neighbors for their own well-being, but neither does their well-being depend on others. Justice is about how persons whose happiness and well-being depends primarily on the pursuit of their own ends will live with others who are similarly motivated. They may need rules to protect them from the egoists, as the altruists may need rules to be protected from themselves, but justice is about the terms that mutually disinterested persons establish to regulate their relations as they pursue aims that are important to them individually.

For Niebuhr, the pursuit of justice requires that we understand what it would mean for real persons to live well. We must know what we would want for them if we loved them. This is necessary to formulate the requirements of justice, even if what we are actually prepared to give is a good deal less than love requires, and also if what love requires proves to be quite different from what the others actually want.

For Rawls, by contrast, mutual disinterest begins with a respect for the fact that the other person has aims and goals, although you need not care at all whether these particular goals are realized. The important thing is not that you agree that the aims and goals are crucial to the other person's good, but that you do not arbitrarily deprive any person of the capacities and resources needed to achieve his or her purposes, whatever they may be.

---

[12] Niebuhr, incidentally uses the term 'disinterested' in a quite different, almost opposite, sense. For Niebuhr, the "disinterested" persons are those who do not cling to their own interests, those who are willing to sacrifice their own interests for the good of others. See, for example, Reinhold Niebuhr, "The Ethics of Jesus and the Social Problem," in Robertson, ed., *Love and Justice*, p. 31.

Rawls' interpretation of liberal democracy is controversial, in part because his principles of justice would severely limit the entitlement of persons to forms of wealth and power that they might accumulate in the course of their freely chosen activities.[13] Nevertheless, political freedom, or liberty, is central to Rawls' political philosophy, as it is to other versions of liberalism.[14] The whole point of formulating principles of justice is that persons be free for a good life of their own choosing, that they not be required to pursue certain goals or acquire certain virtues just because someone else judges that these are good.

For recent versions of liberalism, then, justice sets the boundaries within which freedom may pursue goods of its own choosing. Whether these boundaries are relatively more narrow, as they are under Rawls' "difference principle,"[15] which limits the acquisition of goods by the requirement that advantages gained must also help the least well off, or relatively more wide, as in libertarian versions that allow virtually any acquisition that is not obtained by fraud or coercion, justice marks off that area of our lives that we must yield to the determinations of others, precisely so that those others cannot determine for us what we will call good.

In the years since Niebuhr and his contemporaries called attention to the cultural roots of a "realistic liberalism" in Western traditions and values that are older than liberalism itself, liberal theorists have thus tried to formulate a liberalism that would not require those roots. The premises of a liberal theory of justice adequate to that task have become more explicit than they were in Niebuhr's day, and the differences between Christian Realism and political liberalism on matters of justice have become correspondingly more clear. To understand Niebuhr's position as an alternative to, and not merely as a clarification of, the prevailing political consensus, we must attempt a more systematic statement of his understanding of justice. A complete Christian Realist theory of justice, if such a

---

[13] See, for example, the criticism of Rawls' difference principle in Robert Nozick, *Anarchy, State, and Utopia* (New York: Basic Books, 1974), pp. 192–209.

[14] Freedom of choice is central to this political freedom, which makes it somewhat different from 'freedom' as Reinhold Niebuhr uses the term. See pp. 123–26 above.

[15] Rawls, *A Theory of Justice*, p. 75.

thing were possible, is clearly beyond the scope of this chapter. Nor can we expect to mount a thoroughgoing defense of the Christian Realist perspective against the liberal alternatives. What we can do is to show how the connection between justice and the human good that contemporary liberalism seeks to render unnecessary provides the basis for a more realistic, and sometimes more demanding, picture of what it means to do justice.

BENEVOLENCE

Throughout this book, we have seen in Niebuhr's thought a political realism that seeks to unmask distortions of justice caused by self-interest. Often, this is the most prominent feature of Niebuhr's political analysis, and it is the aspect of his thought that is perhaps most often identified as "Niebuhrian." Nevertheless, we will be unable to grasp Niebuhr's understanding of justice and its relevance for a contemporary Christian Realism unless we also remember his moral realism, which finds alongside the forces of self-interest a real sense of moral obligation, which also has its effect on human action. People continue to appeal to justice, not because they cannot find a more effective language to promote their selfish aims, but because their aims are not *only* selfish. They also feel a sense of obligation that both affirms and limits their individual aspirations in relation to a larger whole, and that binds them to one another.

The "mutually disinterested" contracting parties in Rawls' original position are clearly abstractions from this more complete account of human interdependence and mutuality. That is something that Rawls himself would freely admit. His strategy is to deal with self-interest precisely by constructing an abstraction that shows how it can be contained without violating its own terms. Niebuhr's aim, consistent with the Realist's admonition to take *everything* into account, is to show how self-interest is limited by an equally fundamental sense of mutuality and obligation.

Obligation is, in the first instance, experienced in our

relationships with particular others for whom our affection overwhelms the calculation of personal advantage. Those particular affections, however, can also become the basis for a more general understanding of what others want and need. Indeed, without the primary knowledge of other persons that comes from loving some particular others, we will be ill-equipped to understand what justice requires that we render to all persons, whether or not they are known to us, and whether or not we love them.[16]

The love that is relevant to justice is not primarily an emotional response. It is the disposition to seek the well-being of persons generally that theologians and moral philosophers have called "benevolence."[17] Love draws our understanding of what justice requires in a more and more inclusive and generous direction, rather than allowing us to settle into a mutually disinterested, minimalist definition of justice. Without love, Niebuhr observed, the determination of justice quickly deteriorates into "mere calculation of advantage."[18]

The identification of love as the primary moral norm is drawn directly from the biblical witness to what Niebuhr calls "prophetic religion," and the specification of what love requires is formulated by reference to what the New Testament says about *agape*.[19] Niebuhr's insistence on this point drew criticism from more consistently humanist or naturalist[20] philo-

---

[16] Reinhold Niebuhr, *Man's Nature and His Communities*, p. 107. Niebuhr's thinking on this point was significantly influenced by Erik Erikson. See Brown, *Niebuhr and His Age*, p. 232.

[17] See, for example, Frances Hutcheson, "An Inquiry Concerning Moral Good and Evil," in D.D. Raphael, ed., *British Moralists, 1650–1800* (Oxford: Clarendon Press, 1969), I, 272–80.

[18] Niebuhr, *Faith and History*, p. 193. It may also be the case, as Niebuhr observes, that this calculation will "tend to weight the standard of justice on the side of the one who defines the standard" (*ibid.*, p. 190). However, we should not, as Niebuhr sometimes does, treat this tendency to perpetuate the distortion of moral standards by power as a defect of moral rationalism. The rational standard, consistently applied, aims to defeat special pleading concealed by ideology, as well as more obvious self-seeking exceptions.

[19] Niebuhr, *An Interpretation of Christian Ethics*, pp. 22–28; *Faith and History*, pp. 173–79.

[20] "Naturalism" was the label that some of Niebuhr's most important critics, including John Dewey, preferred for their own philosophy. In this context, of course, "naturalism" refers to the position I called "reductive naturalism" in Chapter Two. See Rice, *Reinhold Niebuhr and John Dewey*, p. 153.

sophers, who argued that the theological claims in Niebuhr's ethics were unnecessary, divisive, and unpersuasive to many who could otherwise agree on the practical requirements of justice.

It would be a mistake, however, to suppose that the biblical interpretation of the connection between justice and love precludes a more general humanistic argument about the requirements of justice. The requirements of *agape* exceed the possibilities of discursive formulation and can be grasped only in myth and symbol, but *agape* is approximated in history by a certain clarity and honesty about my needs, which in turn allows me to see the needs of my neighbors on their own terms, rather than in terms of what I want and need from them. For these purposes, the best evidence that I have achieved some understanding of what love requires is that I can talk about the good of others in terms that they can recognize.

To love another is to wish that person's good. To speak about that love in socially shared terms requires a concept of what that good is. We may reassure the beloved in person without getting very specific, but we will not be able to discuss our love with her doctor or with his children, much less to create a community in which the beloved will find justice, unless we have an idea we can share of what would allow her or him to flourish.

A search for justice that is related to love must include an understanding of human good. Indeed, the theological emphasis on love for the neighbor shares with other versions of moral realism and ethical naturalism the basic idea that the neighbor's good has an objective reality, independent of the neighbor's preferences and desires. So it is possible to want the good of the neighbor without wanting simply what the neighbor wants.

Much of love's anguish results from situations in which we seek another person's true good in opposition to his or her own desires. Those whom we do not love we are likely to leave to their own devices. We may even take a certain grim satisfaction in seeing the ambitious co-worker who subordinates relationships to career achieve the lonely success he so earnestly desired. By contrast, love impels us to try to show people what they are doing to themselves, even when they make it clear that they do not want to know. Love makes moral realists of us all. We cannot avoid telling those whom we love – and the bosses, helpers, friends, and physicians who participate in their lives along with us – what is really good for them.

There is, of course, a significant danger of exploitation and oppression in that love. History supplies many examples of persons whose idea of seeking the good of others included providing them with ample opportunities to serve those who were looking out for their good. We also recognize many instances in which persons with a dull and prosaic notion of happiness have tried to express their love by relieving the creative tensions and the passions for truth that shape the lives of their more venturesome companions. The fact that others have a good that is independent of their wishes does not, in itself, insure that my notion of their good will be the correct one, nor does love alone authorize me to impose my notion on them.

This problem, however, is inherent in all forms of moral realism, including the versions of ethical naturalism that insist on conducting moral arguments strictly in human terms, with no appeal to biblical ideas about God. The only alternative is complete subjectivism, which today frequently results when an appropriate reluctance to impose our notion of good on others shades over into an uncritical affirmation of all their traditions, values, and preferences.[21] Moral realism cannot avoid the risk that it will impose alien values on others under the guise of promoting a general human good. Responsible moral realism must therefore pay particular attention to critical principles that help to distinguish egocentric or ethnocentric thinking from a genuine account of the human good. Responsible moral realists will also retain a healthy respect for the probable contamination of self-interest in even our most objective efforts to apply those critical principles. But the responsible realist will

---

[21] See Martha Nussbaum, "Human Functioning and Social Justice: In Defense of Aristotelian Essentialism," *Political Theory* 20 (May 1992), 202–5, for examples of this uncritical subjectivism in current academic debates about cultural diversity.

not find in these limitations a reason to give up moral judgment altogether.

"*JUSTITIA ORIGINALIS*"

Benevolence, the steady disposition to seek the good of others as love understands their good, clearly distinguishes the Christian Realist's starting point from the mutual disinterest of Rawls' original position, but benevolence alone does not solve the problems of justice. Justice is concerned with how the goods that make up the human good are to be distributed, whether these are material goods, such as food and clothing, or less tangible, but equally necessary goods, such as self-respect.

The classical formula for Western thinking about distributive justice is *suum cuique*: render to each person what is due. That formula provides no real guidance, of course, until it is linked with a determinate understanding of how persons are related so that each knows what is owed to any given other. In Aristotle's Athens, the honor due to persons was sharply differentiated by rank and achievement, so that what one person should receive by way of both social deference and material goods might be very different from what was due to a more humble neighbor.

Aristocratic understandings of justice, such as Aristotle's, prize the achievements of certain talented persons, and allocate society's resources to insure that these talents will be developed. Similarly, an oligarchic view of justice suggests that the necessary conditions of order and prosperity depend on concentrating the wealth and power in the hands of a few persons, while the mass of the people is excluded. Oligarchic justice is satisfied if goods are distributed to sustain the power of the few.

Aristocratic and oligarchic conceptions are not in much favor today as *theories* of justice, though they are perhaps more widely believed and practiced than they are defended by argument. What they share with Christian Realism is a moral realism that distinguishes them from modern liberal theories of justice. Like all moral realisms, they have a definite idea of what the human good is, which in turn determines what goods are important to distribute. What distinguishes oligarchic and aristocratic versions of moral realism from the Christian Realist's interest in justice and human good is the Christian Realist's theological realism. Aristocratic and oligarchic accounts presuppose a competition for limited resources in which justice is done when recognized goods are distributed to individuals in accordance with a recognized scale of values. For Christian Realism, by contrast, life culminates in "the ideal possibility of perfect love, in which all inner contradictions within the self, and all conflicts and tensions between the self and the other are overcome by the complete obedience of all wills to the will of God."[22]

In this theological perspective, justice is less a matter of the distribution of specific goods and is more closely related to *justitia originalis*, the "original righteousness" in which persons live in freedom without the anxious denials of their finitude that lead them to assert their invulnerability by dominating others, or to seek escape from their own contingency by submitting to the will or the plan of another.[23] To do justice to another person, to render to that person what is due, is, in the context of original righteousness, no less than to seek the person's good. Niebuhr spends no time on a definition of justice,[24] because if such a definition were more than the formal *suum cuique*, it would have to specify the entirety of the human good as the due to which an individual is entitled. Absolute justice is identical with love.

THE CIRCUMSTANCES OF JUSTICE

In the real world in which we live, however, we anticipate that we will not be able to do for everyone everything that love requires. This is not simply the result of our inability to summon the reserves of concern and care that love requires for everyone we meet, although that is part of the problem. We

---

[22] Niebuhr, *The Nature and Destiny of Man*, II, 246.

[23] See Niebuhr, *The Nature and Destiny of Man*, I, 182–86, and, generally, the discussion of freedom and sin in Chapter Three.

[24] Gordon Harland, *The Thought of Reinhold Niebuhr* (New York: Oxford University Press, 1960), p. 23.

also lack the resources to meet everyone's needs, even if we were willing to do so.

Rawls clarifies these limitations by describing what he calls the "circumstances of justice." These include both objective and subjective conditions that lead human beings to be concerned about justice. Human beings want and need things that are in limited supply. Everything is not available simply for the taking, but neither are the basic goods that make life possible so scarce that we have little hope of obtaining them. Because we are time-bound, finite persons who cannot wait forever to obtain what we need and want, we are concerned about the distribution of these scarce goods. The facts of our finitude and the limited supply of things are among the objective circumstances of justice. The subjective circumstances include the basic fact that we do care whether our wants are satisfied or not, and the fact that, for the most part, any interest we have in the well-being of others is tempered by a more immediate concern for our own.[25]

The absolutism of Jesus' ethics in the Gospels ignores these circumstances of justice. As Niebuhr observed in his early work, *An Interpretation of Christian Ethics*, Jesus sets aside all the egoism in human life, and even every element of prudent self-concern.[26] So much for the subjective circumstances of justice. What Niebuhr does not add is that Jesus also sets aside the objective circumstances, the limits on material resources that constrain love for others. In response to the Disciples' anxious query about how they should provide for the multitudes, Jesus feeds five thousand people with five loaves and two fish.

Jesus, of course, also lives in a world where weariness and the excessive demands of others take their toll, and it is of the utmost importance that, in the end, love of persons in that world requires complete self-sacrifice. Still, the point of both the teaching and the miracles in the Gospels seems to be to

[25] Rawls, *A Theory of Justice*, pp. 126–30, *Political Liberalism*, p. 66. As Rawls himself notes, David Hume was the first modern philosopher to examine the circumstances that make questions of justice relevant and important.

[26] Niebuhr, *An Interpretation of Christian Ethics*, pp. 22–23.

show us what love would do, without the mental and material constraints that limit it in our ordinary experience.[27] As Niebuhr observes, "The ethical demands made by Jesus are incapable of fulfillment in the present existence of man. They proceed from a transcendent divine unity of essential reality, and their final fulfillment is possible only when God transmutes the present chaos of this world into its final unity."[28]

It appears, then, that the New Testament calls attention to the circumstances of justice principally by denying them. Miracles suspend the objective circumstances that make us worry about distribution and create a space in which persons have what they need and are relieved of diseases that keep them from fullness of life, while Jesus' unyielding insistence on love abolishes the self-interest that leads us to care about our share in comparison with that held by another.

Denying the circumstances of justice, however, appears to have the effect of abolishing justice itself. As Rawls observes, "justice is the virtue of practices where there are competing interests and where persons feel entitled to press their rights on each other. In an association of saints agreeing on a common ideal, if such a community could exist, disputes about justice would not occur."[29] As there would be no need for justice if our objective circumstances provided everything we want, so there would be no reason to think about justice if our subjective circumstances were such that we did not care whether it was ourselves or another who enjoyed whatever goods the circumstances made available.

RELATIVE JUSTICE

One might suppose, then, that Christians would have little to say about the problem of justice as Rawls understands it. Christian thinking about justice becomes more interesting as the Christians become less faithful, i.e. less committed to their common ideal and more concerned to secure their own inter-

---

[27] See Mark 6:35–44, compare Mark 6:30–32.
[28] Niebuhr, *An Interpretation of Christian Ethics*, p. 35.
[29] Rawls, *A Theory of Justice*, p. 129.

ests. Only then do they come to grips with the circumstances of justice, which concern the objective realities of scarcity, and also with the subjective circumstance that persons have a plurality of interests and rarely subordinate all of their aims to one common ideal, even when they profess it as their highest good.

Niebuhr, however, sees a more complex relationship between the ideal and the requirements of justice. Justice is concerned not only with the problems of scarcity and conflict, but also with the aspiration to harmony with our neighbors that leaves us dissatisfied with the interim resolutions of conflict. We pursue our desires and we protect our interests, but that is not all we want. We also want to have those aims recognized and protected by our neighbors, as well. We want some confirmation that what we have chosen for ourselves is truly good, meaning that it can also be valued by others and incorporated into an understanding of their own good. We cannot pretend to accomplish what complete justice requires, but neither can we settle for a version of justice that simply offers adequate protection for existing interests.

The biblical myths of creation, fall, and consummation enable us to grasp this complex relationship between the requirements of "original righteousness" and the balance of competing interests that is possible in history, while a strictly rational account of the circumstances of justice sunders it. The story of creation enables us to imagine human relationships in which the circumstances of justice do not obtain, while Jesus' words and miracles anticipate the eschatological fulfillment in which "God transmutes the present chaos of this world into its final unity." In this way we recognize the contingent and provisional character of the hold which the circumstances of justice have upon us, despite the fact that they must constrain all of our historical choices.

There are forms of Christianity which, by separating the Gospel from the circumstances of justice, deprive our efforts to do justice of theological significance. An example of this is "orthodox Christianity," as Niebuhr describes it in *An Interpretation of Christian Ethics*. This version of Christian ethics "failed to derive any significant political–moral principles from the law of love."[30]

Christian Realism, however, points to the biblical suspension of the circumstances of justice, not to set up an alternative moral reality for Christians to dwell in, but precisely to redefine the circumstances of justice for everyone. The biblical account of human sin and the requirements of original righteousness are "maintained not purely by Scriptural authority but by the cumulative experience of the race."[31] To the subjective circumstances of justice, among which Rawls identifies the factual pluralism of human aims and the concern that we all have to protect our own interests, Niebuhr would insist that experience – and not just Christian faith – requires us to add a disposition not to be satisfied with any system of justice that only balances competing interests. To the objective circumstances of justice, which Rawls links to the conditions of scarcity that require us to be concerned about distribution in the first place, Niebuhr adds that the objective circumstances of justice must include the impossibility of a system of justice that fully satisfies the subjective circumstances of justice.

In place of the incommensurability which Rawls' liberal theory finds between the law of love and the circumstances of justice, Niebuhr's Christian Realism establishes a complex, dialectical relationship of affirmation and negation. There is an absolute justice which renders to each person what is required for full participation in the human good, but this justice is never realized in history. There is also a justice that is relevant for social choices, that turns on degrees of good and evil, but this justice is always a relative justice. As Karen Lebacqz observes, "Relative justice involves the calculation of competing interests, the specification of rights and duties, and the balancing of life forces."[32]

Relative justice stands in both a positive and a negative

---

[30] Niebuhr, *An Interpretation of Christian Ethics*, p. 87. Niebuhr's criticism of "orthodox Christianity" is, of course, directed against a version of dogmatic Protestantism, not against the theology and ethics of Eastern Orthodoxy.

[31] *Ibid.*, p. 283.

[32] Karen Lebacqz, *Six Theories of Justice* (Nashville: Abingdon Press, 1986), p. 86.

relationship to the ultimate law by which it is ordered. As Reinhold Niebuhr puts it:

Love is both the fulfillment and the negation of all achievements of justice in history. Or expressed from the opposite standpoint, the achievements of justice in history may rise in indeterminate degrees to find their fulfillment in a more perfect love and brotherhood; but each new level of fulfillment also contains elements which stand in contradiction to perfect love.[33]

The law of love thus becomes available as a guide to choice and action in history through a relative justice which expresses its meaning only partially. The law of love provides the norms for relative justice, but it also provides "an ultimate perspective by which their limitations are discovered."[34]

Relative justice must be assessed in relation to both the law of love and the more self-interested and exploitative conditions which they have overcome. As Niebuhr put it succinctly, "Equal justice is the approximation of brotherhood under the conditions of sin."[35] Perhaps we might rephrase the aphorism with the less pithy, but more precise, statement that relative justice is love expressed within the bounds of finitude. The rephrasing not only acknowledges the more recent require- ments of gender justice, but avoids any confusion of relative justice with sin. Relative justice is achieved under the specific conditions in which our finite lives, with their limited resources and limited reserves of care, have been cast. These conditions, to be sure, include the patterns of discrimination and exploita- tion that our past sins have created. The "conditions of sin" thus define relative justice in the sense that every attempt to do justice must struggle against specific evils, and every achieve- ment of justice will be limited by other evils which it leaves untouched, and perhaps unnoticed.

Finitude, however, is not sin,[36] and the achievements of relative justice must not be rejected because they are less than perfect justice, nor can we evade the demands to do justice in some particular way with the excuse that this way leaves some

---

[33] Niebuhr, *The Nature and Destiny of Man*, II, 246.
[34] Niebuhr, *An Interpretation of Christian Ethics*, p. 85.
[35] Niebuhr, *The Nature and Destiny of Man*, II, 254.   [36] See page 132.

other injustice intact, or creates some lesser injustice in its execution. We are, as Niebuhr put it, "responsible for making choices between greater and lesser evils, even when our Christian faith, illuminating the human scene, makes it quite apparent that there is no pure good in history; and probably no pure evil, either."[37]

JUSTICE IN CONTEXT

Niebuhr's insistence on the importance of these limited choices between degrees of good and evil reflects the engagement with issues of justice that marked the start of his career and continued alongside his more reflective, academic treatments of the subject for the rest of his life. During his years as a pastor in Detroit, Niebuhr was a staunch advocate of unionization in the automobile industry, especially during a protracted public controversy with Ford in 1926. As chair of Detroit's Interracial Committee during the same year, he also worked to improve race relations in the city and to provide more opportunities for the growing African American population.[38] His ideas about justice were not formed in reflection on abstract considerations of fairness, but in the context of specific, local grievances, expressed more often in outraged protests and angry demands than in reasoned arguments.

His own broad knowledge and his wide range of personal contacts enabled him to sympathize with the claims and counterclaims, but also to see their limitations. Workers in the industrial cities of the United States were not merely demanding better wages and hours and a larger share of the profits of their labor. They were part of a global proletarian movement that would shortly transform the exploitative relations between labor and capital that grew out of the industrial revolution. Yet one could not be swept away by their enthusiasm for the illusion that they were about to create a system of perfect

---

[37] Niebuhr, "Theology and Political Thought in the Western World," in *Faith and Politics*, p. 55. See page 73 above.
[38] On this see especially Fox, *Reinhold Niebuhr*, pp. 88–100; and Brown, *Niebuhr and His Age*, pp. 23–35.

justice. Employers in the United States were, on the whole, more attentive to their workers than their counterparts in other countries. Yet they inevitably claimed a greater reward for their leadership and their generosity than was strictly warranted. The commitment of white leaders to greater racial harmony and their attentiveness to the grievances of the African American community were applauded. Yet black and white were both reminded that no group willingly gives up real power unless confronted by real force.[39]

Judgments about relative justice begin with this assessment of claims and counterclaims, against the backdrop of a particular society, at a particular time in history. The demands for justice that call for attention do not arise because persons have measured their situations against a standard of justice and found them wanting. Rather, the experience of local deprivations and exploitations becomes the standard of justice. Often, what emerges is not a general principle, but simply the wider extension of the local claim. Justice becomes identical with, say, the forty-hour week, or with the principle of one person, one vote. The issues have changed since Niebuhr wrote his first major works on social ethics in the 1930s, but still today most persons who seek justice understand it in very specific terms.

The dialectic of claim and counterclaim is what determines relative justice. What people ask for in specific situations, what they identify as proximate political goals, and what they think they may demand from others define justice for them in practical terms. What the others refuse to grant, what they insist on holding on to as their own, and what demands they find unacceptable provide an alternative understanding of justice. The prevailing standard of justice will be set in these actual experiences of conflict, and the more successful efforts to determine what the society will call just at any point in time will be those that follow this dialectic carefully and attend to the details of the claims and counterclaims, not those that attempt

---

[39] These themes are found throughout Niebuhr's early work, especially in the final chapter of *Moral Man and Immoral Society*, pp. 257–77.

to generalize social norms out of the clash of unreconciled expectations.

The brilliance of Niebuhr's political analysis has never been in doubt. The question for ethics, however, is whether the normative implications of this study of the dialectic of justice come to something more than a warning to pay attention to the details. Every society strikes some balance between contending forces. The powerful will rarely yield, except on issues that do not affect their underlying control of events, and the powerless can never be entirely ignored, if only because they pose a threat to the leisurely enjoyment of power. So there will be a balance based on oppositions that an astute observer can identify. If this equilibrium is all that real societies know of justice, how do we distinguish the Christian Realist's relative justice from the anomic relativism for which, as Duncan B. Forrester puts it, "justice is a weapon, a tool, and instrument for getting what we want"?[40] Is the Christian Realist a skilled dialectician who knows what is likely to happen next, or an ethicist who can identify the difference that separates what is and what is likely to be from what *ought* to be?

The question becomes more difficult when we consider the very different directions in which recent writers have developed Niebuhr's thought and its implications for contemporary political issues. Some find in Christian Realism what John Bennett has called "the radical imperative" to join forces with those who raise the most fundamental questions about economic and political power, especially when these forces are at work on a global scale.[41] Michael Novak, by contrast, portrays Niebuhr as the forerunner of a conservative ethic of "democratic capitalism."[42] Between these points toward the extreme ends of the spectrum of interpretations there are many others also to be noted. Most of the interpreters are keen

---

[40] Duncan B. Forrester, "Political Justice and Christian Theology," *Studies in Christian Ethics* 3 (1991), 2.

[41] John C. Bennett, *The Radical Imperative* (Philadelphia: Westminster Press, 1975). Also Glenn R. Bucher, "Christian Political Realism After Reinhold Niebuhr: The Case of John C. Bennett," *Union Seminary Quarterly Review*, 41 (1986), 43–58.

[42] Michael Novak, *The Spirit of Democratic Capitalism* (New York: Simon and Schuster, 1982), pp. 313–29.

observers of events, and it is possible to conclude that this keenness is all they have in common as a legacy from Reinhold Niebuhr.[43]

Niebuhr's most severe critics, in fact, are those who find his dialectic actually subversive of the claims of the poor. The charge is often made by proponents of liberation theology, who, like Niebuhr, begin with the recognition that all claims about justice are historical and contextual. We cannot begin to evaluate them until we know who is making them and what place these persons occupy in the society in question. What we can know, however, is that the preponderance of power, including the power to manipulate intellectual systems of analysis and the media of communication and persuasion, will lie with those who have economic control and occupy the prestigious social roles. Reinhold Niebuhr would accept all of that.

The liberation analysis diverges at the point where Niebuhr appears to attempt an evenhanded assessment of the claims and counterclaims at work in social conflict. For liberation theology, Christian ethics does not begin with objectivity. It begins with a "fundamental option for the poor."[44]

Because the preponderance of power lies with those who already have it, any analysis that does not seek to overturn the existing order effectively counsels that it be left in place. José

[43] Harlan Beckley, *Passion for Justice: Retrieving the Legacies of Walter Rauschenbusch, John A. Ryan, and Reinhold Niebuhr* (Louisville: Westminster/John Knox Press, 1992), pp. 340–41. Beckley develops a nuanced account of Niebuhr's legacy that takes these criticisms into account while leaving Niebuhr's role as a reformer intact, but he notes that Niebuhr "seemingly lacked grounds for advocating specific policy reforms."

[44] The idea of an "option for the poor" has been basic to Roman Catholic social ethics in the years since Vatican II. Originating with Latin American liberation theologians and enunciated by the Conference of Latin American Bishops at Medellin, Colombia, in 1968, the idea was subsequently adopted in the document *Justice in the World*, issued by the Synod of Bishops meeting in Rome in 1971. While the idea receives a variety of interpretations with more or less radical implications for the church's social role, the basic point that Christians are required by scripture to side with the poor in situations of moral choice may now be regarded as an accepted norm in Catholic social ethics. See, in general, Joseph Gremillion, ed., *The Gospel of Peace and Justice: Catholic Social Teaching Since Pope John* (Maryknoll, N.Y.: Orbis Books, 1976), and Donal Dorr, *Option for the Poor: A Hundred Years of Vatican Social Teaching* (Maryknoll, N.Y.: Orbis Books, 1983).

Míguez Bonino characterizes this "Constantinian" theology as one which says, in effect, "whenever an alternative emerges, the Christian ought to work for the best possible solution, the most just and generous one, *short of endangering the existing order*."[45] The contextual nature of all claims to justice leaves no neutral position for an observer, not even the neutrality of one who traces a dialectical movement in which equality and freedom gradually advance. In the framework of this analysis, Niebuhr's evenhanded dialectical position, which emphasizes equally the social necessity of power and the tendency of power to become inordinate, the rightful resentment of inequality by the poor, and the impossibility of perfect equality, becomes nothing more than an apology for the status quo.[46]

The contextual understanding of justice with which Reinhold Niebuhr begins thus proves to be a source of criticism among more recent students of his thought. This is not, in general, because they reject the contextualization of ethics. Few today would maintain that there is any method of ethical analysis that can arrive at significant moral judgments without some preliminary social and moral commitments. The question seems to be whether Niebuhr's contextualization of justice offers any real normative guidance. Critics insist, with the liberation theologians, that the contextual analyst who wants to work for justice must also make a fundamental choice for one side in the conflict.

GENERALIZATIONS ABOUT JUSTICE

The criticisms have a point, but the normative element that often turns up missing in Niebuhr's dialectical analysis of the forces at work in a social context is nothing so obscure as an unspoken normative principle, nor is it as arbitrary as a "fundamental option" that is taken outside of the framework of analysis. Niebuhr's norm of justice is the law of love.

---

[45] José Míguez Bonino, *Toward a Christian Political Ethic* (Philadelphia: Fortress Press, 1983), p. 83.

[46] For general studies of this controversy, see Ruurd Veldhuis, *Realism vs. Utopianism* (Assen: VanGorcum, 1975), and Dennis McCann, *Christian Realism and Liberation Theology* (Maryknoll, N.Y.: Orbis Books, 1981).

Clearly, however, justice cannot be as simple as prescribing what love requires, even when love takes the more realistic and critical form that Niebuhr's account gives it. The determination of relative justice in a particular social context can never proceed with precision.

Rules of justice do not follow in a "necessary manner" from some basic proposition of justice. They are the fruit of a rational survey of the whole field of human interests, of the structure of human life and of the causal sequences in human relations. They embody too many contingent elements and are subject to such inevitable distortion by interest and passion that they cannot be placed in the same category with the logical propositions of mathematics or the analytic propositions of science. They are the product of social wisdom and unwisdom.[47]

Part of the work of those who called themselves "theological realists" in the early decades of this century was to apply this social wisdom to the search for justice, moving away from the Social Gospel's general identification of the Kingdom of God with the progress of democracy, and providing more specific guidance on questions of public policy. From the Oxford Conference on Church, Community, and State, held in 1937, emerged the concept of "middle axioms." John C. Bennett later used this approach to Christian social ethics extensively in the United States.

Middle axioms lie between the most general principles of justice and the details of public policy.[48] The claim that "justice requires a universal system of education available to all persons" is such a middle axiom, which falls somewhere between the very general claim that a just society is concerned with the welfare of all its citizens and the policy decisions which specify that such education shall be provided by locally elected school boards, or shall extend through the twelfth grade, or shall be financed by property taxes.

Other Christian Realists made extensive use of this method of cautious generalization. Niebuhr, though he praised the

---

[47] Niebuhr, *Faith and History*, p. 193.
[48] John C. Bennett, *Christian Ethics and Social Policy* (New York: Charles Scribner's Sons, 1946), pp. 59, 76–77.

work of his colleague, did not.[49] For him, the important generalizations have less immediate application to policy and a
broader historical scope. The wisdom that guides judgments
about justice comes from understanding the claims that are in
the center of present controversy in light of a global awareness
of claims that are being made in other parts of the world, and a
historical consciousness of how these claims have developed
over time.

The essay "Liberty and Equality" illustrates Niebuhr's
method.[50] A sweeping review of Western political history, with
sideward glances at other parts of the world, is brought to bear
on the pressing question of the moment, the problem of racial
equality in United States constitutional law. The "regulative
principle" of equality provides no simple rule of justice that
can be applied to the constitutional questions, but the astute
observer nonetheless arrives at an understanding of equality to
guide legal arrangements that is more than a report of the
current balance of social powers. Equality governs the future
development of rights and duties, within the practical limits of
what social order requires.

The "American dilemma" is on the way of being resolved, and one of
the instruments of its resolution has proved to be the constitutional
insistence on equality as a criterion of justice, an insistence which the
Supreme Court has recently implemented after generations of hesitation in regard to the application of the principle to our relation
with a minority group, which has the advantage of diverging obviously from the dominant type in our nation and which still bears the
onus of former subjugation in slavery. At last the seeming sentimentality of the preamble of our Declaration of Independence – the
declaration that "all men are created equal" – has assumed political
reality and relevance. It is not true that all men are created equal,
but the statement is a symbol for the fact that all men are to be
treated equally, within the terms of the gradations of function which
every healthy society uses for its organization.[51]

---

[49] See Brown, *Niebuhr and His Age*, p. 136.
[50] Reinhold Niebuhr, "Liberty and Equality," *The Yale Review* 47 (September, 1957),
 1–14. This important essay has been reprinted in several places, including Reinhold
 Niebuhr, *Pious and Secular America* (New York: Charles Scribner's Sons, 1958),
 pp. 61–77, and *Faith and Politics*, pp. 185–97. The page references for "Liberty and
 Equality" in these notes are to *Pious and Secular America*.
[51] "Liberty and Equality," pp. 76–77.

Niebuhr is at this point perhaps less cautious than elsewhere to note that "the gradations of function" that exist in every society always include a disproportionate reward for the powerful, and he would later admit that racial justice proved more elusive than he had anticipated following the first series of public school desegregation orders by the Federal courts in the 1950s.

Nevertheless, the sentences quoted aptly illustrate his approach to normative questions of justice. As a political realist, he is always attentive to the forces that "offer resistance to established norms."[52] He has a sociological and historical explanation for the "hesitation" to apply the norm of equality in questions of race. (His formulation of that explanation reveals the assumption, probably unnoticed, that he and his readers, if not the Supreme Court as well, share the perspective of the white majority reflecting on "our" relation to the African American minority and its claims.) Yet the norm of equality has real effect in this context. The ideal of the Declaration of Independence, the principle that "all men are created equal," cannot be taken literally or treated as a simple historical possibility, but it does direct the course of constitutional interpretation. A claim to justice put forward on this basis may be resisted by political maneuvering, or even put down by force. Certainly we should not assume that the dominant groups in society will arrive at a commitment to equality on the basis of a dispassionate examination of their foundational political documents. The minority will have to find advocates to make the argument, and perhaps muster some raw power to insure that the argument will be heard. Once made, however, the moral basis for the claim cannot be evaded.

After several decades, Niebuhr's judgment here reveals some hesitation of his own that may not have been evident in context. Despite this, all of the elements of the Christian Realist's approach to questions of justice are here. A specific claim is interpreted in the context of larger social and historical

---

[52] Niebuhr, "Augustine's Political Realism," p. 119.

developments, and this investigation yields not only a catalog of opposing forces and interests, but also a dominant idea of justice, which is itself embedded in the history and the myths of the society in question. Symbolic expressions of the requirements of justice cannot be perfectly realized, but they can be rendered into practical norms that will determine how we should apply our efforts in the struggles over concrete issues. Moral commitment alone will not determine the outcome, and political realism will never confuse what is right with what is probable, especially in the short run. Moral realism, however, will never decide where to risk commitment simply on the basis of power. Christian Realism must include both moral and political realism.

REGULATIVE PRINCIPLES

Justice is not simply the dialectical ebb and flow of power. It requires us to align ourselves in certain ways in the dynamics of historical conflicts, choosing loyalties and policies that make for greater equality, rather than widening the differences between individuals and groups; and choosing greater liberty, rather than policies that limit persons to preassigned social roles and possibilities. These "regulative principles" of liberty and equality provide the principal norms of justice,[53] though any hope that they will easily tell us what we must do to be just is dashed by the obvious fact of history that the requirements of liberty and the requirements of equality often conflict.

Like the law of love, which is the most general moral norm, regulative principles state ideals which no choices in history can fully realize. Those who attempt to treat the principles of justice as simple historical possibilities are as doomed to failure

---

[53] This concept is clearly stated in *The Nature and Destiny of Man*, II, 254. There, however, Niebuhr speaks of "transcendent principles." The terminology of "regulative principles" appears in later works, especially "Liberty and Equality," p. 61. See also *Man's Nature and His Communities*, p. 26. Beckley suggests that the concept, though not the terminology, of the regulative principle emerged in the early 1930s, though at that time Niebuhr treated equality alone as the regulative principle of justice. See Beckley, *A Passion for Justice*, p. 214.

as those who think they can live in history guided only by the law of love.

Regulative principles are general, not only in the sense that they are broadly formulated, but also in the sense that they are widely acknowledged. Equality, the principle that persons are to be treated as equals, and liberty, the principle that they are to be allowed as much freedom as possible within the limits of social cohesion, thus qualify as regulative principles. "Stiff upper lip," the principle that one's private problems are not to be displayed in public, may be equally broad, but it is specific to certain social classes and cultures, and so is not a regulative principle.

Indeed, regulative principles must have a "practical universality" or be "essentially universal."[54] What Niebuhr means by those qualifiers, apparently, is that the universality of regulative principles can only be tested in history, by interpretive methods that synthesize a number of culturally and historically specific ideals into a more inclusive one. There is "no universal reason in history," and therefore no rational test by which the universality of a principle could be determined once and for all.[55] Regulative principles are "practically universal," in the sense that thoughtful interpretation and a broad knowledge of history and cultures must not show them to be limited to a specific time and place. Their universality is not guaranteed by their place in some logical system of justice. Indeed, it is implicit in the historical, interpretive method by which the regulative principles are identified that further investigation might show us that our identification of some idea as a regulative principle was mistaken, or might turn up additional principles that have not yet been recognized.[56]

---

[54] Niebuhr, *The Nature and Destiny of Man*, II, 254.   [55] *Ibid.*, II, 252.

[56] In an essay first published in 1963, Niebuhr provides an expanded list of "the various regulative principles of justice," which here includes "equality and liberty, security of the community or the freedom of the individual, the order of the integral community and, as is now increasingly the case, the peace of the world community." See Niebuhr, "The Development of a Social Ethic in the Ecumenical Movement," in *Faith and Politics*, p. 177. On the other hand, Niebuhr sometimes reduces the regulative principles to one, as when he wrote in 1955 that "the Supreme Court has made us aware of the great moral resource we possess in our Constitution in its insistence on equality as the regulative principle of justice." See

Regulative principles are "practically universal," but they are not absolute. The realization of a regulative principle by actual communities and individuals is limited not only by the exigencies of history, which do not allow us to treat them as simple possibilities, but also by the limitations of the principles themselves, which may be in conflict with other valid principles that also apply to the situation in which we find ourselves.

Regulative principles, then, form a complex normative system in which they are in a dialectical relationship of affirmation and negation both to the law of love and to other regulative principles. Niebuhr's treatment of these moral principles is broadly similar to other non-foundationalist, non-relativist versions of moral realism which we reviewed in Chapter Two. Our present purpose, however, is to understand the practical implications of thinking about justice in this framework. A general knowledge of how "regulative principles" work in Niebuhr's ethics makes it easier to understand the relationships that he sets up between "liberty" and "equality," and reminds us again of the relationship both of affirmation and negation that is crucial at every point to his understanding of the law of love as a rule for human life.

EQUALITY

The "practical universality" of equality is evident in its prominence in demands for justice from the ancient Greek philosophers to modern times.[57] Persons who seek justice want to be treated equally with others in their opportunities for education, in their access to jobs and housing, in the way that their votes are counted, or in the resources they have available to meet their needs. Unfortunately, when this dominant feature of the demands for justice is given a normative formulation, there is no obvious way in which all people *are* equal that would easily prescribe how we should treat them equally. As

Niebuhr, "The Race Problem in America," *Christianity and Crisis* 15 (December 26, 1955), 170.
[57] Niebuhr, *The Nature and Destiny of Man*, II, 254.

the Swiss theologian Emil Brunner observed, justice necessarily deals with an abstract concept of human dignity, not with concrete persons and their individual needs. Justice "knows no 'thou'; it knows only the intellectual value, the intellectual thing – the dignity of man."[58]

Equality, taken by itself, is not realistic. Persons are not equal. They are different. But when we must deal with persons in large groups and in whole societies, equality becomes an instrument of love by opposing all the inequalities that do not result from love, but from the exercise of power over those in need. When equality is a regulative principle of justice, the generalization and abstraction from real personality that elsewhere renders persons subject to exploitation now establishes the conditions under which they can flourish. For any particular person, these conditions can be stated quite specifically, but it is also possible to generalize about the things that persons need in order to live well.

People who are flourishing are able to recognize and enjoy their own capacities. They take pleasure in their accomplishments and enjoy doing things well, especially those activities at which they are, as a result of aptitude and practice, noticeably more talented than others. They thrive on challenges that require them to use these talents and to develop them further. To flourish in this way, persons require opportunities to test their capacities, and the assistance of others who will help them with these processes of discernment and development.

These people also understand their individual gifts in ways that give them a place among other persons. They seek out ways to make a distinctive contribution to the good of their neighbors, which in turn contributes to their own individual sense of identity and value. They develop their talents in ways that are attentive to how their accomplishments are understood and received by others, rather than in self-absorption

---

[58] Emil Brunner, *Justice and the Social Order*, trans. Mary Hottinger (New York: Harper and Brothers, 1945), p. 127. For Niebuhr's positive evaluation of this work by Brunner, see Brown, *Niebuhr and His Age*, p.135. See also, however, a criticism of Brunner's earlier work in Niebuhr, *The Nature and Destiny of Man*, II, 255n.

that concentrates only on their own awareness and enjoyment. For this, they require a community of persons that genuinely needs at least some of the things they have to offer, and that is prepared to reward them appropriately for their accomplishments, not least by providing them with the means to continue and to enhance those achievements in the future. In other words, people thrive in a community that provides them with opportunities for creative work and that rewards them for their efforts, rather than exploiting their abilities.

All this is, as we noted, very general and abstracted from the details of individual persons and their needs. It means one thing for a child who has learning difficulties, seeking to master the skills that bring a measure of autonomy and enjoying the mastery of tasks that other children perform routinely. It means something quite different for a talented musician or for a master teacher, and something else again for a middle-aged factory worker whose job is threatened by technological and economic changes. It is, however, this ability to generalize about the requirements of the good life that enables us specify what it means to say, as Niebuhr does, that all persons "are to be treated equally, within the terms of the gradations of function which every healthy society uses for its organization."[59] We can hardly say that the gifted teacher and the talented musician should be treated equally in the sense that society should provide them with the same conditions under which to exercise their individual gifts and goals. Nor can we say that the musician and the child with learning difficulties should be equally rewarded for their efforts. An equal opportunity to compete for a place in medical school is probably equally irrelevant to both the child and the factory worker, yet we can specify in some general way the conditions that each of these, and other persons, too, require from their communities in order to live good lives.

Formulated in these terms, true equality among persons would require that they all live equally well. It is obvious that people are not "created equal" in this sense. Circumstances of

[59] "Liberty and Equality," p. 77. See page 215 above.

birth and accidents of history result in very different outcomes, even for persons of similar natural gifts, to say nothing of the fact that the clever or the strong are likely to find it easier to make their lives good than others who are less well endowed. Moreover, differences in temperament often result in two persons of roughly equal gifts feeling markedly different levels of satisfaction with their lives. Even persons who enjoy similarly favorable circumstances are not created equally happy, as anyone will know whose job requires him or her to respond to the complaints of customers, rectify employee grievances, or assign unpopular tasks.

Still, we are required to treat them equally. The persons who answer their complaints or assign tasks to them must do so impartially. That does not mean that they will all be treated alike. Some will receive far more attention than others, absorbing more of our time and limited resources, not because their querulous personalities demand it, but because the complexities of their situations require it, if we are to equalize the possibilities for them to live well to the extent that this depends on the resources we have under our control.

To put the matter more generally, justice does not require that we make everyone happy, although love conceives the possibility that they will all be so, "when God transmutes the present chaos of this world into its final unity."[60] What justice does require is that insofar as we control the resources that affect the well-being of others, whether these are material goods, or the attentions they need to develop and flourish, or the costs and burdens that must be allocated to meet individual and community needs, we must strive to insure that each person is equally able to enjoy a good life. Occasionally, we will be able to do this simply by treating all of them alike, but more often, we will have to be attentive to their individual circumstances – determining the excellences of which they are individually capable, compensating for different abilities, and correcting the effects of past injustice.

Equal justice reduces distinctions between persons. Using

---

[60] Niebuhr, *An Interpretation of Christian Ethics*, p. 35. See page 205 above.

differences of wealth, rank, gender, or ethnicity as indicators to exclude persons from opportunities to develop talents and enjoy the exercise of their capabilities in ways that are available to others result in inequalities of human good, and advances of justice throughout history have been marked by challenges to these distinctions. Requirements of birth, religious affiliation, and gender that once determined access to higher education in the United States and in Europe are today for the most part illegal in those places. While there are differences between persons that appropriately influence their access to opportunities and resources, equal justice prompts a strict scrutiny of such claims. Thus, while good eyesight is deemed relevant to the opportunity to become an airline pilot, owning property is no longer regarded as a qualification for voting.

The struggles for justice with which Reinhold Niebuhr was primarily concerned had to do with ending discrimination between persons, especially, in the United States, on the basis of race. His analysis of the meaning of equal justice bears the marks of this context, even when he does not allude specifically to the problems of desegregation and sets the analysis in a larger historical framework. Equal justice is about challenges to privileges that cannot be justified by the requirements of social function or by genuinely different needs.[61]

While these challenges are important, it would be a mistake to suppose that equal justice is always about eliminating differences. Sometimes, in order to secure justice, it is necessary that differences be preserved. Because persons truly are different, and not equal, treating them equally requires us to acknowledge distinctive abilities, varieties of wisdom and beauty, and different forms of cultural creativity. Otherwise, equal justice is reduced to an equal opportunity to approximate some type that is identified, subtly or explicitly, as the norm. Equal opportunity is an important part of justice, but it is not the whole of it. It serves the needs of a woman whose skills and temperament enable her to express herself well in traditionally

---

[61] Niebuhr, *The Nature and Destiny of Man*, II, 254–55.

male preserves like the symphony conductor's podium or the trial lawyer's courtroom. It offers less hope to the African American writer or artist who wants to speak in the cadences of the Mississippi Delta or to paint in colors and figures rooted in West Africa.

A large part of the struggle for justice since Niebuhr's time has sought to value and preserve this diversity. Although the issues are in many ways similar to those at the heart of the earlier Civil Rights Movement, these claims to justice are also new in important ways. Failure to understand that newness accounts for much of the confusion that now attends the struggle for justice.[62] The Civil Rights Movement provoked outrage and violence because those who launched it defied white Americans' cherished sense of superiority. They insisted that African Americans were, in ways that racist whites could never accept, the same as Americans of European ancestry. Today, by contrast, Black Nationalists, radical feminists, gay and lesbian activists, and hosts of others claim a justice that rests precisely on protection for their differences. The Civil Rights Movement demanded acceptance on terms that resistant whites found uncomfortable because the terms were so familiar. Movements of liberation and empowerment are often uninterested in acceptance and demand instead the freedom to live out a quite different identity. A powerful desire to escape the constraints of stigma and predetermined social roles underlies both sorts of demand for justice, but one demanded access, while the other demands control of its own exclusions. Is it any wonder that a generation of whites and African Americans, who once struggled to find a place in one another's workplaces and neighborhoods, and eventually in each other's homes and hearts, now shake their graying heads over this new justice? And is it not also understandable that those who demand recognition of their difference look back on the Civil Rights Movement as a kind of sell-out, or at best a part of the prehistory of the struggle for real equality?

---

[62] Charles Taylor, "The Politics of Recognition," in Amy Gutman, ed., *Multiculturalism and "The Politics of Recognition"* (Princeton: Princeton University Press, 1992), pp. 25–73.

What links these two chapters from our recent past in the larger historical struggle for equal justice is the idea that justice is a claim to the human good. The persistent theme of justice is that those who have been ruled ineligible for the good life, or dismissed as incapable of it, are in fact equally entitled to it. Initially, that claim is vindicated simply by achieving the good on the prevailing terms; but eventually, to the extent that there are *real* differences between the parties in the struggle for justice, success in achieving equal access will result in new versions of what that good really is. What begins simply as an extension of the group considered eligible for the good life yields a proliferation of the types of human good available to be sought.

Alongside the dialectic that renders equal justice both an affirmation and a negation of the ultimate law of love, then, we must include an internal dialectic of equality that both affirms difference and calls it into question. Niebuhr was most familiar with the equal justice that questions differences, but Christian Realism may also require us to risk preserving them. No formula settles the direction of our efforts in advance, nor can we identify differentiations based on race, gender, education, or ability as just or unjust, categorically. We can only examine the claims as they are raised, and ask whether the situation that would ensue if the claims were met would be more, or less, like the human good that love persistently seeks.

LIBERTY

Niebuhr grants a certain priority to equality in his account of justice. "A higher justice always means a more equal justice," he asserts.[63] Equality is, however, only one of the two important regulative principles of justice. The other is liberty.

Alongside the claims to equality, which are always artificially secured in the face of the real differences that render us in some respects unequal, there are also claims to political liberty. Persons demand not only fairness from their political communities, but also a measure of freedom.

[63] Niebuhr, *The Nature and Destiny of Man*, II, 254.

[L]iberty is the "due" of each man because man has an essential freedom as spiritual personality which makes it monstrous for any community to use him merely as a tool. The community cannot be merely the fulfillment of man. It is also his frustration. An adequate ethic consequently insists on a degree of freedom which acknowledges the individual as a "child of God" and as able and encouraged to say "we must obey God rather than men."[64]

Niebuhr sets up the regulative principle of liberty in dialectical opposition to the principle of equality, confident that over the long run, justice will appear in the balance that is struck between these two incomplete and partial realizations of it. At first glance, however, the opposition appears to be more complete than that. Resistance to the requirements of equal justice usually takes the form of a reassertion of liberty. Those who wish to maintain racial separation demand freedom of association, in opposition to the open access that equal justice provides. Those who oppose a more equal distribution of resources demand freedom in the use of their property, in opposition to the taxes that equal justice requires.

Because perfect justice is an impossibility, partial efforts at justice tend to become coercive. They force us to give up a portion of our freedom to choose our neighbors, co-workers, and employees. They require us to spend our resources on equipment to provide equal access for those whose abilities are different from the majority. They limit the advantages of wealth and influence that we are able to pass on for the benefit of our children, friends, and favored causes. Also, they tend in a modern, bureaucratic state to bury us under mounds of paperwork by which we prove that we have met the requirements of equal justice. The exercise of liberty does not usually require such extensive documentation.

As we approach the limits of equal justice in history, coercion becomes more necessary if such justice as we are able to secure is to prevail. The dialectic of liberty and equality approaches its antithesis as the measures we employ to enforce equality become so oppressive that they threaten the human

---

[64] Reinhold Niebuhr, "The Problem of a Protestant Social Ethic," *Union Seminary Quarterly Review*, 15 (November, 1959), 9.

good that justice seeks. This point will be reached earlier for those whose positions in society are relatively privileged, and they will be the first to reassert the claims of freedom.

The underlying problem, however, does not depend on class interests. Even a perfectly docile citizenry living under a perfectly just government cannot be said to live well if they live entirely according to someone else's plan. Self-transcendence results in a measure of creativity and autonomy. Political systems must incorporate these expressions of human freedom in their table of political freedoms, if they are to make possible the human good that is the aim of justice.

So liberty, like equality, is a regulative principle of justice. The linking of liberty and justice in our political thinking is not as ancient as the connection between justice and equality. Niebuhr dates it from the English sectarian movements of the seventeenth century.[65] Here, the freedom of conscience to disobey secular authorities who strayed into the area of religious belief becomes a political principle as well. Some parts of life ought to be free from external constraints, and persons are treated justly only when they are free in these matters.

Actually, all that is cherished in the standard of an "open society" in Western civilization had some roots in a curious blend of left-wing Calvinism and sectarian perfectionism of the seventeenth century. In addition it was necessary to garner those aspects of truth in the political policy of the English Reformation, particularly of the Elizabethan Settlement, so clearly elaborated in Hooker's *Laws of Ecclesiastical Polity* in which the conservative monarchism of Edmund Burke and the liberal theories of John Locke were both present in embryo.[66]

The connection between liberty and justice in Western thought thus had to do specifically with limits on the powers of government, and had less to do with persons in their relations to one another. In contrast to the active measures required to create and sustain equality, liberty could be secured by devising a government that did not intervene in the natural freedom of its people.

[65] Niebuhr, "Liberty and Equality," p. 68.
[66] Niebuhr, "The Development of an Ecumenical Social Ethic," in *Faith and Politics*, p. 172.

It is primarily this freedom of persons in relation to their government that Reinhold Niebuhr had in mind when he wrote about liberty. If equality was the principal internal question for the United States, facing the realities of racial separation, liberty was the global issue, as totalitarian governments, equipped with modern technical means to control public opinion and action, attempted to subordinate individual freedom completely to the purposes of the state.

Niebuhr was not so unrealistic as to suppose, however, that unchecked freedom would secure human well-being. The ambiguous potentialities of self-transcendence, which can be used for good or evil purposes, require some limitation if society is to function in the regular, orderly way that human well-being requires. "Nevertheless, the tendency of the community to claim the individual's devotion too absolutely, and to disregard his hopes, fears, and ambitions which are in conflict with, or irrelevant to, the communal end, makes it necessary to challenge the community in the name of liberty."[67] Maintaining a steady, critical attitude toward all government seemed to be the only secure way to prevent the sudden eruption of totalitarian systems that would sweep aside all liberties in their drive to aggrandize the state.[68]

The freedom of conscience against the demands of overbearing state power is essential, but a longer view of the problem of liberty will suggest that the state is not the only thing that threatens it. Persons not only need to be free *from* their communities at times; they also require the freedom to be *for* them. The creative possibilities of interpersonal cooperation and institution building must be engaged if they are to rise in more than momentary ways above the constraints of their situations. Black South Africans, for example, certainly understand the restrictions on liberty that the policy and practice of apartheid imposed. Their demand for freedom, however, was not only a demand for the abolition of apartheid. It involved full participation in government. Those who take political participation

[67] Niebuhr, "Liberty and Equality," p. 66.
[68] See especially Reinhold Niebuhr, "Do the State and the Nation Belong to God or the Devil?" in *Faith and Politics*, pp. 99–101.

for granted may be especially alert to the ways in which community frustrates the individual and see their liberty primarily in terms of a secure knowledge that those frustrations will be constitutionally checked and limited. Those who have been excluded from politics know about frustrated liberty, but they are often quite willing to risk those frustrations in order to be free to build their future, as well as to dream it.

Just as the liberty that is essential to our humanity leaves us unsatisfied with a good that others have chosen for us, so liberty also requires that once the good is known, we must be free to participate in its creation. Indeed, we must be enabled to participate, if we are to receive what recent Roman Catholic ethics has called "social justice." Karen Lebacqz explains:

> Rights are not simply claims to be attributed to individuals apart from community. Because human beings are social by their very nature, human dignity will be addressed in social relationships. "Justice" is not simply a matter of proper distribution of good (distributive justice) but also of permitting and indeed requiring each person to participate in the production of those goods (social justice).[69]

We are not free simply because someone else has elected to give us the goods that freedom seeks, not even if these are the goods we ourselves would choose to pursue.

It is on this point that some of Niebuhr's accounts of human rights and racial justice fail to mirror the anger and frustration that mounted in the African American community even after the end of legal segregation.[70] The freedom to enjoy public facilities and services, and even the freedom to participate in public life by voting, could hardly count as full freedom when they had to be achieved by the action of courts and legislative bodies in which African Americans were minimally represented, and when they pointedly ignored the question of the economic resources that would be necessary to achieve the power to shape these political processes for themselves.

By the end of his life, Niebuhr had begun to revise the

[69] Lebacqz, *Six Theories of Justice*, p. 69.
[70] Herbert O. Edwards, "Racism and Christian Ethics in America," *Katallagete*, (Winter, 1971), pp. 15–24.

formulations that sometimes appeared to limit the positive side of the government's role in liberty to the power to grant a bare political freedom.[71] The constructive treatment of politics in Christian Realism, however, had long provided the basis for such a move. As we saw in Chapter Four, political participation is a basic form of human creativity, without which our freedom has no definitive aims and no lasting results. To seek the good of others requires that we empower them for this participation in their own right. Because justice requires both liberty and equality, we cannot render to persons what they are due simply by giving them a full share of their entitlements – though that is important. They must also be free to take part in the deliberations that determine what those entitlements are, and they must resist in the name of this more complete liberty any version of liberty that offers freedom without participation, or any version of equality that offers entitlements without deliberation.

As with equality, a fully developed Christian Realism requires a more complex understanding of liberty, introducing a new dialectic between participation and autonomy within liberty, alongside the dialectic between liberty and equality that shapes the concrete requirements of justice. Christian Realism has historically been more alert to the dangers that governments can pose to autonomy. Its future effectiveness may depend on a new attentiveness to the importance of participation.

JUSTICE, HOPE, AND HUMAN GOOD

This chapter began with an effort to clarify Reinhold Niebuhr's understanding of justice in the light of recent developments in liberal political theory. Niebuhr's assumption, typical of the public theology of his generation, was that American democracy rested implicitly on important propositions that were drawn from Christian reflections on human nature and

---

[71] Reinhold Niebuhr, "The Negro Minority and Its Fate in a Self-Righteous Nation," in Charles C. Brown, ed., *A Reinhold Niebuhr Reader* (Philadelphia: Trinity Press International, 1992), pp. 118–24.

human communities. Liberal philosophy of the last two decades, by contrast, has sought to construct a moral consensus on more minimal agreements, independent of any but the most general claims about humanity's present character and ultimate destiny.

There are large differences between Reinhold Niebuhr's interpretation of justice and contemporary liberal theories. For Niebuhr, love is essential to prevent the search for justice from deteriorating into an assertion of self-interest, and the ultimate harmony of individual goods is the presupposition of our more immediate moral obligations. For John Rawls, justice makes sufficient sense as the pursuit of individually chosen goods, governed by agreed rules of fairness. More extensive presuppositions are unnecessary, and they may even threaten the mutual tolerance that is essential to social peace.

We must, however, avoid overstating the practical differences between these widely divergent understandings of justice. Certainly Christian Realism has more in common with political liberalism than either shares with the relativist and historicist accounts of justice which reduce its requirements to assertions of particular interests or to customary practices weighted with the legitimacy of traditional authority. Both political liberals and Christian Realists hold that the norms of justice extend across the boundaries of nations and interest groups, and though they differ sharply over the role that beliefs about human nature and destiny may play when conflicts are resolved in accordance with those norms, both agree that such resolutions are possible.

In 1944, Niebuhr drew the lines to divide "the children of light," who believe that "self-interest should be brought under the discipline of a higher law," from "the children of darkness," who "know no law beyond their will and interest."[72] Liberals, Niebuhr believed, belonged among the children of light, although they were "foolish" children for their tendency to believe that the victory of justice over self-interest could easily be accomplished, either in their own lives or in their democratic nations.

[72] Niebuhr, *The Children of Light and the Children of Darkness*, p. 9.

Much has changed in our world and our thinking since then, but the most important intellectual dividing lines remain where Niebuhr drew them. In 1944, the battle lines were real, as well as metaphorical, and the children of darkness represented an evil that even staunch relativists usually take pains to deplore.[73] Today's children of light are perhaps less clear about what they believe, and less confident about their formulations of it. Those who acknowledge "no law beyond their will and interest," by contrast, are often not so much self-willed cynics asserting their power over others as they are disillusioned seekers who have earnestly desired another, more encompassing law, but failed to find it. The differences between today's children of darkness and their predecessors at the middle of the century are important, but the fundamental choice remains to be made between the two kinds of children that Niebuhr himself distinguished.

The important contribution that Christian Realism made to an earlier generation of the children of light was to introduce a probing, skeptical unmasking of hidden interests that was designed to keep the foolish children of light from falling victim to sentimental, idealized versions of their own moral commitments. False hopes for an easy realization of justice in history would only prove too weak for the struggle against a cynical foe who harbored no such illusions. Today, it may be that Christian Realism best serves the children of light, especially the political liberals among them, by reintroducing the motive power of moral and religious ideals to those who learned too well the earlier lesson against sentimentality.

Niebuhr's reference to the "sentimentality" of the affirmation of equality in the Declaration of Independence[74] should not be taken to imply that such symbols are irrelevant to the pursuit of justice, or that they become important only when a pragmatist reformulates them as realizable norms. We have already seen that Christian theology depends on the same sort of attractive, but impossible, formulations of the human

---

[73] See, for example, Gilbert Harman, "Moral Relativism Defended," *Philosophical Review*, 84 (1975), 3–22.

[74] See page 215 above.

good that appear in the Declaration of Independence. The myths of the law, like the myths of faith, grasp possibilities that can neither be formulated in strictly rational terms nor perfectly realized in actual human communities. So, too, the utopian illusions of revolutionaries symbolize aspirations based on real human needs, even if the sober, rational observer understands that their promises can never be kept.[75]

Myths, utopias, and dreams of perfect justice provide the energy that keeps the struggle for justice going. They have power to motivate people who would otherwise remain absorbed in the details of their personal struggles. More important, these images of what perfect justice would be like provide the basis for the specific claims and demands that are the stuff of controversy in daily social and political life. Persons and groups who nourish dreams of perfect justice make demands for specific, realizable approximations of their goal. The dream of the "beloved community" in which each person's needs are met and each person's gifts are valued becomes the basis, not only for a community of care and respect among those who share the dream, but also for a demand for equal rights in the wider society. Richard Bernstein describes a civil rights gathering in Hattiesburg, Mississippi, in 1964 in terms that echo this point:

[T]here were two things that deeply impressed me – that I was witnessing the creation of just one of those public spaces that Arendt describes, and that what gave the participants the courage, hope, and conviction to participate was informed by their communal religious bonds ... We know how rare and fragile such events can be – how they occur in extraordinary circumstances when individuals feel a deep sense of crisis and injustice, and are motivated to come together. But the danger that we face today is one of forgetfulness and an overly "sophisticated" cynicism that erodes what Ernst Bloch called the principle of hope.[76]

Bernstein is no doubt correct that a moral realist at the end of Reinhold Niebuhr's century must worry about "overly 'sophisticated' cynicism" as Niebuhr worried about "senti-

---

[75] Cf. Niebuhr, *Moral Man and Immoral Society*, p. 277.
[76] Richard Bernstein, "The Meaning of Public Life," in Robin W. Lovin, ed., *Religion and American Public Life* (New York: Paulist Press, 1986), pp. 48–49.

mentality." Both the sentimental wish that dreams may become reality and the cynical assumption that what people dream is a thinly disguised report on their immediate interests obscure the real relationship between the symbols of ultimate good and the claims people make in political situations.

The utopian or mythical ideas that shape concrete political demands connect the struggle for justice to the human good. Persons demand as equal justice a reality they conceive in freedom, and what they conceive in freedom, they regard as good. It may be that a system of justice can be elaborated in theory on more minimal assumptions, but that will not reduce the hopes that people bring to politics.

Conclusion

Historical epochs do not conform to the calendar. Someone has remarked that the twentieth century began in 1914, when World War I shattered the political assumptions and social stabilities of nineteenth-century Europe. Future generations may well say that the twentieth century ended in 1989, when the sudden collapse of communism in Eastern Europe signalled the end of the bipolar world, divided between two hegemonic superpowers.

The years between, what we will remember as the twentieth century, were a time of nation-states that dominated large sections of the globe and took to arms in the name of even larger values. It was a century that needed realism, if its leaders were to escape moral pretensions that would tempt them to crusades, and if its people were to resist concealed powers that threatened to put their lives at the service of other people's interests.

It was Reinhold Niebuhr's century. A young man at its start, he learned its illusion-shattering lessons well. He first found his intellectual center with a group of "younger theologians" for whom the expectations of Jesus' ethics could not be a "simple historical possibility," but who also understood "the truth in myths" that was more enduring than the rational expectations of scientific progress.

When Niebuhr turned his critical realism on religious hope itself, in *Moral Man and Immoral Society*, some of his theological colleagues thought that he had surrendered Christian hope

235

and handed the power of social transformation over to fanatical revolutionaries.[1] In time, Niebuhr would come to expect much less from revolutionaries, and his greatest work, *The Nature and Destiny of Man*, concentrates precisely on the power of the Christian view of human nature to sustain hope without yielding to pride.[2] *Moral Man and Immoral Society* is an incomplete statement of Christian Realism, but in writing it, Niebuhr learned to trace the power of ideas, illusions, and self-deceptions in the movement of large historical forces, and so he came to interpret the events of his century for a much wider audience than other theologians could command.

His was a world of mass movements and great powers. What the leaders who controlled these forces believed about their place in the world was important, if for no other reason than that they would act to achieve their supposed destiny. As Niebuhr understood the realist's task, however, it was not to weigh the truth of these claims, but to assess the power that lay behind them, so as to construct the delicate balance of forces under which human survival, and even human flourishing, might be possible. In a world divided between sharply conflicting ideologies, the triumph of any one of them would inflict costs that human civilization could not bear.

Ronald Stone has aptly summarized Niebuhr's global political realism, especially in the Cold War years:

> He envisaged the competition extending for decades or even longer. There could be no resolution through war, but neither partner in the competition could be expected to surrender its respective myths or ideologies. Wise statesmanship was the most important element in maintaining the uneasy partnership in preventing nuclear war. He had no great confidence in education, cultural exchanges, religious impulses, or disarmament plans eliminating the tension caused by the two continental empires competing for influence and interests in the world. This view of the world, essentially of two nuclear-armed scorpions locked in a small bottle, was not a world he would have wished for, but it was the world he perceived.[3]

---

[1] See Fox, *Reinhold Niebuhr*, pp. 142–43.
[2] Niebuhr, *The Nature and Destiny of Man*, II, 321.
[3] Ronald H. Stone, *Christian Realism and Peacemaking* (Nashville: Abingdon Press, 1988), p. 38.

It was also a world he was well prepared to explain, especially to a younger generation of theologians and political leaders who might wish to make it more congenial to their own hopes and dreams, the way young men in Niebuhr's generation had tried to make it a "world safe for democracy." It was not a world that most people actually wanted, but it proved to be sufficiently stable to avert catastrophe, and Niebuhr had cogent reasons why apparently higher aspirations had to be postponed or foregone to insure that stability.

Niebuhr feared that if this world ceased to be, it would disappear in a nuclear holocaust. In the end, it fell apart because the people who had been persuaded or coerced into maintaining the pressure from the East simply walked away from it, leaving a startled West to contemplate how much of its supposedly free way of life had actually been structured by the exigencies of the conflict.

When Niebuhr died in 1971, the forces that would bring about this dissolution were just barely visible. Christian Realism confers no predictive powers. (It was, after all, Reinhold Niebuhr who predicted in 1933 that the German industrialists who had supported Hitler against the socialists would quickly rein him in if his nationalistic ambitions started to impinge on their commercial interests.)[4] So it is little wonder that readers who today come new to Niebuhr's work are often struck by what is missing.

In the basic texts of Christian Realism, there is much about the truth in myths, and little about ordinary, empirical truth. Niebuhr's realism takes account of ideological self-deception, but says little about the inability of totalitarian systems to sustain the flow of information that a modern, technological society requires. Propaganda does overwhelm common sense, especially when conditions are unfamiliar and dangerous, but its staying power proves very limited. What we now know both about the life of people in the former Soviet Union and about the reading of scripture in communities of the oppressed suggests that ordinary people form a remarkably accurate picture

---

[4] Reinhold Niebuhr, "The Opposition in Germany," *New Republic* 75 (June 28, 1933), 169–71.

of what is going on around them, even when there are powerful forces at work to conceal it from them.[5]

Niebuhr, more than many of his contemporaries, did understand the bonds of ethnicity, territory, and language that seem to be replacing ideological commitments as the principal sources of violent conflict in the post-Cold War world. But he regarded these evidences of "tribalism" as important principally when they become entangled with more modern differences based on class and economic power, and in any case, he anticipated that these forms of pluralism would be "digested" by democratic nations which achieved legal formulations of universal human rights.[6] As we have seen in the more extended discussion of Niebuhr's ideas about justice, he gives little thought to an equality that would sustain differences between persons, rather than rendering them irrelevant.[7]

Because the balance of power was so important to the world Niebuhr knew, stability assumed a normative role in its own right. "Security," "order," and "peace" are mentioned as possible "regulative principles" of justice, alongside liberty and equality.[8] The risks of disorder, both to those who hold power and to those who may be crushed in the effort to obtain it, often temper the search for justice with a realistic respect for the opposition.

REALISM AND ITS CRITICS

It is hardly surprising, then, that some contemporary observers find the classic texts of Christian Realism largely irrelevant to a global community based on rapid transfers of goods and information, and shaped by economic forces that governments are often unable to control. Others find Niebuhr's work actually opposed to their demands for recognition and justice. His

---

[5] On these points, see, for example, Hedrick Smith, *The New Russians* (New York: Avon Books, 1991), pp. 21–25; and Gustavo Gutierrez, *We Drink from Our Own Wells* (Maryknoll, N.Y.: Orbis Books, 1984).

[6] Niebuhr, *Man's Nature and His Communities*, pp. 86–88, 99.

[7] See pp. 228–30 above.

[8] Niebuhr, "The Development of a Social Ethic in the Ecumenical Movement," in *Faith and Politics*, p. 177. See page 218, note 56 above.

emphases on the ambiguity of all moral claims and the importance of political stability summarize attitudes they must overcome to achieve their goals. For them, Christian Realism has
become part of the ideology of conservatism.[9]

Today's Christian Realist, however, may prove surprisingly
responsive to these criticisms of the classic formulations. After
all, what the critics are describing are the results of technical
developments and economic changes that had barely begun in
Niebuhr's time. The Christian Realist's commitment "to take
all factors in a social and political situation ... into account"[10]
supports these new understandings. The Christian Realist has
no *a priori* commitment to the particular set of social, political,
and economic forces that proved decisive in the situations that
Reinhold Niebuhr analyzed.

Feminist theologians have a slightly different criticism that
goes closer to the heart of Niebuhr's thinking. For them, the
understanding of human nature that shapes Christian Realism's hopes for human fulfillment and its characteristic warnings about the temptations of power is too narrow. It depends
too much on the excesses of pride that accompany positions of
power and understands too little of the loss of selfhood that
befalls women and others who are taught to seek fulfillment by
denying their own hopes and plans. It is important to note that
in his more systematic statements, Niebuhr does balance his
emphasis on pride with a warning against the dangers of
"sensuality."[11] Still, the critics are right to correct the limitations of the masculine, agential humanity that provides most of
Reinhold Niebuhr's "human nature."

Today's Christian Realist will not defend a narrow conception of human nature. He or she will be as concerned to
understand the moral life of those whose choices are limited
and denied as to point out the dynamics of pride. She will not,
however, overlook the fact that the contemporary feminist
critics, no less than the Christian Realists of the mid-century

---

[9] Bill Kellerman, "Apologist of Power: The Long Shadow of Reinhold Niebuhr's
Christian Realism," *Sojourners* 16 (March, 1987), 15–20.
[10] Niebuhr, "Augustine's Political Realism," in *Faith and Politics*, p. 119.
[11] See the more extended discussion of this point on pp. 142–47 above.

whom they criticize, make an argument that turns on how we understand human nature. A conception of human nature that includes the aesthetic as well as the agential, the emotional commitment as well as the rational calculation of consequences, and that spreads these characteristics across both the male and the female members of the human species will provide a richer understanding of human fulfillment on which to base our moral principles and our political goals. This new assessment, however, shares with earlier versions of Christian Realism a conviction that the human good is the proper subject of ethics, and that we cannot settle our disagreements about what we ought to do without reference to our understandings of a fully human life.

Implicit in many of the critiques of Christian Realism, then, are the Christian Realists' own patterns of argument: Prescriptions for action are based on attention to the complexity of forces at work in a situation, especially the trends that go unnoticed because they are pervasive, and the interests that go undetected because they are concealed by appeals to more general values. Understanding how a social system ought to function rests on understanding how to meet the needs of human nature and how to avoid the distortions to which it is susceptible. To see what Christian Realism is, we need to attend not only to the works of those who chose the label for themselves, but also to those who have used its methods to move beyond the limitations of its first practitioners.

APOLOGETIC THEOLOGY

The question about Christian Realism at the end of Reinhold Niebuhr's century is not a question about whether we can apply Niebuhr's political principles directly to new problems. Especially, the question is not a counterfactual speculation about what Reinhold Niebuhr would say and do if he were here today. The question about Christian Realism is about the most general convictions of those who sought a "realistic theology." They believed that the truth about God must in the end prove consistent with every other kind of truth we can know,

and they believed that by attending to reality, without insis
in advance that it conform to faith's expectations, we would in
the end find "whatever ground of courage, hope, and faith is
actually there, independent of human preferences and
desires ..."[12] They believed, partly on the basis of their study
of Christian history, and more out of their experience of life in
Christian communities, that this realism has been a persistent
characteristic of Christianity, so that attentiveness to what
Christians have thought about human life is likely to prove
more accurate as a guide to present possibilities than any of the
alternative understandings of the human condition.

The subject matter of this book has been Christian Realism,
rather than the specific judgments about public policy and
international affairs with which Christian Realists have been
preoccupied. We have examined a loose family connection of
realisms – political, moral, and theological. Christian Realists
have typically held versions of all three of these sorts of realism,
although holding one of them does not rigorously entail
holding the others. Certainly there have been those readers
who applauded their political realism, but were baffled by
their theology, and others who believed that moral realism
requires stricter adherence to principles than the political
realists would admit. The Christian Realists, however, tried to
hold all three sorts of realism together.[13]

For them, each realism was a search for the truth about an
aspect of reality, guided by a pragmatic method and starting
from naturalistic evidence. Niebuhr and his counterparts
among the Younger Theologians would not at first have been
satisfied with either of those labels, but from a broader perspective on the options in twentieth-century philosophy we find in
pragmatism and naturalism important ways to characterize
the Christian Realists' way of choosing courses of action and
understanding reality.

Niebuhr himself eventually adopted "Christian pragmatism" as an appropriate name for "the firm resolve that inherited dogmas and generalizations will not be accepted, no

---

[12] Horton, *Realistic Theology*, p. 38.
[13] See the more extended discussion of this point on pp. 3–31 above.

matter how revered or venerable, if they do not contribute to the establishment of justice in a given situation."[14] Justice is measured by how well a solution works in context. We assess the gains in relation to particular historical antecedents, and we determine the risks posed by specific obstacles. Practical justice is achieved as the principles of justice become coherent with the rest of the requirements of life in an organized society, for such justice can be done, not merely imagined.

Niebuhr was always suspicious of naturalism understood in a narrow and reductive way. Nevertheless, the term is appropriate to Niebuhr's ethics and theology, for which human experience is a primary point of reference for understanding both the requirements of morality and the reality of God. For Christian Realism, there can be no claims to moral and religious truth that stand in simple contradiction to the rest of what we know.

Ideally, there should be a constant commerce between the specific truths, revealed by the various historical disciplines and the final truth about man and history as known from the standpoint of the Christian faith. In such a commerce the Christian truth is enriched by the specific insights which are contributed by every discipline of culture. But it also enriches the total culture and saves it from idolatrous aberrations.[15]

It is this pragmatism and naturalism that relates Christian Realism to all forms of human knowledge which also relates it at once to other ways of thinking about ethics and politics. While Reinhold Niebuhr's authority in American intellectual and political life is sometimes cited as evidence that the mid-century decades were still under the sway of a Protestant, Christian culture, Niebuhr himself knew better. As early as 1937 he declared, "For the past two hundred years the Christian Church has been proclaiming the gospel in a world which no longer accepted the essentials of the Christian faith."[16] Obviously, one cannot tell such a world that the Christian faith

---

[14] Niebuhr, "Theology and Political Thought in the Western World," in *Faith and Politics*, p. 55.

[15] Niebuhr, *Faith and History*, p. 167.

[16] Niebuhr, *Christianity and Power Politics*, p. 203.

is simply what it already knows; but one can make a case for the Christian faith in terms consistent with the way in which that world settles questions of truth. Pragmatism and naturalism speak in those terms to the modern world, especially in America.

It is this approach to the questions of ethics, politics, and theology that marks a Christian Realist in the 1930s or the 1990s. In Niebuhr's day, it set the defense of the biblical worldview that he undertook apart from the return to the "world of the Bible" proclaimed by Karl Barth and his followers. Today, it sets Christian Realism apart from systems of theology that concentrate on the meaning internal to Christian belief and reject the task of vindicating its claims before a more general critical audience.[17]

That is not to say that Christian Realists simply accept their assignment on the terms laid down by secular critics. Part of the task of a naturalistic Christian ethics is to broaden the understanding of nature, incorporating complex human aspirations and religious affections into our understanding of what is natural, and rejecting the reductive naturalism that simplifies the account of our lives by ignoring the complexity of the evidence. Part of Christian pragmatism is to question a coherence theory of truth that ignores the incoherences that are essential marks of the limits of our understanding.

The Christian Realist ventures into apologetic theology not simply to answer questions, but also to challenge the terms in which the questions are put. The Christian understanding of human life and its fulfillment is not just a summary of conventional wisdom. Indeed, it is at many points contradictory to ordinary notions of happiness, and because the Christian cannot *prove* its validity short of a final assessment beyond history, its validation in terms of pragmatic, natural reason always remains limited and incomplete.[18]

Still, the apologetic task is important, if only because the apologist is always also the skeptic and the critic. One of the clearest insights of Christian Realism is that those who hold to

---

[17] For a more extensive discussion of this topic, see Placher, *Unapologetic Theology.*
[18] Niebuhr, *Faith and History*, p. 152. See above, pp. 38–41.

Christian faith do not live only in Barth's "strange new world of the Bible," but also in the modern world whose assumptions have made the Bible's world strange to us. Perhaps the Bible's world has always been strange,[19] but it will be strange to each age in its own way. Unless we can explain the Bible, at least provisionally, in terms that are coherent with the rest of what we know and believe, we will never know what its strangeness means for us.[20]

CHRISTIAN REALISM IN A NEW CENTURY

When we turn from theology to the tasks of ordering our political life together, the Christian Realist proceeds with humility and with confidence. As we have observed, Christian Realism confers no predictive powers. A habit of attention to all the forces at work in a social and political situation does not always allow us to plot their trajectories accurately. Nor does the Christian Realist escape the distortion of insight by interest. No one does. The marks of ideology and gender, race and class will be inscribed in every judgment, in ways that will often be most evident to those whose interests differ.

All that should make the Christian Realist humble. The confidence comes from the awareness that, sooner or later, those who see matters differently will have to make their own case in realistic terms. It will then be possible to bring the insights of the biblical view of human nature to bear on the inadequacies of the alternative proposals, whatever the limitations of the Christian Realist's position may be at the outset.

The architecture of Christian Realist political thought that Reinhold Niebuhr sketched provides the starting point for a political presentation of the biblical alternative. Politics begins with the good that individuals in their freedom conceive for themselves.[21] While freedom is shaped by community, and may, under unfavorable circumstances, all but disappear for particular individuals, the capacity to claim for oneself more

---

[19] "For Jews demand signs and Greeks desire wisdom, but we proclaim Christ crucified," I Corinthians 1:22–23 (NRSV).

[20] See pp. 158–61 above.   [21] See above, pp. 123–27.

than what is simply given is basic to human life, and the recognition of these claims in one another is the starting point for all politics. This idea of human dignity seems to lie behind all modern doctrines of human rights. However difficult it may be to identify specific, substantive rights that truly have universal applications, political arrangements derive their legitimacy from the recognition that everyone has *some* claims that deserve to be honored by any community.

From this freedom of human consciousness to imagine a good that transcends circumstances, many different political arrangements may follow. It is important for Christian Realism that there is rarely a straight line from individual aspiration to social reality. Politics is a dialectical process, in which aspirations are constantly tested and revised in relation to material limits and competing goals. The judgments we make about politics are inevitably contextual.[22] We assess specific demands against a specific existing order, measuring the requirements of justice not only against the ultimate law of love, but also against the costs and risks of change.

The freedom inherent in human nature and the ambiguity of every political expression of that freedom provide the dynamics of Niebuhr's approach to politics, and they will no doubt endure despite the changes in our circumstances. A future Christian Realism must, however, view the relations between these elements quite differently from the mid-century Realism that sought social stability and a balance of power between two competing ideologies.

The Cold War gave occasions for a rehearsal of the values of freedom against the limitations of a closed society. The meaning of freedom could be explicated by contrast to the places where it was denied, even if political realism also required the occasional limitation of freedom for security reasons. Today, in large parts of the world, the liberal freedoms of speech, press, and association and the values of multi-party democracy are generally affirmed. It is less likely that freedom will be deliberately restricted than that it will be trivialized by

[22] See above, pp. 209–13.

excessive familiarity. The risk is that freedom will come to mean nothing more than free choice among a range of options that the market provides. We are free because we can choose detergents or careers without the constraints of centralized planning, and because we can change either if a more attractive alternative comes along.

In that context, the role of Christian Realism is not to talk about realistic limits, but to expand political imagination. People need to envision not just another career, but whole new ways of organizing work and new systems of economic security. Traditions that have been suppressed and kept out of the political discourse need to be explored, and new ways of leading and sharing power must be tried. Practical constraints and competing visions will, of course, remain, and Christian Realists are not likely to forget this. When no one any longer dares to be utopian, however, the role of the Realist may be to recall that the human reality also includes the capacity for such dreams.[23]

Expanding our political imagination in this way might lead in turn to a rediscovery of the importance of politics in our lives. Among the lessons of this extended study of Christian Realism is the fact that our human nature is profoundly political. We need the negotiations and the arguments, the cooperation and the oppositions that an inclusive political community provides, not only to get anything done, but also to know anything about reality and how we are related to it.

When we think about the human need for community, our attention is usually focused on intimate relationships and on the family, where strengths are built and where devastating distortions of personality can happen. 'Community,' where it extends beyond these intimate bonds at all, tends to refer to the face-to-face interactions of neighborhoods, small towns, and social groups. 'Politics' refers to what happens in the depersonalized space beyond community. In fact, however, politics, with its demands for recognition and its search for cooperation,

---

[23] Cf. Roger Shinn, "Realism, Radicalism, and Eschatology in Reinhold Niebuhr: A Reassessment," in Nathan A. Scott, Jr., ed., *The Legacy of Reinhold Niebuhr* (Chicago: University of Chicago Press, 1975), pp. 98–99.

goes on even in the intimate communities, and the need to be part of a community where recognition and cooperation take place extends far beyond the limits of our personal relationships. Politics, as we have understood it here, encompasses the search for knowledge of the self and knowledge of God that Calvin identified as the two parts of true wisdom.[24]

The usual contemporary views of politics are strikingly at variance with this Christian Realist assessment. For some, who find their humanity limited and denied by the dominant political powers, politics is an oppressive reality to be named, first, and then broken. The political task is to unmask the forms of political oppression that sustain the interests of the powerful. Then we shall enter a new era, which will be somehow post-political, at least in the sense that the opposed interests that now structure our human communities will no longer exist. The failure of the institutionalized Marxist versions of this vision have not diminished its attractions for those who have experienced political repression.

For others more comfortably situated, politics is not something to be broken, but something to be avoided. Knowledge of self and God are something they seek in private life, where the results are more clearly under their own control. Public life is important only as a place to obtain the resources for private life, and politics serves to insure that one's access to the resources is not restricted and that one's freedom in their private use is not limited.

These two contemporary views, in different proportions in different places, characterize much of the thinking about politics as we come to the end of Reinhold Niebuhr's century. Niebuhr's warnings, directed first at liberal optimists and Social Gospel idealists, not to expect too much from politics come too late for these contemporaries, who in their different ways expect from politics exactly nothing. In a new century, Christian Realism must teach us to think again about politics, so that we will not expect too little of it. Because we are so constituted as to hope for the perfect harmony of life with life,

[24] John Calvin, *Institutes of the Christian Religion*, I, i, 1.

there is no way in which politics can give us all of what we seek. But there is no way to achieve any of what we hope, no way, indeed, even to know what it is that we hope, that does not pass through politics.

Select bibliography

Audi, Robert. "The Separation of Church and State and the Obligations of Citizenship." *Philosophy and Public Affairs* 18 (Summer 1989):259–96.

Barth, Karl. *Church Dogmatics.* Translated by G. W. Bromiley. Vol. IV/2. Edinburgh: T. &. T. Clark, 1958.

The Epistle to the Romans. Translated by Edwyn C. Hoskyns. New York: Oxford University Press, 1968.

Beckley, Harlan. *Passion for Justice: Retrieving the Legacies of Walter Rauschenbusch, John A. Ryan, and Reinhold Niebuhr.* Louisville: Westminster/John Knox Press, 1992.

Benne, Robert. *The Ethic of Democratic Capitalism.* Philadelphia: Fortress Press, 1981.

Bennett, John C. *Christian Ethics and Social Policy.* New York: Charles Scribner's Sons, 1946.

Christian Realism. New York: Charles Scribner's Sons, 1941.

Bernstein, Richard. "The Meaning of Public Life." In *Religion and American Public Life*, edited by Robin W. Lovin, 29–52. New York: Paulist Press, 1986.

Brink, David. *Moral Realism and the Foundations of Ethics.* Cambridge: Cambridge University Press, 1989.

Brown, Charles. *Niebuhr and His Age.* Philadelphia: Trinity Press International, 1992.

ed. *A Reinhold Niebuhr Reader.* Philadelphia: Trinity Press International, 1992.

Durkin, Kenneth. *Reinhold Niebuhr.* Harrisburg, Pa.: Morehouse Publishing, 1991.

Finnis, John. *Fundamentals of Ethics.* Washington, D.C.: Georgetown University Press, 1983.

Fox, Richard W. *Reinhold Niebuhr: A Biography.* New York: Pantheon, 1985.

Frankena, William K. "Love and Principle in Christian Ethics." In

Faith and Philosophy, edited by Alvin Plantinga, 203–25. Grand Rapids: Eerdmans, 1964.

Gewirth, Alan. *Reason and Morality*. Chicago: University of Chicago Press, 1978.

Green, Ronald M. *Religion and Moral Reason: A New Method for Comparative Study*. New York: Oxford University Press, 1988.

Religious Reason: The Rational and Moral Basis of Religious Belief. New York: Oxford University Press, 1978.

Habermas, Jürgen. *Reason and the Rationalization of Society*. Vol. 1 of *Theory of Communicative Action*. Translated by Thomas McCarthy. Boston: Beacon Press, 1984.

Harland, Gordon. *The Thought of Reinhold Niebuhr*. New York: Oxford University Press, 1960.

Harries, Richard, ed. *Reinhold Niebuhr and the Issues of Our Time*. Grand Rapids: Eerdmans, 1986.

Hauerwas, Stanley. *Against the Nations: War and Survival in a Liberal Society*. Minneapolis: Winston Press, 1985.

Character and the Christian Life. Trinity University Studies in Religion. San Antonio: Trinity University Press, 1975.

A Community of Character. Notre Dame, Ind.: University of Notre Dame Press, 1981.

Hershberger, Guy F. *War, Peace, and Nonresistance*. Scottdale, Pa.: Herald Press, 1944.

Horton, Walter Marshall. *Realistic Theology*. New York: Harper and Bros., 1934.

James, William. *The Writings of William James*. Ed. John J. McDermott. New York: Random House, 1967.

Kegley, Charles W., and Robert W. Bretall, eds. *Reinhold Niebuhr: His Religious, Social, and Political Thought*. New York: Macmillan, 1961.

Lebacqz, Karen. *Six Theories of Justice*. Nashville: Abingdon Press, 1986.

Lindbeck, George. *The Nature of Doctrine*. Philadelphia: Westminster Press, 1984.

McBrien, Richard P. *Caesar's Coin: Religion and Politics in America*. New York: Macmillan, 1987.

McCann, Dennis. "Reinhold Niebuhr and Jacques Maritain on Marxism: A Comparison of Two Traditional Models of Practical Theology." *Journal of Religion* 58 (April 1978):140–68.

Macintosh, Douglas Clyde, ed. *Religious Realism*. New York: Macmillan, 1931.

MacIntyre, Alasdair. *Whose Justice? Which Rationality?* Notre Dame, Ind.: University of Notre Dame Press, 1988.

Morgenthau, Hans J. "The Influence of Reinhold Niebuhr in American Political Life and Thought." In *Reinhold Niebuhr: A Prophetic Voice in Our Time*, edited by Harold R. Landon, 97–116. Greenwich, Conn.: Seabury Press, 1962.

Murray, John Courtney. *Religious Liberty: Catholic Struggles with Pluralism*. Edited by J. Leon Hooper. Library of Christian Ethics. Louisville: Westminster/John Knox Press, 1993.

We Hold These Truths: Catholic Reflections on the American Proposition. New York: Sheed and Ward, 1960.

National Conference of Catholic Bishops. *Economic Justice for All: A Pastoral Letter on Catholic Social Teaching and the U.S. Economy.* Washington, D.C.: United States Catholic Conference, 1986.

Niebuhr, H. Richard. *Radical Monotheism and Western Culture*. New York: Harper and Row, 1960.

The Responsible Self: An Essay in Christian Moral Philosophy. New York: Harper and Row, 1963.

Niebuhr, Reinhold. "An American Approach to the Christian Message." In *A Traffic in Knowledge: An International Symposium on the Christian Message*, edited by W. A. Visser 'tHooft, 55–56. London: Student Christian Movement Press, 1931.

Beyond Tragedy: Essays on the Christian Interpretation of History. New York: Charles Scribner's Sons, 1937.

The Children of Light and the Children of Darkness. New York: Charles Scribner's Sons, 1972.

Christian Realism and Political Problems. New York: Charles Scribner's Sons, 1953.

Christianity and Power Politics. New York: Charles Scribner's Sons, 1940.

Does Civilization Need Religion? New York: Macmillan, 1928.

Faith and History: A Comparison of Christian and Modern Views of History. New York: Charles Scribner's Sons, 1949.

Faith and Politics. Edited by Ronald Stone. New York: George Braziller, 1968.

An Interpretation of Christian Ethics. New York: Seabury Press, 1979.

"Liberalism: Illusions and Realities." *New Republic* 133 (July 4, 1955):11–13.

Man's Nature and His Communities: Essays on the Dynamics and Enigmas of Man's Personal and Social Existence. The Scribner Lyceum Editions Library. New York: Charles Scribner's Sons, 1965.

Moral Man and Immoral Society. The Scribner Lyceum Editions Library. New York: Charles Scribner's Sons, 1960.

The Nature and Destiny of Man. New York: Charles Scribner's Sons, 1964.

Pious and Secular America. New York: Charles Scribner's Sons, 1958.
"A Reorientation of Radicalism." *The World Tomorrow* 16 (July 1933):444.
The Self and the Dramas of History. New York: Charles Scribner's Sons, 1955.
The Structure of Nations and Empires. New York: Charles Scribner's Sons, 1959.
"The Truth in Myths." In *The Nature of Religious Experience: Essays in Honor of D.C. Macintosh*, 117–35. New York: Harper and Bros., 1937.
Novak, Michael. *The Spirit of Democratic Capitalism*. New York: Simon and Schuster, 1982.
Nussbaum, Martha. *The Fragility of Goodness: Luck and Ethics in Greek Tragedy and Philosophy*. Cambridge: Cambridge University Press, 1986.
"Human Functioning and Social Justice: In Defense of Aristotelian Essentialism." *Political Theory* 20 (May 1992):202–46.
Putnam, Hilary. *Reason, Truth, and History*. Cambridge: Cambridge University Press, 1981.
Ramsey, Paul. "Love and Law." In *Reinhold Niebuhr: His Religious, Social and Political Thought*, edited by Charles W. Kegley and Robert W. Bretall, 79–123. New York: Macmillan, 1956.
Rauschenbusch, Walter. *Christianity and the Social Crisis*. Louisville: Westminster/John Knox Press, 1992.
Christianizing the Social Order. New York: Macmillan, 1912.
Rawls, John. *Political Liberalism*. New York: Columbia University Press, 1993.
A Theory of Justice. Cambridge, Mass.: Harvard University Press, 1971.
Reeder, John P., Jr. *Source, Sanction, and Salvation: Religion and Morality in Judaic and Christian Traditions*. Englewood Cliffs, N.J.: Prentice-Hall, 1988.
Rice, Daniel F. *Reinhold Niebuhr and John Dewey: An American Odyssey*. Albany: SUNY Press, 1993.
Robertson, D. B., ed. *Love and Justice: Selections from the Shorter Writings of Reinhold Niebuhr*. Louisville: Westminster/John Knox, 1992.
Sayre-McCord, Geoffrey, ed. *Essays on Moral Realism*. Ithaca: Cornell University Press, 1988.
Stone, Ronald H. *Professor Reinhold Niebuhr: A Mentor to the Twentieth Century*. Louisville: Westminster/John Knox Press, 1992.
Stout, Jeffrey. *Ethics After Babel*. Boston: Beacon Press, 1988.
Strawson, P. F. *Skepticism and Naturalism: Some Varieties*. New York: Columbia University Press, 1985.

Sullivan, William M. *Reconstructing Public Philosophy*. Berkeley: University of California Press, 1986.

Taylor, Charles. *Sources of the Self: The Making of the Modern Identity*. Cambridge, Mass.: Harvard University Press, 1989.

Tietje, Louis H. "Was Reinhold Niebuhr Ever a Marxist? An Investigation Into the Assumptions of His Early Interpretation and Critique of Marxism." Dissertation, Union Theological Seminary. 1984.

Tinder, Glenn. *The Political Meaning of Christianity*. Baton Rouge: Louisiana State University Press, 1989.

Tracy, David. *Plurality and Ambiguity*. San Francisco: Harper and Row, 1987.

Troeltsch, Ernst. *The Social Teaching of the Christian Churches*. Translated by Olive Wyon. With an introduction by Richard Niebuhr. 2 vols. Library of Christian Ethics. Louisville: Westminster/John Knox Press, 1992.

West, Cornel. *The American Evasion of Philosophy*. Madison: University of Wisconsin Press, 1989.

White, Morton O. *Pragmatism and the American Mind*. New York: Oxford University Press, 1971.

What is and What Ought to Be Done. New York: Oxford University Press, 1981.

Whitmore, Todd D. "Christian Ethics and Pragmatic Realism: Philosophical Elements of a Response Ethic." Unpublished Ph.D. Dissertation, University of Chicago. 1990.

Yoder, John Howard. *The Politics of Jesus*. Grand Rapids: Eerdmans, 1972.

The Priestly Kingdom: Social Ethics as Gospel. Notre Dame, Ind.: University of Notre Dame Press, 1984.

Index

254